GET•THE
Interview
EVERY TIME

Fortune 500 Hiring Professionals' Tips
for Writing Winning Résumés and Cover Letters

Brenda Greene

Dearborn™
Trade Publishing
A **Kaplan Professional** Company

This publication is designed to provide accurate and authoritative information in regard to the subject matter covered. It is sold with the understanding that the publisher is not engaged in render-
ing legal, accounting, or other professional service. If legal advice or other expert assistance is
required, the services of a competent professional should be sought.

Vice President and Publisher: Cynthia A. Zigmund
Acquisitions Editor: Jonathan Malysiak
Senior Project Editor: Trey Thoelcke
Interior Design: Lucy Jenkins
Cover Design: Depinto Designs
Typesetting: the dotted i

Published by Dearborn Trade Publishing
A Kaplan Professional Company

Printed in the United States of America

04   05   06   10 9 8 7 6 5 4 3 2

Library of Congress Cataloging-in-Publication Data

Greene, Brenda.
      Get the interview every time / Brenda Greene.
         p.   cm.
      ISBN 0-7931-8302-2
      1. Resumes (Employment)   2. Job hunting.   3. Employment interviewing.   I. Title.
HF5383.G7235 2004
650.14—dc22

                                                                              2003023853

Dearborn Trade books are available at special quantity discounts to use for sales promotions, employee premiums, or educational purposes. Please call our Special Sales Department to order or
for more information at 800-245-2665, e-mail trade@dearborn.com, or write to Dearborn Trade
Publishing, 30 South Wacker Drive, Suite 2500, Chicago, IL 60606-7481.

To Charlie

Contents

*"Résumés that garner interviews exhibit these three qualities: there are no spelling
or grammatical errors; they are neat and professional in appearance;
and they show relevant experience."*

LISA A. WHITTINGTON
Human Resources Director, Host Marriott

You just sent your résumé out and, taking stock of yourself, realize that your good looks, tailored suit, and charming demeanor don't count for much at this pivotal moment. The only thing that really matters is what you have said about yourself—in writing—to a total stranger.

Think about it: You have two minutes to make an impression that can determine the quality of your life for the next three, five, or maybe even ten years. Your résumé is one of hundreds that are sent to a big company on any given day. A lot is riding on that first impression. So what actually happens when your résumé lands in the human resources (HR) department of a major corporation?

If the company software doesn't bounce your résumé back into cyberspace because there aren't any keywords that match its needs, it might get a quick once-over. And if there are no errors and your qualifications don't sound overstated, the résumé might get a second look, and then the HR specialist might even read your cover letter. It's a two-minute judgment call that will determine the outcome of your job search.

How do I know this? I recently conducted a comprehensive survey of 50 Fortune 500 professionals who said basically the same thing. Your résumé has a two-minute opening to make the grade—not a lot of time to sell yourself to a company.

Without a doubt, getting in the company door can be a challenge, especially in an economy that, according to David Leonhardt of the *New York Times,* "seems like a lukewarm bowl of mush" (June 15, 2003). It takes a good résumé to win an interview at most companies, but it also helps to know how America's biggest companies recruit the best talent.

If you're like most job seekers, you want to know what catches an employer's attention. Is it talent? Work history? Education? Relevant experience? And what are the best practices for targeting desirable positions at big companies? How do you even go about it in the digital age, when everyone is scanning, attaching, e-mailing as they've never done before?

There was a time when all you had to do was sit down and write a standard résumé. Depending on your temperament, you either sweated through this exercise or you relished every minute. And the process was relatively straightforward:

Either you followed the format the career counselor gave you or you found a résumé book in your local library that contained samples you could use as a model. You then printed your new résumé on quality stationery, mailed it to 50 of your favorite companies, and waited impatiently for the telephone to ring to set up the sought-after interview.

Things have changed dramatically since then. That's one of the reasons this book was written.

Get the Interview Every Time: Fortune 500 Hiring Professionals' Tips for Writing Winning Résumés and Cover Letters relies extensively on the feedback of 50 Fortune 500 professionals who participated in this study about their hiring practices. These professionals—specialists, managers, directors, vice presidents—answered a detailed questionnaire on what Fortune 500 companies want to see in applicants' résumés and cover letters and how they recruit the best talent. These hiring professionals see thousands of résumés a month (sometimes even a week). Some of the data will surprise job seekers—and even career consultants.

A NEW BODY OF KNOWLEDGE

The first thing a prospective employer sees is a candidate's résumé. It's your ticket to an interview. Knowing what the expectations are in America's biggest, most profitable companies gives you a competitive edge. The results of the study provide insight directly from the people who make thousands of hiring decisions every year. More than 2 million people work for the 50 companies represented in this study—an extensive amount of hiring experience.

Although plenty of information is available for the newcomer to the job market, this book sorts through the conflicting information on a successful job search. The collective wisdom contained in the Fortune 500 survey represents a new body of knowledge on the subject of a successful job search because these companies are the standard-bearers and leaders on the business front. Smaller companies are bound to adopt the same practices (if they haven't already) in the near future.

THE PLUGGED-IN RÉSUMÉ

Because Fortune 500 companies are the companies most likely to employ the latest technologies and software, classified ads and networking are only part of the equation in securing a job in the digital age. You need to master the electronic job market to take advantage of the innumerable opportunities available to those who know how to navigate this new territory. And you need to know that a one-size-fits-all résumé in this highly competitive job market will not make the cut.

Most résumés today are delivered to human resources departments via e-mail, so if you're not familiar with all the variables of the electronic résumé, your two-minute opportunity could evaporate on the spot. Every participant in my study said that most recruiting takes place on the company Web site. In fact, a representative from J.P. Morgan Chase & Co. noted in a recent *Wall Street Journal* article that 77 percent of its hires so far this year started on the corporate Web site, and that includes entry-level jobs up to some vice president positions (June 24, 2003).

It's essential to have a résumé that is cyberready. *Get the Interview Every Time* provides simple, step-by-step guidance for posting electronic résumés.

STRATEGY BASED ON FIRSTHAND ADVICE

Finding the right job is a priority, especially because the average American spends between 56 and 61 hours per week at work. Add to that figure the 1.5 hours per day commuting and the math is easy: working takes up a significant amount of time in an adult's life. Because almost everyone who works needs a résumé, it makes sense to have a sound strategy based on firsthand advice from the experts inside the human resources departments of America's biggest companies.

That's one of the reasons I've included so many sample résumés for you to examine. Most of these samples are actual résumés that have passed the two-minute acid test. They have opened the door to rewarding positions at excellent companies. The résumé samples can guide you in the preparation of your own targeted résumé.

Get the Interview Every Time covers all the essentials for launching your résumé and winning an interview in today's competitive market. It will help you do the following:

- Research and target your next job.
- Write dynamic cover letters.
- Launch an Internet-ready cover letter and résumé.
- Customize your résumé for a targeted job.
- Prepare for an interview.
- Get the job.

Get the Interview Every Time covers everything you need to know about finding the right job with a targeted cover letter and résumé. Whatever your profession, you need this book to navigate job seeking in the 21st century. Also remember that whatever you do, don't sit back and lament the difficulties of finding a good job in a sluggish economy. You're wasting valuable time that could be spent researching your prospects on a company Web site. The new economy, or what some cynics call the "new stagnation," still holds innumerable opportunities for those who know how to focus their job search. Don't shortchange yourself: rewarding jobs are available when you know how to navigate today's job market. Let *Get the Interview Every Time* help you refine your résumé and cover letters so that you can target the job that will provide you with meaningful and rewarding work.

Detailed surveys were sent to executives at 50 Fortune 500 companies. The responses from the 50 Fortune 500 hiring managers/directors/vice presidents are the crux of this book. *Get the Interview Every Time: Fortune 500 Hiring Professionals' Tips for Writing Winning Résumés and Cover Letters* quotes extensively from the information these insiders provided.

Since the survey was conducted, some companies have merged or no longer rank among the Fortune 500. Some individuals, meanwhile, have moved to other companies or have been promoted. Participants are from companies on the 2002 Fortune 500 list that appeared in the April issue of *Fortune* magazine. The list, for the most part, reflects the status of companies and individuals at the time I received responses to the survey. It needs to be mentioned here that the respondents' participation in the survey does not necessarily indicate an endorsement of this book.

I would like to extend my appreciation to the following professionals for their time and thoughtful contribution:

- **Albertson's, Inc.:** Stacy Harshman, employment administrator
- **Allied Waste Industries, Inc.:** Kathy O'Leary, human resources generalist
- **ALLTEL Corporation:** Julie Ruesewald, senior human resources generalist
- **Aquila, Inc.:** Carol Eubank, human resources manager
- **Avon Products, Inc.:** Robin Fischer, director of talent acquisition
- **The Bank of New York Company, Inc.:** Ken Dean, assistant vice president, human resources
- **Bank One Corporation:** Jeremy Farmer, senior vice president, human resources
- **BB&T Corporation:** Michael Tyree, human resources specialist
- **BJ's Wholesale Club, Inc.:** Paula Axelrod, manager of staffing
- **The Chubb Corporation:** Mary Powers, assistant vice president, human resources
- **Continental Airlines, Inc.:** Mary Matatall, director, global recruiting
- **Darden Restaurants, Inc.:** Susan Lock, human resources manager

- **Deere & Company:** Sherri Martin, human resources director, consumer and commercial equipment division
- **Dollar General Corporation:** Gary Moore, recruiting director
- **Energy East Management Corporation:** Sheri A. Lamoureux, director, human resources planning
- **Engelhard Corporation:** Rocco Mangiarano, human resources director
- **Enterprise Leasing Company:** John Tomerlin, vice president, human resources
- **Fannie Mae:** Trang Gulian, manager of staffing
- **Federal-Mogul Corporation:** Jackie Coburn, manager of staffing
- **FMC Corporation:** Kenneth R. Garrett, vice president, human resources
- **Gannett Co., Inc.:** Stacey Webb, human resources representative
- **Georgia-Pacific Corporation:** Chris C. Collier, group manager of corporate recruiting
- **Health Net, Inc.:** Cherri Davies, manager of staffing
- **H.J. Heinz Company:** Tom DiDonato, human resources vice president for Heinz NorthAmerica
- **Host Marriott Corporation:** Lisa A. Whittington, director of human resources
- **Household International, Inc.:** Brian Little, human resources group director
- **Idaho Power Company (subsidiary of IDACORP, Inc.):** Dawn Thompson, human resources specialist
- **International Truck & Engine Corporation (Parent: Navistar International Corporation):** Bill G. Vlcek, manager of strategic staffing
- **Jabil Circuit, Inc.:** Heather McBride, senior human resources generalist/recruiting manager
- **J.C. Penney Corporation, Inc.:** E. Humpal, manager of employment services
- **JDS Uniphase Corporation:** Stephen Heckert, human resources senior manager
- **Jones Apparel Group, Inc.:** A. Tejero DeColli, human resources senior vice president
- **Kellogg Company:** Cydney Kilduff, director of staffing and diversity
- **Kindred Healthcare, Inc.:** Donna Campbell, manager of recruiting services
- **Lucent Technologies, Inc.:** Sherry Rest, manager, process and technology, recruiting and staffing solutions
- **Marathon Oil Corporation:** R.T. Beal, manager of talent acquisition
- **The McGraw-Hill Companies:** David Murphy, executive vice president of human resources
- **Merck & Co., Inc.:** Tracy L.S. Grajewski, senior director, corporate staffing
- **The Mutual of Omaha Companies:** Dan Bankey, manager of strategic staffing

- **Pepsi Bottling Group:** Cecilia McKenney, human resources vice president
- **Phelps Dodge Corporation:** David Pulatie, human resources senior vice president
- **Saks Incorporated:** Roland Hearns, vice president of recruitment placement
- **Southern California Edison Company:** Susan Johnson, human resources manager
- **State Farm Insurance Companies:** Leslie Humphries, human resources specialist
- **SYSCO Corporation:** Amy Moers, senior staffing manager
- **Teachers Insurance and Annuity Association—College Retirement Equities Fund (TIAA-CREF):** Carol F. Nelson, second vice president, staffing and relocation services
- **Tesoro Petroleum Corporation:** Janie Lopez, human resources consultant
- **Thrivent Financial for Lutherans:** Debra Palmer, manager of staffing
- **United Parcel Service, Inc.:** Stacy R. Wilson, human resources administrator
- **Unisys Corporation:** Patrick Dunn, director of workforce planning

In addition to the Fortune 500 individuals listed above, others contributed to the book as well. I would like to thank Helen Cunningham, my coauthor of *The Business Style Handbook, An A-to-Z Guide for Writing on the Job with Tips from Communications Experts at the Fortune 500,* who painstakingly reviewed this manuscript to make sure it was accurate and relevant and also researched Chapter 9 in this book. In addition, I am indebted to Dan Bankey, a manager of strategic staffing at Mutual of Omaha, for his thoughtful and extensive comments as well as his insight in Chapter 9 on what the future holds for job seekers. I would also like to thank Heather McBride of Jabil Circuit, Lisa Whittington of Host Marriott, and Donna Campbell of Kindred Healthcare for adding great value and insight to Chapter 10 in their critiques of a sample résumé.

In addition, I would like to thank my family and friends for their support, encouragement, and sample résumés: Charles Greene, Myles Greene, Rose Anna Greene, Marie Elena Greene, Rose Greene, Mary Ellen Caputo, Nick Caputo, Marissa Caputo, Nicholas Caputo, Rosemary Chiavetta, Phil Chiavetta, Cathy Chiavetta, Amy Bennett, Terry Byrne, Mary Adele Byrne, Mary D'Annibale, Al D'Annibale, Doreen Murray, Ray Murray, Patty Leonard, Sylvester Leonard Jr., Alice Good, Joel Good, Coleen Byrne, Megan Byrne, Suzann McKiernan-Anderson, Sabina Horton, Kim Horton, Mary Ward, Martin Ward, Peggy Gaines, Sheila Nadata, Mary Lou Adelante, Robert Edward Barlow Jr., Mary Beth Barlow, Sharon Ambis, Luke Kallis, Tom Anderson, Michael Barry, Esther Brandwayn, Debra A. Brodsky, Jaclyn Cashman, Kathy Murphy, Min Chen, Isabel Cunningham Uibel, Steven Felsenfeld, Angelo Guadagno, Andrea G. Preziotti, Izabela

Karlicki, Suzanne M. Lanza, Michelle N. McKenna, Mark McLaughlin, Sasha Oblak, Cheryl S. Peress, Rhonda Price, Alma Rodriguez, Michael J. Rosch, Nicholas Seminara, Andrea Caryn Sholler, William Berde, Lorna Milbauer, Muriel Krell, and Paul Krell.

And, finally, I would like to thank my agents, Joelle Delbourgo and Jessica Lichtenstein; my editor, Jon Malysiak; my project editor, Trey Thoelcke; and my copy editor, Lois Sincere.

1

FORTUNE 500 RESULTS

"Focus your energies on the specific jobs that match the talents and interests you have—and individually tailor your efforts toward convincing the candidate companies that you can provide measurable ROI when hired."

DAN BANKEY
Manager of Strategic Staffing, Mutual of Omaha

Recruiting practices at large corporations have changed dramatically in the last five years. The basic, one-size-fits-all résumé and cover letter—standard entry into the 20th-century work world—have gone through innumerable transmutations. Today job seekers are expected to maneuver their way around the new hiring landscape electronically. They must target their individually tailored résumés and cover letters to specific *open* positions that are, more often than not, posted on company Web sites.

In the 21st century, pounding the pavement has given way to scouring the Internet.

According to the survey of 50 Fortune 500 hiring professionals conducted in 2002, hiring practices at major companies have undergone an overhaul. Even though it is still essential to network and prepare a professional-looking résumé and cover letter, it's also necessary to know that most companies recruit new employees via the Internet at company Web sites. In fact, a 2002 study conducted by iLogos Research, a division of Recruitsoft, claims that "81 percent of Fortune 500 companies are posting job openings on their corporate Web sites." Moreover, 70 percent of the Fortune 500 hiring professionals surveyed for this book said résumés sent electronically are preferred. Knowing what the expectations of Fortune 500 hiring professionals are gives job seekers the competitive edge when seeking employment at both large and small companies.

Experts who participated in the survey were virtually unanimous in stating that résumés need to be not only individually tailored for targeted jobs but skill specific and results oriented as well. And it must be immediately obvious to a prospective employer that the job seeker is a "good fit" for the company and its culture.

In a two-page, 24-question survey, Fortune 500 hiring professionals answered questions regarding their respective hiring practices. Their responses to the survey provide job seekers an inside view of what Fortune 500 employers look for when acquiring new talent. Here are just a few of the survey questions.

- How are most résumés delivered to the HR department?
- Is a cover letter attached to every résumé?
- Does a computer program screen résumés?
- What is the ideal length of the standard résumé?
- What's the single most important piece of information on a résumé?
- How much time is spent reviewing a résumé for the first time?
- What are the grounds for sending a résumé to the unwanted pile?
- Where should applicants seeking employment begin their job search?
- What does the company do with blind (unsolicited) résumés?

Some of the responses confirm what you already know, but most answers will surprise you. Did you know, for instance, that most résumés at Fortune 500 companies are delivered via e-mail? As already mentioned and shown in Figure 1.1, 70 percent of the respondents prefer this method (11 respondents prefer snail mail and 4 prefer fax; all percentages were based on the number of respondents who answered the particular question).

One thing is for certain: a job search in the 21st century requires access to a computer as well as to the Internet.

FIGURE 1.1 *Résumé Delivery Preferences*

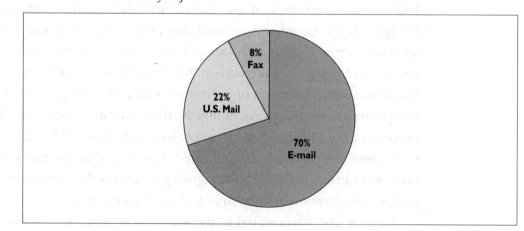

WHAT THE EXPERTS SAY ABOUT COVER LETTERS

That electronic cover letter you agonized over for three hours may not be read unless your résumé jumps out of the pack and catches the attention of the recruitment officer. In fact, most e-mailed résumés are submitted without cover letters: 74 percent of the respondents claimed that no cover letters were attached at the time of submission, whereas only 13 respondents said that cover letters were included. In the case of an attached cover letter, only 40 percent of the respondents read the cover letter *before* they read the résumé. The remaining respondents read the cover letter only if they were interested in the candidate. Trang Gulian, a manager of staffing at Fannie Mae, said she "only reviews a cover letter if more information on the candidate is needed."

But just because hiring professionals don't read all cover letters doesn't mean they don't expect to see one. On the contrary, the data suggest that although the first thing hiring professionals look at is the résumé, the next thing they look at (if they are interested) is the cover letter. Cutting corners and blasting a solo-flying résumé out into cyberspace may not produce good results.

Taking a casual approach toward writing the electronic cover letter may be counterproductive as well. In fact, 84 percent of the survey respondents expected the e-cover letter to conform to their high writing standards, which are the same as those of a standard cover letter; only two respondents indicated that it's not a strike against the candidate if the electronic cover letter is informal.

And what about the standard cover letters sent by snail mail? Are they considered dinosaurs? Not yet. If they are well written and insightful, these cover letters could help you to stand out above the rest. Tracy Grajewski, a senior director of corporate staffing at Merck, said she wants the cover letter to "tell [her] how focused the person is on his or her job search and give [her] an idea where to refer the résumé."

So what (at the very least) do Fortune 500 professionals expect from both standard and electronic cover letters?

- That they accompany every résumé you send
- That they are brief but error free and accurate
- That all pertinent contact information is included (name, address, telephone number, e-mail address)
- That accomplishments are highlighted in a short paragraph
- That the position being applied for is specified

The Fortune 500 participants had a good deal more to say about what they expected to see in cover letters, but Chapter 5 goes into more detail.

If you're wondering whether your résumé and cover letter get the human touch, you can be assured that only 36 percent of the companies use computer programs to initially screen applicants. If, however, the company does screen, those résumés and cover letters should include keywords that company programs can pick up. Even though the majority of respondents don't yet have the capability to screen (64 percent don't), it's just a matter of time before they jump on board. Why? Because manually screening thousands of résumés is labor intensive, especially for Fortune 500 companies.

Eighteen of these companies receive between 50 and 100 résumés a day, twelve receive more than 100 résumés a day, and four of the 50 companies claimed they receive more than 500 résumés per day (ALLTEL, Chubb, Continental Airlines, Unisys), as depicted in Figure 1.2. Only 22 percent of the Fortune 500 companies receive fewer than 20 per day. The competition for jobs at Fortune 500 companies is stiff.

The survey results, which represent a new body of knowledge on hiring practices in the 21st century, clearly indicate that the momentum in recruiting is shifting swiftly toward the Internet. It's safe to assume that what Fortune 500 companies do today, smaller businesses will do tomorrow. Why? For the simple reason that it makes good fiscal sense. According to Cambria Consulting's Bernie Cullen, a partner at the Boston-based human resource consulting firm, companies can "cut their costs [finding] new employees by nearly 90 percent compared with traditional recruiting techniques" via the Internet.

FIGURE 1.2 *Résumés Received per Day*

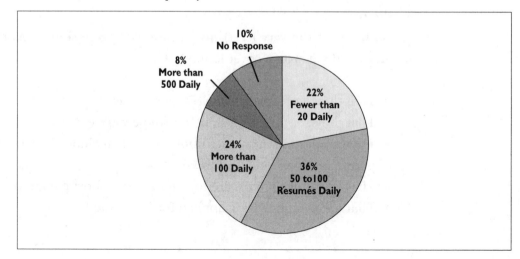

THE CRUX OF THE RÉSUMÉ

When asked what they looked at first when reviewing a résumé, 80 percent of the respondents said it was "related experience." Human resource professionals are *primarily* concerned with filling *open* positions. When an applicant can match the experience of the person leaving the company, the transition is smoother and less costly (according to a 2002 Beta Research Corporation Study featured in the *New York Times,* it costs on average "$10,350 to replace an employee who leaves for another job").

Surprisingly, neither educational background nor applicants' previous place of employment was a top priority. In fact, only one respondent said educational background was the first thing he looked at, and only one respondent said where the applicant worked before was the first priority. Four of the respondents stated they look at the format and style of the résumé. If that meets their expectations, then they proceed to further examine the qualifications. One respondent said that he checks the grammar and spelling before proceeding, and two said they look at a combination of the four factors mentioned.

Another surprise is that the category of "accomplishments" was not checked off by a single survey participant. Although a candidate's prior accomplishments may be a deciding factor in whether the candidate will be asked to interview, this category seems to come into play only once other criteria are met. As was made clear by many respondents, accomplishments must be backed up with verifiable numbers, results, or promotions. These hiring professionals are wary of overblown accomplishments and "hype."

If you're wondering how much time is spent reviewing your résumé for the first time, make note of the fact that you don't have all day to capture a recruiter's attention. Most—36 percent—said they spend 2 minutes; 34 percent said they spend 1 minute; 22 percent said they spend 30 seconds, and 6 percent said 5 minutes. One respondent said it depended on the résumé.

This information should actually encourage you because it differs slightly from conventional thinking on the subject. For example, according to the résumé design page in OWL, the online writing lab of Purdue University, "Employers will usually take, at most, only 35 seconds to look at this one-page representation of yourself before deciding whether to keep or discard it." And in an April 29, 2003, *Wall Street Journal* article, Joann S. Lublin wrote: "Employers overlook significant experiences because they typically scan a résumé for just 15 seconds."

Whether it's 15 seconds or 2 minutes, you still must grab the recruiter's attention quickly. That's why it's important that your "related" experience is immediately evident on the résumé. The best possible way to capitalize on this experience is to make sure your résumé contains relevant keywords and a focus statement. (See later chapters for more detailed information.)

As for the length of your résumé, the survey indicates a general consensus. When applying for a management position, the standard is two pages, according to 74 percent of the respondents. Taking a minority view, 18 percent of the respondents thought one page was standard and only 8 percent thought three. Only two respondents said it "depends."

The preference for brevity makes sense when you consider that recruiters at large corporations look at hundreds of résumés each week. They need to zero in on the pertinent information quickly. Creating a ten-page résumé is almost certain to diminish your chances of getting a thorough examination by a recruiter.

START SEARCHING THE COMPANY WEB SITE

It's best to begin your job search by first narrowing down the companies you're interested in and then going to their Web sites. But before you go to the career page and start filling out a profile or searching for a specific job in the accounting department, spend some time getting a feel for what the company is all about. Research is crucial to gaining an edge, according to the Fortune 500 respondents.

When asked where applicants should begin, 74 percent said to start at the company Web site. Surprisingly, only 18 percent said networking should be the first option, a finding that flies in the face of the commonly held belief that networking is the most important key to beginning a successful job search. One respondent advised reading the classifieds, another said to go to job fairs, and two advised, "all of the above."

When asked where their companies advertise jobs, 60 percent said these jobs can be found on the company's Web site; 12 percent said they use newspaper classifieds; 6 percent said they use online job boards; and 20 percent said they used all of the areas previously mentioned. One respondent said that an agency was his company's primary source.

Although the survey results reinforce the fact that time spent on a company Web site is highly advantageous, you do need a strategy. Surfing haphazardly through innumerable company Web sites and job boards could be counterproductive if you neglect other strategies. Try to aim for balance, and add some job fairs, networking, and even cold calling to the mix.

Developing a strategy before sitting down at the computer is crucial. Pinpoint the companies that interest you and target specific jobs. Once you've narrowed your target, you'll be able to make the best use of your time on the Internet.

AVOIDING THE PITFALLS

As obvious as this may sound, it is essential that before posting your résumé on a company Web site or even an online job board you make sure that your information is accurate and error free. Run everything through the spell checker—twice. For extra insurance, you should even have another person read your material for grammar and spelling errors or inaccurate gaps in your employment history. The margin of error in putting together this information is greater than you think.

When asked what the percentage of errors was for submitted résumés (see Figure 1.3), 36 percent of the respondents said that 10 percent have errors; 44 percent said 25 percent have errors; 16 percent said 50 percent have errors; and two respondents said 75 percent of the résumés they see contain errors!

Errors are one reason your résumé flounders; in fact, 14 percent of the respondents said spelling and grammar errors disqualify even the most accomplished candidates, but there's another important reason you may not get a response.

When asked what the grounds were for sending a résumé immediately to the unwanted pile (see Figure 1.4), 54 percent of the respondents reported a lack of computer skills, 18 percent said applying for a position that isn't *open* doesn't work, and 12 percent said stipulating a specific salary is a negative. Only one respondent considered a gap in work history a serious issue.

Most recruiters in human resources departments at Fortune 500 companies are practiced at detecting incongruities in the information you provide. Even if the information seems straightforward and direct, many verify the facts, especially when a candidate gets past the first stage of the process. In fact, exactly 50 percent said they "always" verify information on résumés, 28 percent "usually" check, and only 22 percent "sometimes" check.

FIGURE 1.3 *Résumés Received with Errors*

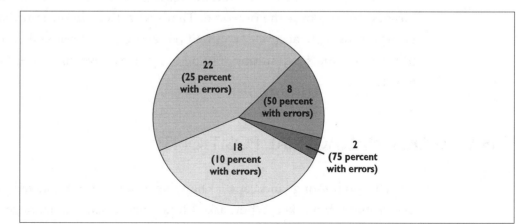

FIGURE 1.4 *Reasons for Refusing Résumés*

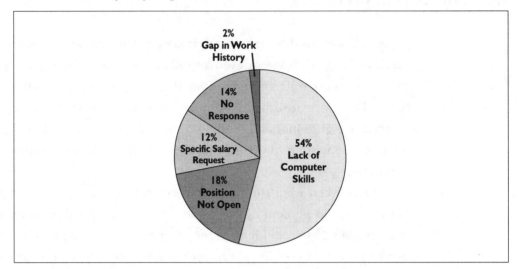

And what about the ubiquitous personal information and interests sections on many résumés? According to the Fortune 500 respondents, if the information isn't relevant, don't include it. Twenty-one respondents said they prefer not to read about applicants' outside interests, 14 said such information was "acceptable," and 7 advised including it only if those interests are applicable to the job. Mentioning your love of poker and mountain climbing activities could work against you, so remember to keep *all* the information on your résumé relevant.

Once you send the résumé, there's a good chance it will be acknowledged; at least the majority of respondents (27) always acknowledge receipt of your résumé. Of the rest, 15 acknowledge receipt only if they are interested in you as a candidate, and 5 said that acknowledgment depends on the method of submission (which generally means that if you e-mail a résumé, an automatic response is generated). Only 3 of the respondents said they never acknowledge receipt of résumés.

Whether you receive an acknowledgment or not, once the résumé is sent, you have no control over the outcome. That's why it's so important that your initial effort is thorough, accurate, and well researched. And remember: don't sit back just because you sent out one résumé to a prospective employer. Continue your efforts.

WHAT ABOUT MANAGERIAL POSITIONS?

The job hunting landscape is changing as much for managers as it is for newbies to the job market. When asked how they recruit for managerial positions, according to the survey, 40 percent said résumés are still used; 26 percent said they rely on a recruitment agency; 18 percent said management positions are filled by a referral from someone in the company; 12 percent said they use the company Web site; and 4 percent rely on the classifieds. Based on the cost savings and momentum, you can expect the percentage recruited via the company Web site to grow steadily during the next few years.

What was particularly interesting about the survey results was that your dream job may present itself up to a year after you submit a résumé. Most of the Fortune 500 respondents keep your résumé on file for a year or more; in fact, exactly half of the respondents confirmed this. And 24 percent said they keep them for up to six months, whereas 6 percent said three months, and one respondent said one month. For those applying for an open position at the company, the odds are better. Your résumé stays on file until the open position is filled, according to 10 percent of the respondents.

Sometimes you may have the urge to send a résumé blindly to a company that you would like to work for with the hope that eventually a suitable position will open up. The good news is that only 12 respondents said they would not consider such résumés at all. Half said they file them for an eventual need they may have, and six route them to the appropriate departments. Four hold on to them indefinitely, especially if the candidate is recommended by either a personal friend or someone within the company.

When asked if they ever filled a position by using a résumé from their files, 76 percent said they do (even though this does conflict with how they view less recent résumés on online job boards). Only 12 percent said they prefer new résumés.

FIGURE 1.5 *Recruiting for Managerial Positions*

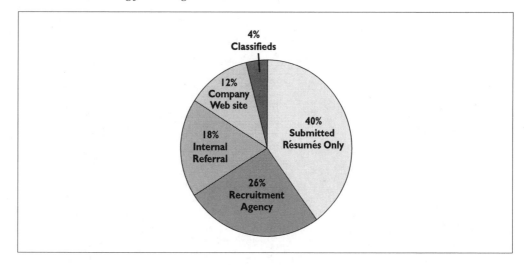

The survey results cover the basics for launching your résumé and winning an interview in today's competitive market. The findings provide insight directly from the people—HR specialists, managers, directors, vice presidents—who make thousands of hiring decisions every year. Cutting through the conflicting information about the best tactics for finding a job is that much easier now that you have firsthand information from these Fortune 500 hiring professionals.

2

HAVE YOU DONE
YOUR RESEARCH?

"Determine how the company fills job openings and pursue the method it prefers."

CAROL EUBANK
Human Resources Manager, Aquila, Inc.

Before you brush off your résumé and sprinkle it with innumerable keywords, create a strategy and target several companies on your dream-job list. Plan to spend about half of your time on the Internet looking at the Web site of each of these companies.

This is the planning stage and, according to the Fortune 500 participants, may be the most essential step in the job-seeking process. All major corporations today expect their applicants to be familiar with the company's Web site. They want to see that you've done your research. And why shouldn't they? Never before have job seekers had such easy access to a company's business, culture, and employment opportunities.

Companies have spent millions and dedicated significant resources to ensure that their Web sites have valuable content and are user friendly, and for good reason: when it comes to hiring—company Web sites are incredibly cost effective. Merck, for instance, has saved "several million dollars over the past year by relying more on its corporate Web site to find candidates" (*Wall Street Journal,* June 24, 2003). Web sites enable companies to hire from a broad range of candidates without using expensive search firms and advertisements.

Once you've decided to pursue a certain company, it's also helpful to examine its literature from previous years as it will give you a good idea of how the company has evolved. Annual reports, press kits, brochures, price lists, and other publications are readily available online. If you already submitted your résumé and are waiting for the telephone to ring, put this in-between time to good use by reading every piece of literature you can find on the prospective employer.

That way you have all the information you need in the event that you are asked to interview.

This kind of preparation tells the company you are interested in becoming a part of the team. In addition, you don't want to go into an interview and ask questions that could have been easily answered just by reading the Web site.

Brian Little, a group director in human resources at Household, reaffirms this in the survey: "Research before you send a résumé. Nothing wastes more time than looking at résumés that should have never been sent in the first place."

GETTING STARTED

Even in cyberspace you may need paper and pen (especially if you don't have a handheld device to make notes). Dedicate a small notebook to your job search and start jotting down relevant information on each company to which you plan to submit a résumé. Carry this notebook around with you to jot down important information, such as the names of contacts, companies you want to research, and the like. Having this information in a notebook saves you the trouble of backtracking in case you are suddenly called in for an interview. It's a time-saver, and you can enter the information in the job data file on your computer at a later time.

I once attended a seminar on corporate communications. The teacher of the class must have found grammar and syntax a little too dry for her tastes because she exhibited an endless penchant for self-help tangents. On one of her many excursions, she advised us to boost our self-esteem by writing our résumé. I looked around the room and noticed I wasn't the only person in the class who looked dumbfounded. In fact, by the look on everyone's face, I think I can safely say that the idea of writing a new résumé sounded as inviting as joining the Jacksonport Polar Bear Club for its annual dip into the icy waters of Lake Michigan on New Year's Day. Not one of us welcomed the idea of writing a résumé to boost our confidence, which is one reason why the temptation to get off track when searching for a job is so strong. If you're like most people, it's a challenge to whittle your work history down to two pages of relevant, but dynamic, material.

The good news is that before you pull out the paring knife, you can still make headway in the job hunt by conducting research. Jump-start the process by clicking onto the Web sites mentioned in *Time* magazine's "50 Best Sites on the Web" (July 3, 2003). Devote a few hours to the following career sites to get the brain in gear: flipdog.com, careerjournal.com, monster.com, salaryexpert.com, and wetfeet.com. Not only will you pick up useful keywords, but the sites may actually inspire some enthusiasm for the task at hand. Besides recommending job boards where you can plug into a listing of nationwide opportunities, these sites provide guidance to job seekers on such topics as interview techniques, salary scales, and résumé-writing tips.

At this point, it is not advisable to post your résumé on the big job boards. The most efficient use of your time lies in scouring company Web sites because that's where you'll find the majority of open positions. Moreover, doing your own research at a company's Web site keeps you in the driver's seat—you're targeting the company instead of jumping at a possible job lead that you may eventually turn down. It's early enough in the job search so that you can do the choosing rather than jumping at whatever comes along.

Keep the job boards in reserve for when you've exhausted most of your other options. But something to keep in mind when you do post your résumé on a job board: many recruiters look only at recent entries. If your résumé lingers too long on a job board, you cut your chances of being seen, so don't rush to put a résumé out there. Do some prep work instead.

Another caveat is that matching skills between employer and employee is more difficult on mainstream job boards. Many recruiters are switching to job boards operated by professional groups because the chances of a match improve significantly. According to one health care technology recruiter: "About 15 percent of people who respond to a job posting [on the professional group job board] have the right skills, compared with the 2 percent results . . . at mainstream job boards" (Adelson, *New York Times,* October 29, 2002).

Another excellent Web site (but not a job board) for company profiles and research is www.hoovers.com. (Everyone can access the profiles, but you have to be a paid subscriber for more in-depth information.) And you will get more information than you can handle by putting a company name through the Google search engine.

So keep in mind that exploring these career Web sites should be for informational purposes at this stage of the job hunt.

VIRTUES OF SIMPLICITY AND HUMILITY

When you go to the career page on a company's Web site, take a look at the company's mission statement or its profile of its "archetypal employee." Not only will you find useful keywords, but you'll also get a good idea of whether the company is a suitable fit for you.

It shouldn't come as any surprise that the mood of employers has shifted significantly in the new millennium. The ego-driven résumés of the 1990s no longer find a home at many of America's largest corporations. In his book *Good to Great,* Jim Collins contends that the values embraced by the companies he profiled and the words they use to describe the corporate culture include "disciplined, rigorous, dogged, determined, diligent, precise, fastidious, systematic, methodical, workmanlike, demanding, consistent, focused, accountable, and responsible." Use these words as a guideline for the tone of your résumé. And remember, as David Brooks wrote in the *New York Times Magazine* (June 29, 2003) about *Good to Great:* "The culture at these companies encourages the Lincolnian virtues of simplicity and humility."

Most of the recruiters at Fortune 500 companies have examined thousands of résumés, so you can be fairly certain they are adept at detecting sensational claims of glory. Rocco Mangiarano, a director of human resources at Engelhard who sees between 50 and 100 résumés per day, said in the survey that applicants should be honest about who [they] are and what [they've] done." And David Murphy, an executive vice president at The McGraw-Hill Companies, said in the survey, "Hype does not pay." He added that "exaggerated claims about skills and/or achievement" are his personal grounds for sending a résumé to the unwanted pile.

So resist bombast. Go instead to the company Web site and look up its mission statement; most Fortune 500 companies have one (even if they call it by another name). Many of them are simple statements about a company's goals and values; others are more elaborate texts; but all of them have keywords that you can use in either your cover letter or résumé.

To cite one example, the H.J. Heinz corporate Web site has a section called "Vision and Values" that is loaded with clues about its culture and values. It says about its vision: "Being the best premier food company does not mean being the biggest, but it does mean being the best in terms of consumer value, customer service, employee talent, and consistent and predictable growth. . . . Our vision will be supported by our VALUES, which define to the world and ourselves who we are and what we stand for." The company then lists its values, based on the adjective *premier,* that are important to it. Paraphrased, they are passion, risk tolerance, excellence, motivation, innovation, empowerment, and respect.

If you were to write a cover letter to this company, you might want to refer to its Web site material and show how these values are exhibited in your own work history. Remember, hundreds—and sometimes thousands—of résumés are sent to large corporations on a weekly basis. David Pulatie, a senior vice president in human resources at Phelps Dodge, said in the survey: "You must create personal uniqueness. When hundreds apply for the same job, you must stand out."

One way to distinguish yourself so that your résumé is pulled from the pack is by knowing about a company's culture and values. It also helps you to decide whether the company would be a good fit for your interests and background. Stephen Heckert, a senior manager in human resources at JDS Uniphase, reaffirms this idea: "Search company Web sites for the companies that are a personal fit culturally and careerwise."

GETTING DOWN TO THE NITTY-GRITTY

After you have scoured the more general pages of a company Web site, proceed to the "career" or "job opportunities" page (but only if you are sure you have a current résumé that reflects what the company needs). Once there, you will see directions on how to apply for an open position. Generally, you will be asked to send your résumé directly to the company, or you will be asked to fill out the company's employee profile (which usually utilizes much of the information already on your résumé).

If you decide to fill out the company profile, *do not rush through this process.* Have a dictionary on hand and be prepared to double-check the accuracy of your information—from spelling and grammar to dates and company names. Human resources personnel are evaluating your communication skills, so do everything in your power to make sure that any information you provide the company is accurate and error free. One more gentle reminder: *Take your time.* If you are going to be interrupted a few times because you have to pick up your daughter from soccer or you expect the telephone to ring with a call from a recruitment agency, then it's better to fill out the company profile late at night or early morning. It's essential that all your communication with a prospective employer is 100 percent professional.

Most companies expect you to have an e-mail address, but if you don't, create one before you go to the company Web site. On the PepsiCo career profile page, you are given a link and the option of creating an e-mail address with Yahoo!. My advice, however, is that you get your own e-mail address from Yahoo! or Hotmail. Many times company Web sites require you to log on before proceeding to a specific job. Sometimes your e-mail address acts as your username during log-in, so there's no getting around the need for an e-mail address. Even if you already have one, you may want to set up a new account to use specifically for the job search. Furthermore, to avoid electronic glitches, get used to your new e-mail before using it.

It is essential you follow directions precisely; several Fortune 500 survey participants stressed this fact again and again. Dawn Thompson, a specialist in human resources at Idaho Power Company, said this in the survey: "Pay close attention to the application procedure of the company. One who doesn't follow procedures usually isn't considered." So when PepsiCo requests in its career profile that your résumé attachment not exceed 16,384 characters, do not send one that has 18,000 characters.

This may sound simple to most of you, but many applicants don't follow basic instructions. Don't be one of them. You are ready to go to the career page of a company Web site only when you have a current, accurate, and succinct résumé as well as an e-mail address and a dictionary. A few hours of quiet time is also recommended.

It is also helpful to be armed with a list of action words (see Chapter 4 for more information) to use in the event that you are asked to describe your career objective. A consistent reason Fortune 500 participants reject a résumé was that the applicant's objective was fuzzy or too general. Either applicants did not determine what positions were open and available or they lacked any real direction in seeking specific employment. If you have to fill out an employee profile rather than send your résumé, you may be asked to write a career objective in your profile. If you don't have one on your résumé, then you'll have to compose one on the spot before submitting your profile. That's when the list of action words comes in handy.

J. Michael Farr, author of *The Quick Résumé and Cover Letter* (see "Resources"), has this to say: "One of the worst things you can do with your résumé is to try to make it work for 'any' job. While it is acceptable for you to consider a broad range of jobs, applicants who don't seem to know what they want to do impress few employers. This means that all but the simplest résumés deserve to include a job objective."

On some company Web sites, you may only apply for open positions. Make sure you read the job description, which is usually more elaborate than the one you find in a classified advertisement, before applying for the job. Pick up some of the keywords from the job description and put them on your résumé (provided you have these skills, of course). If you are sending a "blind" résumé, one that will be held by the company for future positions or jobs not advertised, that's all the more reason to narrow your options. Employers want to see your focus.

An employer wants to match candidates whose credentials meet the criteria of the open positions in his or her company. Job seekers must anticipate those needs and then target their résumés accordingly. Revamping your résumé to reflect this employer-directed focus is essential. Employers want to know how you can solve their problems or meet their needs. The more you know about the company, the better you position yourself to customize your résumé to meet the company's needs.

Take, for instance, the Procter & Gamble career site. Besides allowing applicants to apply for open positions via the standard online job forms, the site gives you an opportunity to click on its career advice center and even participate in its "interactive online courses." Another click and an applicant can discover what it takes to succeed at P&G, something called the "what counts factors." This is valuable information when you are targeting your résumé—as well as when you land the interview.

COMPANIES AS OPEN BOOKS

It used to take three to six months for job seekers to find a new job, but in a competitive job market experts say it can take up to a year, because employers are deluged with résumés for just one or two openings. This can be discouraging unless you spend your time productively—researching your field as well as your career potential.

It's all about matching your qualifications to current job opportunities at a company. Many of the Fortune 500 participants said that if your qualifications don't match, your résumé remains active in the company database from six months to a year. That's not what always happens, though. When A. Tejero DeColli, a senior vice president at Jones Apparel Group, Inc., was asked what the company does with unsolicited résumés, she replied that they just don't accept them. You have to specifically apply for open positions. A few other participants also said their companies don't consider unsolicited résumés.

What this means is that you should do some sleuthing to find out what a company's policy is toward unsolicited résumés. If the information is not readily available on the career page, then either write the HR department an e-mail asking what its policy is regarding unsolicited résumés or call and ask.

Some of you may be puzzled by the suggestion that you call the company. If a company explicitly states that you should not call it, then by all means honor that policy. If, however, you are unsure what the company policy is, then investigate further. Stacey Webb, a human resources representative at Gannett, stated that job seekers need to be "persistent. Contact the HR department to express your interest in opportunities with the company."

If a phone call is permissible, you have the opportunity to find the name of the person to whom you should send your résumé. It's a good idea to have a list of questions ready before calling the HR department, such questions as these:

- What is the standard procedure for applying to the company?
- Are there any openings now?
- Will there be any positions opening up in the near future?
- If a résumé is sent to the department via e-mail, should it be sent as an attachment or as plain text (ASCII, pronounced *askee*)?
- Do you require a career profile (e-form) to be filled out on the company Web site beforehand?

You don't want to sound like a novice in case you do get an opportunity to speak to an HR representative. As with online applications, your communication skills are on display—and being evaluated. You can improve your chances of being hired by being prepared and anticipating an employer's needs.

Of course, a good strategy for finding a job is *networking*. Nearly every one of the survey participants stressed the importance of referrals, contacts, and networking. But even if you do have a contact at the company, you are putting yourself at a disadvantage if you choose to bypass the research stage of the job-hunting process. Chances are that even with a contact at the company, you will have to follow the standard procedure for applying for the job. Don't shortchange yourself: Do your research, become familiar with the company Web site, and know as much as you can about the targeted company. It will not be a waste of time.

AND DON'T BE DISCOURAGED

The Fortune 500 companies surveyed for this book have thousands of employees, anywhere from 3,420 at Thrivent Financial for Lutherans to 360,000 at UPS, with most of the companies falling into the 25,000 to 50,000 range. Their hiring expertise goes a long way when acquiring talent.

Having the relevant skills to match a job opening is the number one qualification mentioned by the Fortune 500 participants. If your skills are not current or not in demand, don't be averse to taking a course to brush up. Finding a new job can take anywhere between three months and a year, and if you aren't presently employed, you probably won't spend more than 20 hours a week looking for a new job. If you have to brush up on your computer or accounting skills, that leaves half the week open and available.

Employers appreciate your dedication, because those who succeed in today's challenging environment are those who never stop learning and are willing to seek the information that will make their job search more productive and fruitful. According to Dan Bankey, a manager of strategic staffing at Mutual of Omaha, "We're looking for lifetime learners."

As already mentioned, it costs a company $10,350 to replace an employee who has left for another job. Because a poor hiring decision can be costly to a company, try not to be impatient if the hiring process takes longer than you would like. You can be assured that the bigger the company, the longer it will take to procure a new position. Cydney Kilduff, a director of staffing and diversity at Kellogg Company, said applicants should "be patient—big wheels turn slowly."

And if you really want to work for a particular company, don't give up. David Murphy of McGraw-Hill said, "Do not rely on simply sending a résumé. Work the headhunter. Network your way into contact with the right hiring authority at the target company." Cecilia McKenney, at Pepsi Bottling, added: "Be persistent with the company you want to work for. Pursue jobs with multiple mediums and follow up."

A one-size-fits-all résumé or dusting off the old résumé and updating it just doesn't work in today's highly competitive job market. Job seekers now must do the following:

- Write concise and skill-specific résumés.
- Target jobs that match their skills.
- Post résumés so they are seen by the appropriate hiring managers.
- Write engaging cover letters that make an applicant stand out.
- Anticipate what a company needs.

Remember that, according to the Labor Department, there are more than 1,200 official job occupations, so determining the best course to take depends on many factors. Your preliminary research helps to narrow your options. It also helps you determine whether the conventional snail mail, hard copy résumé is a requisite or only a posted ASCII résumé will meet a company's requirements. In today's digital environment, you cannot proceed with your job hunt until you determine exactly what is required.

3

RÉSUMÉ FORMAT AND DESIGN

"I prefer résumés that are concise and easy to read."

MARY MATATALL
Director of Global Recruiting, Continental Airlines

Hiring professionals see hundreds, sometimes thousands, of résumés each week, and, generally, they spend no more than two minutes looking at each one. Many Fortune 500 survey participants mentioned that an "easy-to-read" résumé was one of the prerequisites to offering a prospective employee an interview, so choosing the right format and design can make a difference.

SELECTING THE FORMAT: CHRONOLOGICAL OR FUNCTIONAL

Creating an easy-to-read résumé starts with the basics and moves toward the finer points. First, you must decide what format works best for your skills and experience.

Most résumés follow a reverse chronological format: a time history of your work experience, beginning with your most recent position. Many recruiters prefer it simply because it is *easy to read*. A chronological depiction of your work history allows hiring professionals to see how long you were with each company. It also allows them to obtain a good idea of your growth as an employee and learn what companies you worked for as well as assess your increasing responsibilities.

The functional résumé, on the other hand, is more skills based and categorical. It works particularly well if there is a gap in your work history, you have limited paid experience, you worked part-time and/or as an independent contractor, or you are changing careers. For instance, if you want to emphasize the skills for a sales management position that you acquired working as a volunteer soccer coach and fundraiser rather than highlight your last short-term job as a programmer, the functional layout may be a better choice.

But functional résumés have their downside. Practiced human resources professionals can easily detect work gaps or camouflage. Even if a recent relocation and a work gap were legitimate, a functional résumé may still send out the red flags to *some* employers. Initially, they may wonder if you are hiding something. The good news is that an unconventional employment history can still be transformed into a virtue if the information is presented in a strong, honest, and deliberate fashion.

Not every work history falls neatly into either a chronological or a functional format. On the contrary, there are quite a few variations—linear, creative, accomplishment, international, keyword, targeted, and curriculum vitae as well as a combination of these formats—that may be more suited to your needs. Basically, though, they are all derivatives of either the chronological or functional format, so these two formats will be the focus of this chapter.

Before you choose a format that works best for your skills and experience, you need to compile key information so that it can be positioned as needed. This is the backbone of your résumé, and you need to spend a good portion of your time in developing it and then, at a later point, revising it. Not only must it be 100 percent accurate and error free, but it must also be vibrant and focused. If the key information is faulty, even the best design will fail. For now, just compile the basic information so that you can begin to build a multipurpose résumé. At this point you may start to transfer all the earlier research you put in your notebook or handheld device into your newly created job data file on your computer. This is where you will also store your key information.

WHAT TO INCLUDE

Every résumé should provide the following data: contact information, focus statement, professional experience, and educational background. Avoid listing the following: personal data (height, weight, age, marital status, photograph), hobbies, references, salary requirement, or history. Your résumé must accentuate the positive. Save any sensitive issues (such as a physical disability or criminal record or your seven children) for later.

Your key information should be arranged as follows.

Contact Information. In the digital age, this information takes up more and more space on a résumé. How much data should you provide? Begin with your name, address, home telephone number, and e-mail address. You have to decide if it's necessary to provide a daytime contact number; if you don't want to include your current work number, cellular numbers are good alternatives. Some individuals may want to include their URL so employers can go to a Web site if they have the inclination. Your URL should be at the top of your résumé, which should resemble the following:

Martha Hempenstall
111 Avenue E
New York, NY 10000
(212) 674-1000
marts@aol.com
www.marts.com

Focus Statement. It's known by many names (*career objective, expertise, skills summary, professional qualifications, key features, accomplishments, background, highlights, professional profile*), but usually it's the brief statement appearing after your contact information. It pulls all of your information together and should tell a prospective employer, in a few sentences, what your level of expertise is or what type of position you are seeking at the new company or what your most significant accomplishments are. Information Technology (IT) professionals often include a skills summary here that details their proficiency in hardware and software. As mentioned earlier, don't shoot for too wide a target. *Try to anticipate what the prospective employer needs* and pepper this statement with employer-directed, attention-catching words. Sometimes a focus statement is as simple as the title of the job you seek. Most are longer. Here's an example of a focus statement (aka career objective), which would follow your contact information (notice that it lists both the position being applied for as well as the candidate's expertise):

OBJECTIVE: Development Associate

Strategic writer with eight years' experience fundraising more than $2 million and developing—from start to finish—successful, long-term nonprofit, government, and corporate campaigns.

Professional Experience. This section is the crux of your résumé. How you list your previous employment or experience will depend on whether you use the chronological or functional format. When preparing the chronological résumé, your most recent experience should be listed first and then earlier professional experience in descending order by date. A functional résumé, on the other hand, emphasizes your skills rather than where you worked and for how long (although it is often recommended that you give dates and where you worked but in a less prominent position). Sometimes you describe a particular position, sometimes you describe just your skills. The first position in the professional experience section in the functional format is often reserved for the work experience that most closely relates to the position being sought at the new company. Your professional experience section in the functional format will be more skills oriented and less specific than it would be in the chronological format.

What's most important to remember, according to a 2002 job market study done by the *New York Times* (February 5, 2002), is that résumés grab recruiters' attention when the "work experience fits the open job." Julie Ruesewald, a senior human resources generalist at ALLTEL, agrees. She said, "Don't apply for jobs you're not qualified for."

In the chronological format, the emphasis should be on the professional experience listed first, as most employers are primarily interested in your current or most recent employment. If it's not obvious what industry you worked for and you are certain the prospective employer won't be familiar with the company, such as CIS Group, Inc., describe it briefly, either right after the name (technology) or in the description of accomplishments or duties. The first entry usually gets the most space on a résumé. A word of caution to those who feel the need to fudge some information: The Internet has made it relatively easy to verify almost anything, so make sure all of the data here are accurate.

Educational Background. List your degrees and professional certifications in this section. How much space you devote to your educational background depends on what you want to emphasize in your résumé. If you graduated within the last five years or have virtually no work experience, you may want to expand on your college coursework or certifications here. Another common option for recent graduates is to rearrange the order of the key information and highlight the educational section by moving it to the top of the page following your contact information. (One Fortune 500 respondent recommended that you list your education first, even if you have a lot of experience.) Whether you place dates next to your completed degrees is a decision you will have to make. Some prefer not to include these dates because they believe it pinpoints their age, even though anti-discrimination laws should protect applicants. But if you feel strongly about how old you are, then don't include dates here.

If you are fluent in languages or have a relevant professional affiliation, you may also include it in this section. If you are in the process of completing a degree, list your anticipated graduation date. Some résumé books and career experts recommend that high school information or unfinished college degrees not be listed, although this issue is not cut and dried. As Dan Bankey of Mutual of Omaha said, "Absolutely include any training and continuing education. It can be a differentiator." You need to decide whether mentioning an incomplete degree will further your cause.

Bankey added: "We sort by years of schooling, so if someone has some college, put it in. High school can be important if it's the highest level one has. We look at the highest level. Falsifying an application can disqualify you; truth and honesty are really important to us. We find that one-third of résumés have something that is not correct, but we'll give a candidate an opportunity to explain it. People really feel the need to have a college degree."

CONTENT IS KING

Your contact information, focus statement, professional experience, and educational background (regardless of where it is placed) form the backbone of your multipurpose résumé. While there's plenty of room for variation in the design of a résumé, this information must be correct, readable, and dynamic. Don't spend hours, however, rearranging the information in a hundred different ways. The more accessible and straightforward your information, the better your chances that your résumé will hit its intended target.

Content is king in a résumé, so it's a good idea to devote most of your time on developing how you present your experience. Some effort, nonetheless, must be directed toward the design of the résumé before you pull all the pieces together, because a good design makes your content more readable.

DESIGN ELEMENTS

What are some of the design features of an easy-to-read résumé? Balance, symmetry, and white space all contribute to the visual impact of a reader-friendly résumé. No one should have to struggle to review your material. And a good design goes a long way toward easing eyestrain, especially when hundreds of résumés must be reviewed.

Adhering to the notion that a résumé should never be more than one page long, some job seekers tend to cram too much information in too little space, making it difficult to find relevant information and perhaps explaining why *74 percent of the survey participants prefer two-page résumés.* Unless you are a newcomer to the job market or have limited experience, plan to write two *full* pages. Several Fortune 500 respondents said the length depends on how extensive your experience is. Use your best judgment, but don't forget that because hundreds of résumés are competing for the recruiter's attention on any given day, you don't want to overwhelm a recruiter with an eight-page résumé.

Choose either full-width spacing or a column approach to achieve the balance needed to display all your key information in a flattering light. As a starting point, allow one inch for your margins—top and bottom as well as left and right. Sherry Rest, a manager of recruiting and staffing solutions at Lucent Technologies, said, "Although résumés are most often reviewed in electronic format, make sure your printed format has margins that will allow a recruiter or hiring manager to make notes."

Experiment with fully justified or ragged-right margins. Full justification, whereby both margins are aligned, may give you more words per line, but a ragged right margin (the right margin has an uneven edge) is faster to read, according to a study by Microsoft and reported in Susan Britton Whitcomb's book *Résumé Magic* (Indianapolis: JIST, 1999). Just remember that the decision to use a fully justified or ragged right margin will not hurt your cause one way or the other. Plan to keep your design as simple and readable as possible. The hours you labor over the design may be an exercise in futility, especially if the only version your prospective employer reviews is your e-mail's plain text version (without formatting and embellishment).

To get a few ideas about indentation, bullets, rules, and columns, take a look at how other résumés are designed (see the samples at the back of this book). You can also browse through online job boards. Choosing a design for your résumé depends on how much information you need to include—and then finding the design that will display it in the most flattering fashion.

If your word processor has résumé templates, experiment with them but don't resort to filling in the blanks. Using templates may encourage you to settle for a run-of-the-mill description of your work history or tempt you to rush through the process of putting the pieces together yourself. The more time spent creating your résumé, the better your objective and design. You don't want to give the recruiter the impression that your résumé was thrown together in a rush with little thought or focus.

Kenneth Garrett, a vice president in human resources at FMC Corporation, said in the survey that you should "know what's on your résumé and be able to articulate it precisely." Your résumé should tell the recruiter that you have thought about who you are as an employee and what your career goals are—and that you have spent time presenting this information in a purposeful manner in your résumé.

MAKE IT INVITING TO READ

Your résumé should be a logical arrangement of key information, which is why order and consistency—or the lack of it—play such a big role in résumé writing. Chances are your résumé won't even be read if the information is presented in a haphazard fashion, so before focusing on the big picture, pay attention to the small details.

One of the trickiest areas of writing a résumé is consistency because of the many variables. Typefaces, indents, bullets, wording—all of these elements have to be presented in a consistent way. You don't want Montana showing up in three different forms (Montana, Mont., and MT) or one job title to be in boldface and the next job title in italics. Because of all these variables, proofread a résumé several times. Make sure verb tense is correct; your punctuation is consistent; your indents align correctly. Take the extra time to do this.

Your computer has a wide array of typefaces. Times New Roman, Courier New, Garamond, and Arial are all good choices (they also convert well). Giddyup, UltraBronzo, and Visigoth will probably send red flags to more conservative recruiters. Mixing up typefaces, such as Arial for one section and Garamond for the next, is hard to pull off unless you're very creative. Err on the side of caution when it comes to typefaces; otherwise, the résumé may look immature, cluttered, or downright unreadable.

You should, however, use bold, italics, and capitalization interchangeably so long as they are used in a consistent pattern (for instance, make sure *all* of the names of the companies are capitalized or use bold to highlight *every* position held). The easiest to read is roman type, so don't overdo it with too much boldface or italic type. Practice restraint.

Start with a font size of 12 for normal text. Some claim you can reduce the size of text to 10, but 10 is hard to read and doesn't print as well as 12. Resist the temptation to squeeze all of your information on one page by going to a smaller font. Instead it's better to rearrange your résumé—or at least the white space—than to go to 10 points. If it's necessary to fit in one or two extra lines, then reduce the text to 11 at the minimum (however, for electronic submissions, 10 points is typical). Going smaller may discourage some readers, especially those who have read innumerable résumés from 9 in the morning until 5 at night.

You may experiment with larger sizes for your headings, but don't get carried away (14 and 16 are adequate). By selectively enlarging the typeface, you are highlighting something you think is important, and it's hoped that the important something is a great job or accomplishment (and not your name).

Positioning your information appropriately is also important. If recruiters have to scour the remote corners of your résumé for pertinent information, the résumé is missing its mark. Your selling points should be placed up front, and don't hide important information in a lot of detail. Short, direct points and paragraphs are better than long ones, so edit rigorously, and try to whittle the résumé down to its essence.

You should invest in quality stationery with matching envelopes if you're mailing your résumé as well as quality stationery for copies of your résumé, which you will bring to your interviews. Stick to white or neutral colors for a professional appearance. Bright-colored paper (florescent pink or iridescent blue, for instance) sends the wrong message to recruiters. Use a laser printer or a photocopy machine for extra copies. In the digital age, it doesn't pay to invest in offset printing (and making 100 copies) because, according to the Fortune 500 participants, it's better to tweak each résumé for a specific job. In many respects, your résumé will be a continual work in progress.

If you don't have access to a computer (or you know for certain that someone else can do a much better job), then you might want to consider hiring a professional résumé writer. You still have to write your key information, but résumé writers can help you with design, keywords, focus, and target. You can find résumé writers in the Yellow Pages. A certified professional résumé writer (CPRW) has passed competency tests, so look for this designation when reviewing his or her credentials. The CPRW certification process is administered by the Professional Association of Résumé Writers & Career Coaches (PARW/CC). Remember that these certified résumé writers will assist you in preparing a multipurpose résumé, but you still may have to revise it each time you apply for a new position.

For those of you who may need additional help, nonprofit career counseling services are available in every state. Also, every college has a career center that reaches out to the college and, sometimes, general population. Don't be afraid to seek help. Career counseling firms and job search companies are also alternatives, but be wary. Not all of these firms are legitimate; some charge advance fees and deliver only empty promises. Before you decide to contract the services of a company, review www.jobscams.com or visit www.execcareer.com, both of which monitor career-marketing companies.

If you go to headhunters, remain proactive. Become as involved in the process as possible, even if they create your entire résumé from scratch and choose each company to which your résumé is submitted. David Murphy of McGraw-Hill recommended that job seekers "work the headhunter." And Ken Dean, an assistant vice president at the Bank of New York, had this caveat: "You cannot rely on [headhunters] to put [your résumé] in front of the correct person." With this in mind, think of the headhunter as a partner.

But chances are that if you are reading this book, you plan to create your own résumé. As long as you have access to the basic tools (computer and the Internet) and follow a few sound guidelines on language, layout, and design, it's not that difficult to create a winning résumé that opens doors.

PUTTING THE PIECES TOGETHER

Once your key information is written and a format chosen, you are ready to build a résumé. This section provides step-by-step suggestions, using "Before" and "After" versions of both chronological and functional formats to illustrate the various points. (See additional sample résumés at the back of the book.) Many of the suggestions are based on feedback from the Fortune 500 participants.

The two "Before" résumés are multipurpose and have wide applications in their respective fields. The "After" résumés are employer driven and job specific, which is what most companies expect today. The first résumé in this chapter uses a chronological format; the second is based on a functional format.

According to Stephen Heckert, senior manager of human resources at JDS Uniphase: "Focus your résumé on a company's current or future job openings. This may mean developing a different résumé for each job opening." If you're worried about writing a new résumé every time you apply for a job, relax. It's not necessary to write 30 different résumés for 30 different jobs. What you ultimately should aim for is a multipurpose, but dynamic, résumé that can be tweaked every time you apply for a specific job. It's easier than you think.

BUILDING A CHRONOLOGICAL RÉSUMÉ

In a chronological format, you describe what you did and how well you did it next to your employer information. You list your work history, beginning with your most recent employer and ending with your least recent employer. It's a winning format because it is simple and direct. If you have a lot of gaps in your work history, this format will reveal every one of them because it is arranged by date. That's one of the reasons employers prefer the chronological format, which easily discloses whether you have a stable work history with a progression of responsibilities and accomplishments.

Creating a fictitious scenario, as shown in Figure 3.1, better illustrates why a chronological format works best for this sample résumé.

Mary relocated to northern New Jersey when her husband was transferred. For a few years, she commuted to her job in White Plains, but then the two hours of bumper-to-bumper traffic each day began to get the better of her. She decided to change jobs, but she wasn't exactly sure how she wanted to proceed in her career path, so she quit her job in White Plains and hurriedly revised her résumé in response to a classified ad she saw in the paper. She got the job at the local library in New Jersey, and although it was not a permanent solution, the position satisfied her on other levels. She worked in that capacity for two years—enjoying the interaction with the public.

When the position of administrative assistant at a large book distributorship came to her attention (by investigating open jobs on a company Web site), Mary decided to make a move. Before she did anything, though, she had to revamp her résumé to apply for the job. She decided to use a chronological format because of her solid work history. What her résumé looked like when she applied for the library position is shown in Figure 3.1.

Mary's résumé indicates she is a competent and loyal employee who worked at a well-known Fortune 500 company for 16 years. She had no trouble securing the position of assistant librarian because she is an enthusiastic and reliable individual with varied interests and talents. Now she wants to set her sights higher—on a position that is more challenging and financially rewarding. She read the description of the administrative assistant position at a Fortune 500 book distributorship on a company Web site and realized it combines her earlier administrative talents as well as her interest in books:

> The Merchandising Department has an excellent opportunity for an Administrative Assistant. The ideal candidate will be responsible for providing administrative support to the Director, Store Inventory management and occasional support to two Vice Presidents, managing routine correspondence for Field Merchandise Department, and coordinating travel schedules and reservations. You will also be responsible for preparing agendas for meetings, acting as liaison with appointments and guests, and assisting the Field Merchandise Department with projects and initiatives. The ideal candidate will be creating reports and schedules using Excel, Word, and other software, performing administrative functions such as transcribing minutes of meetings, arranging conference calls, and providing backup phone support. Additional responsibilities include coordinating filing systems, ordering and maintaining supplies, and arranging for equipment maintenance.
>
> **Qualified candidates** should have some college and at least 4 years of administrative experience. You will also have excellent computer skills, including MS Word, Excel, Access, and Adobe Illustrator, and excellent verbal and written communication skills. Additionally, you must have the ability to multitask, be extremely organized and a team player. Must be responsive to deadlines.

FIGURE 3.1 *Mary Smith's "Before" Chronological Résumé*

Mary E. Smith

1 Lincoln Ave., Ridgewood, NJ 07100, (201) 670-1000

Objective

I am a seasoned professional with excellent administrative and interpersonal skills and am interested in an executive administrative assistant position.

Experience

1985–2001 IBM Corporation, White Plains, NY

Assistant to the Vice President of Marketing–North America
- Extensive travel arrangements, both domestic and international
- Executive meeting planning and coordination
- Heavy calendar and e-mail correspondence
- Follow-up with staff
- Backup to the Americas Vice President's desk

Executive Secretary to the Director of Marketing–Latin America
- Liaison to Latin America assignees
- Travel coordination in the Americas
- Heavy calendaring, conference calls and meeting planning
- Focal point to Latin America secretaries
- Backup to the Vice President of Marketing desk

Marketing Programs Coordinator
- Coordinate customer and sales force mailings
- Brochure production, inventory and design
- Alumni and prospect databases
- E-mailings to customer representatives

Education

Little Flower Catholic School for Girls–Philadelphia, PA
(academic as well as business curriculum)

Interests

Reading, exercise, tennis, gardening, needlepoint

References

Available upon request.

If you are wondering whether Mary can just update the "Before" résumé and have a chance to interview for what she thinks may be her dream job, the answer is *probably not.*

Mary's "Before" résumé is a chronological, multipurpose document with a broad target. She could find a position with this résumé, but it will be difficult to get an interview at a company that can match her skills, her desire to grow, her interests, and her financial needs. She is doing herself a disservice by not substantially revising her résumé.

Let's take a closer look at the "Before" résumé, section by section.

Contact Information. The leadoff font is different from the text font. The italicized contact information isn't the problem; the clashing fonts are. If you are committed to using italics for the contact information, at least use the same italics type as the text. It makes more sense. She should also remove the comma after the ZIP code (no need to put a comma before a parenthesis). Better yet, though, is to drop the telephone number down to the third line because, in this day and age, providing the prospective employer easy access to you means including more information. What about a cell phone number? An e-mail address should definitely be included.

Focus Statement. Mary's "Objective" is not focused. Instead, it is generic and a bit tired—and doesn't do justice to her extensive experience at a Fortune 500 company. She will, of course, need to revise it in her new résumé to include her current position as an assistant librarian. But if she resorts to a broad cliché instead of vividly describing what she hopes to attain and what she has to offer the prospective employer, chances are most recruiters' eyes will glaze over.

Experience. This is the heart of the "Before" résumé. Mary missed an opportunity to show her increasing responsibilities and promotion. Even though assistant to the vice president of marketing was the most current position she held at the Fortune 500 company (that's why she listed it first), she was promoted from executive secretary to marketing programs coordinator. It's not obvious in the "Before" résumé because Mary decided she preferred working for company movers and shakers to working independently in the marketing department, so she shifted the information around—a valid personal decision. She knows herself best, but for now she needs to highlight her increasing responsibilities and promotion in the résumé so recruiters pay attention. By simply providing dates alongside the three positions listed and moving the marketing programs coordinator position to the second slot, she would highlight the steady progression in her career.

Fortune 500 survey participants made the same point. Sherri Martin, director of human resources at Deere & Company, said she likes a résumé to exhibit "a career history of success demonstrated through advancement." David Murphy, executive vice president at The McGraw-Hill Companies, said that "consistent career development" was one of the three qualities that made a résumé stand out.

As for the bulleted description of Mary's responsibilities, it is brief, which is positive, but the sentences should not be fragments (without verbs). It is more dynamic and action oriented when a verb is used in the bulleted sentences (nouns are not necessary, but periods are). A résumé is not a memo but rather a formal introduction to a new company. Recruiters expect you to be professional by following the writing style typically found in most résumés (see Chapter 4 for more information on this topic).

In addition, the description of Mary's duties is vague when it needs to be specific. Cecilia McKenney, a vice president in human resources at Pepsi Bottling Group, said she expects to see a "clear career progression that shows increasing responsibilities and/or skill organization" in a résumé.

Finally, although many excellent keywords (nouns or short phrases that describe your qualifications and will be picked up if your résumé is scanned) are sprinkled throughout the description of Mary's responsibilities, there is room for more. Cherri Davies, a manager of staffing at Health Net, Inc., said her company "screens résumés submitted by e-mail or URL Web site by keyword searches." Make sure your résumé contains enough keywords to make it past the first round.

Educational Background. Most résumé books recommend that you do not include your high school or incomplete degrees, even though most job seekers feel they must put something in this section. Because Mary does not have a college degree, she lists her high school instead. She could strengthen this section by including any continuing education classes that will be relevant in her new position. She should highlight and expand on her computer know-how. Even though working for a large computer company assumes a certain understanding of technology, recruiters (as well as scanners) are looking for specifics on this front. When asked the number one reason for rejecting résumés, 54 percent of the participants said a "lack of computer skills."

There isn't a consensus for the inclusion of "interests" on résumés. Twenty-one of the Fortune 500 participants said applicants should not include outside interests on a résumé; 7 said to include them only if they were relevant to the job; and 14 said it was valid to include them. The safest bet, then, is to include only those interests that may enhance your performance on the job or are applicable to the position being sought. It will not be a strike against you if you forgo including outside interests. Mary can better further her cause if she elaborates on her technical know-how in the preceding section rather than highlight her outside interests in a separate section.

Finally, it goes without saying that references are "available upon request," so there's no need to include this statement on a résumé.

THE "AFTER" RÉSUMÉ

Now take a look at how the "After" résumé shown in Figure 3.2 is designed and targeted so that it hits the mark for the position Mary is seeking at the book distributorship. Compare the wording in the job posting with the words Mary now uses to describe her qualifications in her new résumé.

As noted in Chapter 1, the Fortune 500 survey participants prefer brief résumés; 74 percent said it should be no more than two pages and 18 percent said it should be no more than one. Mary's résumé did not warrant two pages. Instead, it's a one-page, chronological résumé that highlights what the particular employer needs.

Mary has many talents to offer, but she needed to reposition her information and put more emphasis on the positive. She also had to redesign her résumé so that it exhibited more purpose and logic. Here are the changes that made the difference.

- Uses a Garamond font throughout (14-point, bold italics for the heading, 12-point roman for the text).
- Flushes her heading to the right to counterbalance the document.
- Includes a focus statement that describes herself more fully (but doesn't sound like a cliché) and zeros in on what the prospective employer is seeking.
- Drops the first-person *I* from this statement and follows the style of professional résumés.
- Writes brief, but dynamic, statements that fit on one page—without squeezing in irrelevant information.
- Lists her most current position using keywords *(filing systems, administrative support, conferences)* from the prospective employer's job opening description.
- Uses dynamic verbs to begin the bulleted information *(provided, guided, maintained, scheduled, generated, managed, acted, transcribed)*.
- Uses dates in her description of duties at IBM, showing the progression of increased responsibility.
- Inserts more keywords from the prospective employer's job description in her work history at IBM.

FIGURE 3.2 *Mary Smith's "After" Chronological Résumé*

M a r y   E l e a n o r   S m i t h
100 Lincoln Avenue, Ridgewood, NJ 07100
Home (201) 670-1000 • Cell (201) 670-0001 • E-mail mxsmith@yahoo.com

PROFESSIONAL QUALIFICATIONS: Multitalented, team-oriented and experienced support person with excellent computer and marketing skills who can blend creative, interpersonal, and administrative skills that meet and exceed goals in both a Fortune 500 environment as well as a research organization

2001-Present   **Ridgewood Public Library, Ridgewood, NJ**
Assistant Librarian
- Provide courteous and efficient service to patrons at large public library that is ranked one of the "busiest in county."
- Guide students as well as professionals in research.
- Maintain filing systems and provide backup support to technologist.
- Provide administrative support to library director.
- Schedule classes at Habernickel Technology Training Center.
- Generate publicity for events.

1985-2001   **IBM Corporation, White Plains, NY**
1998-2001   *Assistant to Vice President of Marketing—North America*
- Arranged extensive travel arrangements, domestic and international.
- Coordinated and scheduled executive meetings.
- Managed heavy e-mail correspondence.
- Assumed major responsibility in planning and follow-up with staff.
- Acted as backup to the Americas Vice President's desk.
- Transcribed meeting minutes.
- Met tight deadlines and adept at multitasking.

1993-1998   *Marketing Programs Coordinator*
- Coordinated customer and sales force mailings.
- Produced brochure—supplying text and design—met deadlines.
- Maintained alumni and prospect databases.
- Managed extensive e-mailings to customer representatives.
- Ordered and maintained supplies.

1985-1993   *Executive Secretary to Director of Marketing—Latin America*
- Acted as liaison to Latin America assignees.
- Coordinated all travel schedules and reservations in the Americas.
- Arranged conference calls and meeting planning, with heavy calendaring.
- Teamed with other support personnel to maintain several databases.
- Acted as backup to Vice President of Marketing desk.
- Assisted in preparing agendas and reports for meetings.

PROFESSIONAL DEVELOPMENT AND TRAINING: Selected consistently to attend workshops on time management, marketing, business writing at IBM. Completed HTML and Web Page Design courses at the Habernickel Technology Training Center.
COMPUTER SKILLS: Lotus Notes, Excel, Access, MS Word, WordPerfect. HTML. Familiarity with Adobe Illustrator. Adept at learning new computer skills.

- Drops the reference to her high school and instead accentuates her continuing professional educational development. (The job description says the candidate *should* have some college, not *must*.) The HTML and Web design classes were taken at the library, which is called the Habernickel Technology Training Center.
- Emphasizes her computer skills. Even though her knowledge of Adobe Illustrator (another keyword) is not substantial (she never used it on a daily basis at work nor does she have certification in it), she knows she is adept at learning most computer programs. Mary will enroll in a crash course while she continues her job search.

REACH, DON'T SETTLE

In the recent "jobless recovery," competition is stiff and employers are holding out for candidates who match their requirements exactly. But if your other skills are particularly strong, you should at least apply for a position, even if it is a reach. You never know. You may still get a chance to interview.

Mary has done her research, so she knows this job for which she applied would be a good fit for her. She pursues it, and even if she doesn't get an opportunity to interview for this specific position, she's going to keep this company in her job data file and apply for other openings at the company as they arise. Mary's résumé is in good shape now. All that is necessary is a slight revision for the next job posting to include new keywords and possibly a different objective.

Many Fortune 500 respondents encouraged job applicants to keep plugging away, even after a rejection. In other words, you shouldn't necessarily give up after the first try. Not only does your résumé stay in company databases for an extended period of time, but most Fortune 500 hiring professionals surveyed said they want to see a strong interest from the candidate in working at the company. Going out of your way to get the necessary training the next time you apply for a job is certainly a good indication of your interest in a particular company.

THE FUNCTIONAL RÉSUMÉ

The functional résumé presents an applicant's skill set independently from a work history. Most experts suggest that you include a work history so that the recruiter doesn't think you are hiding important information (gaps in employment, limited experience, or short tenures at previous employers). In an article on Monster.com, Norma Mushkat cited a survey of 2,500 recruiters done by ResumeDoctor.com in which the functional format was listed as one of the ten top peeves. In addition to these drawbacks, a functional format is more difficult to write.

Then why is an example of the functional format included in this book? Simply because it works well for those with unconventional work histories. Take a look at the "Before" and "After" examples in Figure 3.3 and Figure 3.4, which apply to the following scenario.

Mikhail is a data processing consultant specializing in information technology. His background is varied and broad: He has worked as an independent consultant at 28 companies in his 30-year work history. Mikhail's résumé is five pages long—and the chronological format of his "Before" résumé excessively details every assignment he ever had; much of the information is repetitive. When he discovered a position for a senior design analyst on a company Web site, he targeted his résumé for this specific opening. He decided to use a functional format and cut his résumé to two pages.

Although Mikhail knows it's important to include at least a bare-bones listing of the companies he has worked for, he also knows a bulleted list of his top projects would work better than a detailed description of each job. Mikhail pares his résumé to two pages by listing all the companies in a separate section without the detailed descriptions of what he did at each company. Because the prospective employer is a technology firm, he wants to highlight his technical skills. If the company wants more detailed information about his earlier work history, it can refer to Mikhail's Web site, where this information is presented in chronological order. Here is Mikhail's résumé before he revised it.

FIGURE 3.3 *Mikhail's Unrevised Résumé*

Mikhail Okdamir   www.okda.com
1 Palisade Avenue
Union City, NJ 07100
Business: (201) 866-1000
Cell: (201) 866-0001

SUMMARY
Successful data processing professional with years of experience in various areas of information technology. Skilled technologist, organizer. Excellent writing and communication skills.

(continued)

FIGURE 3.3 *(continued)*

SOFTWARE
MQ, CICS, COBOL, COBOL II, LE COBOL, DB2, SPUFI, QMF, VSAM, DOS/VSE, MVS, IDMS, INTERTEST, Viasoft, Xpediter (batch and online), Macro CICS Assembler, Assembler, CEDF, ADS, Easy Test, File-AID, Library Management system, Panvalet, Librarian, Endevor, TSO/SPF, ROSCOE, CMS, SDF, Debug, COMPAREX, MS Word, Visio, HTML, ABC FlowCharter, Windows 98

EXPERIENCE
May 2002-Dec 2002. **HIP NEW YORK.** EPO/PPO. Implementation of new health plan. PHCS Interface project that will expand HIP services beyond tri-state ten counties area. Provider Incentive Checks system. Coordinated interface process with Fleet Bank Interface system to clear Claims Benefits Checks (FTP). Developed technical specifications for Geriatrix system. Various supporting claim processing projects. Generated entries for General Ledger for Provider Incentive checks. Converted user requirements into programming specification. Scheduled new jobs and on request jobs. Coordinated implementation of jobs involving banks. Prepared technical documentation. Production support. Coding and testing.
VSAM, CICS, COBOL, FTP, XPEDITER, JCL (batch and online)

Nov 2000-May 2002. **MORGAN STANLEY INC.** Mutual funds support. Managed and supervised File Expansion project. Developed supporting documentation. Converted user requests into formalized programming specifications. Supported 12B1 process. Interfaced with Trust division that supplied input data for 12B1 process. Scheduled new jobs and ran on-request jobs. Prepared and wrote 12B1 Project overview. Generated vouchers for AP system. Balanced AP vouchers before production run. Followed up on daily production. Prepared reports on production problems for management. Conducted meetings with user to resolve various technical questions associated with requirements. Coding and testing of requested JCL and/or program changes.
CICS, DB2, SPUFI, LE COBOL, COBOL II, MQ, VSAM, VIASOFT, INTERTEST, VISIO, TSO/SPF, JCL, MS WORD

Feb 2000-Oct 2000. **BANK OF TOKYO/MITSUBISHI.** Maintained bank accounting system (IMMS). Constructed accounting vouchers. Developed technical specifications form user requirements. Advised user on usage of new online systems. Developed guidelines to reorganize VSAM files. Specifications for program and/or JCL changes presented for approval and walk through. Developed procedure to add new line printer for printing of checks. Installed supporting software. Coded, tested new programs, program enhancements and/or supporting JCL. Developed process to update and enhance system documentation.
VSAM, DB2, CICS, INTERTEST, COBOL II, MVS/JCL, VISIO, MS WORD

Apr 1997-Dec 1999. **DEAN WITTER REYNOLDS INC.** Mutual funds processing. Developed systems specification from user requirements. Developed backup procedures. Coded and tested major system components. Developed new programs. Participated in Y2K Remediation. Assisted in developing audit trails to prove completeness of Y2K changes. Instructed backup employee on 12B1 changes. Proposed audit trails to prove 12B1 process. Scheduled new jobs for production. Followed up on production moves. Generated proper journal entries for AP system. Balanced and proved voucher file before scheduled implementation. Testing and coding of various proprietary mutual fund programs and/or jobs. Assisted in installation of new developer supporting software (Viasoft).
CICS, DB2, SPUFI, COBOL II, VSAM, VIASOFT, INTERTEST, TSO/SPF, JCL, MS WORD

FIGURE 3.3 *(continued)*

Sept 1996-Mar 1997. **PAINE WEBBER INC.** Developed program specification for Taxlot reconciliation system. Ran ad hoc jobs to support user research. Input files were generated on UNIX platform. Assisted user in developing strategies to process data. All proposed changes presented to management for walk-through. Coded and tested programs and/or supported JCL. Developed required journal entries for AP system. Journals were balanced before added to production. Heavy user interface.
CICS, COBOL II, VSAM, DB2, SPUFI, QMF, TSO/SPF, JCL, MS WORD

Aug 1995-Aug 1996. **PERSHING CO.** Mutual fund support. Client support. Coded and tested major enhancement. Interfaced with users. Developed and prepared service requests for the program and/or JCL changes, which were presented to management for approval. Followed up with user on all new implemented changes. Resolved post implementation problems. Prepared required documentation and changes to user manuals. Tested and coded new programs and/or JCL. Scheduled new jobs for production. Verified jobs dependencies. Generated vouchers for company AP system. Balanced voucher file before production.
CICS (Command), COBOL II, VSAM, DB2, QMF, TSO/SPF, XPEDITER, MS WORD

Feb 1995-Aug 1995. **PETRIE RETAIL CO. SENIOR CONSULTANT.** Major enhancements in Fixed Asset System. Designed new approach to generated audit trails for AP system. Designed enhancements. Presented user with proposed changes. User presentations. Organized/suggested improvements for system documentation.
CICS, VSAM, COBOL, ROSCOE, JCL

Apr 1993-Feb 1995. **MEDCO CONTAINMENT CO. SENIOR CONSULTANT.** Designed online Formulary Rebate system. Prepared specifications for batch process. Prepared presentation for users. Developed screens and written programming specifications. Prepared/suggested improvements for system documentation. Assisted junior level programmers with Batch CICS debugging approaches. Coded new programs and/or new JCL streams and added the changes to existing processes. Tested and debugged. Interfaced with management in presentations and walk through.
DB2, QMF, SPUFI, VSAM, CICS, COBOL II, MVS/JCL, TSO/SPF, XPEDITER, MS WORD

Feb 1993-Apr 1993. **BROWN BROTHERS HARRIMAN. SENIOR CONSULTANT.** Developed programming specifications from user requests. Developed program documentation. Developed process to document program and/or JCL changes. Coded and tested all program and/or JCL changes. Maintained existing. Received and delivered system.
CICS, VSAM, COBOL II, MVS/JCL, TSO/SPF

Dec 1991-Jan 1993. **IBJ SCHRODER BANK. SENIOR CONSULTANT.** Designed and tested interface with IECA. Modified various online programs in Auctions System. Designed and implemented new reporting system for federal government. Applied vendor supplied fixes to Custody and Trust programs (Omnitrust). Journal entries.
VSAM, COBOL II, CICS, ADABAS, MVS/JCL

Sept 1991-Dec 1991. **GE INFORMATION SERVICES. SENIOR CONSULTANT.** Vendor. Presented new strategies for functional design approach. Implementation of Batch file transfer and Mailbox system for major investment bank. Coding and testing new programs and JCL.
COBOL II, VSAM, CICS, INTERTEST, MVS/JCL

(continued)

FIGURE 3.3 *(continued)*

June 1991-Sept 1991. **LEVER BROTHERS. SENIOR CONSULTANT**. Warehouse replenishment system. Prepared user requested activity reports. Presented report layouts. Developed programs and JCL to generate required reports. Developed and proved input file for AP system.
VSAM, CICS, COBOL II, MVS/JCL, TSO/SPF

Apr 1991-June 1991. **DRESSER PUMP INDUSTRIES. PROJECT MANAGER.** Planned and supervised conversion from DOS/VSE to MVS. Conducted technical interviews and assembled project team. Monitored and resolved business and technical problems. Project manager. Coordinated activities of group of 13. Conducted status meetings.
MVS/JCL, VSAM, COBO I, TSO/SPF

June 1990-Apr 1991. **SHARP ELECTRONICS. SENIOR CONSULTANT.** Manufacturing applications, tracking and reconciling custom broker payments. Maintained various projects. Testing and debugging.
IDMS, COBOL II, VSAM, CICS, MVS/JCL, TSO/SPF

Feb 1990-June 1990. **IBM PROFESSIONAL SERVICES. SENIOR CONSULTANT.** Worked on client's site. Insurance applications. Interfaced with management. Coding and testing.
COBOL, ASSEMBLER, CICS (Macro), VSAM, MVS/JCL, TSO/SPF

Oct 1989-Feb 1990. **DEUTCHE BANK. SENIOR CONSULTANT.** Trade entry system. Tax reporting system. Prepared system outline for trade cancellations. Interfaced with management. Coding and testing.
WANG/COBOL

July 1989-Oct 1989. **MERRILL LYNCH CO. SENIOR CONSULTANT.** Worked defining the requirements for various projects. Trained junior personnel. Tested and debugged. Interfaced with management.
COBOL II, VSAM, CICS, MVS/JCL, TSO/SPF

June 1989-July 1989. **ADP CO. SENIOR CONSULTANT.** Worked on various projects. Maintenance. Tested and debugged. Interfaced with management.
ASSEMBLER, VSAM, CICS (Macro), TSO/SPF

Mar 1989-May 1989. **DREXEL BURNHAM LAMBERT CO. SENIOR CONSULTANT.** Worked on the implementation of enhancements for multi-currency processing. Tested and debugged.
VSAM, CICS, COBOL II, MVS/JCL, TSO/SPF

Sept 1987-Feb 1989. **BANK OF TOKYO, SENIOR CONSULTANT.** Vista Security Processing system (VSPS). Project manager responsibilities. Resolved production problems in batch and on-line part of the VSPS system. Planned and supervised conversion of FSPS system from DOS to MVS. Interfaced with software vendor suggesting many quality and/or functional improvements. Applied, coded, and tested many vendor-supplied software bulletins.
VSAM, CICS, COBOL II, MVS/JCL, TSO/SPF

Mar 7-Aug 1987. **VISTA CONCEPTS. SENIOR STAFF CONSULTANT.** Worked on securities processing packages for major banks in USA and Canada. Interfaced with clients in USA and Canada. Assisted in defining client's needs and deliverables. Resolved production problems on client site. Interfaced with corporate management. Suggested changes and improvements.
VSAM, COBOL I, MVS/JCL, TSO/SPF

FIGURE 3.3 *(continued)*

May 1986-Mar 1987. **FIRST BOSTON CO. SENIOR CONSULTANT.** Participated in streamlining and improving the night cycle process. Interfaced with DTC. Coding and testing.
VSAM, COBOL, MVS/JCL, TSO/SPF

Feb 1986-May 1986. **FIRST JERSEY NATIONAL BANK. SENIOR SYSTEMS CONSULTANT.** Participated in the redesigning of stock transfer and accounting systems. Assisted in defining user requirements for CICS-based stock transfer system. Interfaced with DTC. Defined software and hardware requirements for installation of transfer agent software package.
VSAM, COBOL I, ROSCOE

May 1985-Feb 1986. **SHEARSON LEHMAN/AMERICAN EXPRESS. SENIOR SYSTEM ANALYST.** Directed and participated in the design, development and installation of computer-based information systems, Clearance system (Cage Processing). Proposed system improvements and provided various alternatives.
COBOL, VSAM, CICS, TSO/SPF

Nov 1984-May 1985. **SPEAR, LEEDS, & KELLOGG. SENIOR PROGRAMMER/ANALYST.** Participated in the design, development and installation of computer-based information systems. Assisted in conversion of various applications from DOS to MVS. Assisted in the development and implementation of new Clearance systems. Wrote programming specifications.
CICS, IDMS, COBOL, TSO/SPF

Aug 1982-Nov 1984. **BRADFORD TRUST. LEAD PROGRAMMER/ANALYST.** System documentation. Wrote programming specifications. Assisted with production problems. Coding and testing.
VSAM, COBOL I, CICS, MVS/JCL

July 1977-June 1982. **MERRILL LYNCH CO. SENIOR PROGRAMMER/ANALYST.** Designed system improvements and provided various alternatives. Prepared programming specifications. Prepared documentation. Project leadership responsibilities.
CICS, VSAM, ASSEMBLER, COBOL I, TSO/SPF

Feb 1974-June 1977. **PERSHING CO. PROGRAMMER/ANALYST.** Prepared programs as necessary. Participated in system analysis.
ASSEMBLER, ISAM, TSO/SPF

HARDWARE
IBM 303x, IBM 308x, IBM 43xx

EDUCATION
IBM: MQSeries Applications Programming (OS/390); MQSeries Introduction (OS/390)

On-line Software International: CICS Command Level coding: CICS Application design; CICS-VS Debugging and internals

Merrill Lynch Co.: Management training courses. BDAM Assembler Interface, CICS Macro Level coding (Assembler); MVS JCL; VSAM coding (Assembler)

New York University: Business Programmer Certificate, "C" language course

Chubb Institute: Visual Basic 3.0

University of Economics, Ljubljana, Slovenia: Degree in Business Administration & Management (BS)

Mikhail's résumé indicates that he is qualified and multitalented, consulting for 30 years as a programmer/analyst, but that many of his jobs were unrelated. Even though he worked primarily at financial services companies, he needs to point out this common thread in his long history. Mikhail examines the job posting for the new job.

> **Senior Design Analyst:** with proven ability to analyze system components against project requirements and produce general design and program specifications. Must have strong verbal and written communication skills. Proven ability to lead large development projects through all phases of lifecycle with emphasis on testing component.
>
> Extensive experience in IBM mainframe development, including: COBOL, MVS, JCL, Mainframe analysis and debugging tools, such as File-AID, Xpediter, etc. Experience with VM operating system a plus but not a requirement. Experience in Order Processing and/or Market Data systems a strong plus but not a requirement.

Mikhail takes note of certain keywords so that he can include them in his revised résumé. He has all of the qualifications necessary for the new position, but he will have to rearrange his key information to reflect that. Let's take a closer look at the "Before" résumé, section by section:

Contact Information. Name, address, and telephone and cell numbers are listed, and, in addition, Mikhail has included a URL to his Web site. He may want to rearrange the contact information so that it doesn't look so lopsided. A flush-left design works well for electronic transmittals of a résumé, but a more balanced distribution of Mikhail's contact information will save space. He will include an e-mail address in the "After" résumé.

Focus Statement. Mikhail's summary does not define the type of position he is seeking nor does it tell the employer what he has to offer. Instead, it is a tired description of just about any garden-variety programmer/analyst. Nothing in this statement stands out to grab an employer's attention. As with Mary's focus statement in her "Before" example, his target is too wide and doesn't anticipate what the employer needs. When he revises this focus statement, he will include keywords as well as highlight his expertise.

Technical Summary. Because Mikhail is a technology professional, he includes a technical summary so prospective employers don't have to search for this expertise. He lists only those programs and applications that he is prepared to talk about in an interview. In the revised résumé, he will move the hardware reference into the technical summary with software.

Professional Experience. The chronological listing is too duty oriented. More emphasis should be placed on measurable outcomes, his leadership skills, and his problem-solving abilities. Throughout his career Mikhail supported, maintained, developed, designed, and implemented systems. The progression of responsibility is hard to find in his description of duties. Repositioning this information will make it easier to read, especially by HR professionals who may not have technical backgrounds. The hiring manager with a technical background can always refer to Mikhail's Web site for a more detailed and chronological description of his background.

Educational Background. Mikhail graduated with a degree from a foreign university but gives the U.S. equivalent (bachelor of science) so employers are not confused. He also lists his certifications, which are especially important for technologists, as they reveal that his knowledge of systems is current. Because he is not a recent graduate (within the last five years), it is not necessary to provide dates in this section. Mikhail has managed to pare the five-page résumé down to two pages using the functional format, emphasizing his skills and accomplishments. Now let's look at the "After" résumé.

Mikhail is a seasoned professional who fits nicely into the prospective employer's opening. He has whittled away the superfluous and repetition, cutting his five-page résumé down to two without sacrificing any key information. Here are the changes that made the difference.

- He uses an Arial font throughout—at full justification. The "After" résumé easily converts into an electronic version when necessary.
- He uses bullets and rules to separate and add balance.
- His focus statement is no longer run-of-the-mill. Instead, he picks up keywords from the prospective employer and inserts them into his own Qualifications Summary.
- His personal achievements are basically the same as they were in his chronological résumé, but now he opens his bulleted information with dynamic verbs *(defined, redesigned, planned, prepared, designed, participated, tested, developed, constructed, managed, and implemented)*.
- His work history is included but in a separate section. It doesn't make sense for an independent contractor to make his work history the focus of the résumé.
- His hardware and software expertise are grouped together. Employers, especially technical or scientific ones, want to see that employees' skills are

FIGURE 3.4 *Mikhail's Revised Functional Résumé*

Mikhail Okdamir
1 Palisade Avenue
Union City, NJ 07100

Telephone: (201) 866-1000, Cell (201) 866-0001, E-mail: MO111@optonline.net
Website: www.okda.com

QUALIFICATIONS:

Self-motivated and experienced senior design analyst with proven track record in design, testing, specifications, development, and enhancement of systems. Adept at solving complex technical problems and communicating to management or team leader status of assignment, including project timelines, issues, and contingencies. Highly skilled technologist with excellent communication and leadership skills can move projects through lifecycle in Financial Services sector

TECHNICAL SUMMARY:

Software MQ, CICS, COBAL COBAL II, LE COBAL, DB2, SPUFI, QMF, VSAM, DOS/VSE, MVS, IDMS, INTEREST, Viasoft, Xpediter (batch and online), Macro CICS Assembler, Assembler, CEDF, ADS, Easy Test, File-AID, Library Management system, Panvalet, Librarian, Endevor, TSO/SPF, ROSCOE, CMS, SDF, Debug, COMPAREX, MS Word, Visio, HTML, ABC FlowCharter, Windows 98.
Hardware IBM 303x, IBM 308x, IBM 43xx

PROFESSIONAL ACHIEVEMENTS:

• Developed technical specifications and guidelines to reorganize VSAM files. Developed program specification for Taxlot reconciliation system. Developed and prepared service requests that were presented to management for approval.
• Managed and supervised File Expansion project while developing supporting documentation. Developed technical specifications.
• Defined software and hardware requirements for installation of transfer agent software. Interfaced with users. Coded and tested all program and/or JCL changes.
• Constructed accounting vouchers and maintained bank accounting system (IMMS). Coded and tested new programs to update and enhance system documentation. Developed supporting documentation.
• Planned and supervised conversion from DOS/VSE to MVS. Conducted technical interviews and assembled project team.
• Participated in Y2K remediation while assisting in developing audit trails to prove completeness of Y2K changes. Instructed backup employee on 12B1 changes. Interfaced with management in presentations and walk-through.

FIGURE 3.4 *(continued)*

- Designed new approach to generated audit trails for AP system. Designed enhancements and organized user presentations.
- Prepared specifications for batch process while assisting junior level programmers with Batch CICS debugging approaches. Coded new programs and/or new JCL streams and added changes to existing processes.
- Redesigned stock transfer and accounting systems while defining user requirements for CICS-based stock transfer system.
- Technical know-how needed for last three positions: VSAM, CICS, FTP, XPEDITER, JCL (batch and online) CICS, DB2, SPUFI, LE COBOL, COBOL II, MQ, VSAM, VIASOFT, INTERTEST, VISIO, TSO/SPF, JCL, MS WORD, MVS/JCL, VISIO, FILE-AID

WORK HISTORY:
HIP (New York) May 2002 to December 2002; **Morgan Stanley,** November 2000 to May 2002; **Bank of Tokyo/Mitsubishi,** February to October 2000; **Dean Witter Reynolds,** April 1997 to December 1999; **Paine Webber,** September 1996 to March 1997; **Pershing Co.,** August 1995 to August 1996; **Petrie Retail,** February 1995 to August 1995; **Medco Containment Company,** April 1993 to February 1995; **Brown Brothers Harriman,** February 1993 to April 1993; **IBJ Schroder Bank,** December 1991 to January 1993; **GE Information Services,** September 1991 to December 1991; **Lever Brothers,** June 1991 to September 1991; **Dresser Pump Industries,** April 1991 to June 1991; **Sharp Electronics,** June 1990 to April 1991; **IBM Professional Services,** February 1990 to June 1990; **Deutche Bank,** October 1989 to February 1990; **Merrill Lynch Co.,** July 1989 to October 1989; **ADP Co.,** June 1989 to July 1989; **Drexel Burnham Lambert,** March 1989 to May 1989; **Bank of Tokyo,** September 1987 to February 1989; **Vista Concepts,** March 1987 to August 1987; **First Boston Co.,** May 1986 to March 1987; **First Jersey National Bank,** February 1986 to May 1986; **Shearson Lehman/American Express,** May 1985 to February 1986; **Spear, Leeds & Kellogg,** November 1984 to May 1985; **Bradford Trust,** August 1982 to November 1984; **Merrill Lynch,** July 1977 to June 1982; **Pershing Co.,** February 1974 to June 1977

EDUCATION AND CERTIFICATION:
IBM: MQSeries Applications Programming (OS/390); MQSeries Introduction (OS/390)
Online Software International: CICS Command Level coding; CICS application design; CICS-VS debugging and internals
Merrill Lynch: Management training courses; BDAM Assembler Interface, CICS Macro Level coding (Assembler); MVS JCL; VSAM coding (Assembler)
New York University: Business programmer certificate; "C" language course
Chubb Institute: Visual Basic 3.0
University of Economics, Ljublijana, Slovenia: Degree in Business Administration and Management (Bachelor of Science equivalent)

current. In his "Before" résumé, it was evident that Mikhail had used certain computer languages recently and that's why it was necessary for him to supplement this information in the certification section.

- All relevant information is accessible and accurate. Mikhail double-checks the spelling of technical information by Googling all hardware and software terminology.
- The functional format is logical and purposeful, exhibiting balance, consistent pattern, and good design.
- Finally, this "After" résumé is much easier to read because Mikhail has eliminated irrelevant information and cut the five pages down to two while still retaining important keywords.

Now you have to decide which format works best for your work history. Even though a chronological format is preferred by hiring professionals, some work histories just won't fit this mold, calling for a functional format instead. Whichever one you choose, though, make sure your résumé conforms to these guidelines.

- Double-check for accuracy. Run it through the spell checker—twice. Ask for objective feedback from outsiders. Your sentences should be direct and brief. Do not exceed two pages in length unless absolutely necessary.
- Make sure you emphasize your accomplishments rather than your responsibilities.
- All of your dates should be accurate and specific.
- Include all contact information, including an e-mail address.
- Make sure you are qualified for the position you are applying for.

WHAT DO EMPLOYERS WANT?

Knowing what an employer wants helps you to design your résumé so that it reflects the employer's needs. To paraphrase a particularly helpful summary of what is typically valued by employers, reported in Susan Britton Whitcomb's book *Résumé Magic* (see "Resources" at end of book), your résumé should illustrate that you can help a company to make money, save time, make work easier, be more competitive, build relationships, expand business, attract new customers, and/or retain customers. If your résumé exhibits these eight qualities (or at least a few of them), you have a good shot at getting that interview.

4

WRITING THAT WORKS

"Be clear and honest and articulate your experience well."

CHRIS COLLIER
Group Manager, Georgia-Pacific

Good communication skills top the list of nearly every employer when considering prospective applicants, so don't underestimate the importance of making sure that *all* your communication with a potential employer is clear, dynamic, and accurate—whether it's the initial e-mail, a résumé, a job application, or a cover letter. You don't get many second chances when applying for a job.

In the Fortune 500 survey, this point was stressed again and again. There is no room for error or inaccuracy in your first introduction—which is usually your résumé with the attached cover letter—to a company.

Hundreds of people may be vying for one job, which means that part of what human resources professionals do is disqualify candidates. They have to narrow the talent pool, so a spelling or grammatical error simplifies the process for them. In most cases, a résumé with errors goes immediately to the unwanted pile, which is why you must make every effort to hone and perfect all your written communication with a prospective employer. Even the most talented and inventive research scientist won't get the chance to light up the Bunsen burner if his or her résumé and cover letter are hurriedly put together and riddled with inaccuracies and/or errors.

For some, writing well is a tall order because their strengths lie in other areas. For those of you who fall into this category, don't be discouraged. Accept the fact that you will have to master this shortcoming—at least as far as résumés and cover letters go. Luckily, it's not as difficult as it seems. The place to start, once again, is with your research.

THE MIND-SET

When you research potential companies, think about your career goals, and then carefully write your résumé and cover letters, you gain the ability to wrap your words around those career goals. One of the problems with many résumés is their lack of focus; in fact, it may be downright unclear what an applicant actually wants.

Job seeking can be stressful under the best of circumstances. Instead of thinking reasonably about the reality of finding a job, some people muddle through—mixing up the advice they got from their uncles in retail with the suggestions they got from the career counselors at the employment center. Clear thinking—which is earmarked by purpose and thoughtfulness—gives way to automatic survival mode. Many applicants copy a résumé that suits their needs, plug in the pertinent information, dash it off to a prospective employer, and hope for the best. They don't take the time to discover what their skills and accomplishments are and how best to match them with an employer.

You may not subscribe to Freudian theory, but Sigmund knew what he was talking about when he said the two ingredients for happiness are meaningful love and meaningful work. So take the time to discover what your skills and accomplishments are and to decide how you can be of service to a prospective employer. Once you do that, you're ready to proceed.

FINDING THE RIGHT WORDS

When conducting your job research, take note of key phrases and words that will be useful in targeting your job. Besides helping you with keywords for your résumé, another plus to doing research is that you begin to adopt those phrases and words as your own—to discover the language and style of your profession. To communicate effectively to prospective employers, you need to know how to reach them in language they understand. Research helps you communicate on a prospective employer's level. Every profession has its own idioms, so you should make an effort to learn them.

Learning a profession's idioms is accomplished by reading trade journals, "Googling" topics specific to your field, and scouring company Web sites. You start to pick up the current lingo related to your profession—and you store all this information for later use. In a May 6, 2003, article in the *Wall Street Journal* directed at people returning to the workforce after an extended absence, it was suggested that "re-entry candidates sprinkle a résumé with the latest buzzwords for a targeted occupation. Doing so shows they know what's hot and helps a company computer scanner catch key phrases." This suggestion is actually valid for any individual applying for a new job. If you haven't done so already, adopt the current language of your profession. Make it your own and use it in your résumé and cover letters.

THE TOOLS

Don't assume anything when it comes to writing. Even the best writers make mistakes. Before you begin to revise your key information, take the dictionary off the shelf and put it next to your coffee cup—just in case you need it. (If you prefer online resources, use the online edition of *Merriam-Webster's Collegiate Dictionary* at www.m-w.com or the online edition of *The American Heritage Dictionary* at www.bartleby.com). Up-to-date dictionaries are indispensable—one of the best investments you can make, provided you use them. Invest in a hard copy of either *Merriam Webster's Collegiate Dictionary* (11th edition) or *The American Heritage Dictionary of the English Language* (4th edition).

Just think of the technology revolution. A plethora of new words is introduced into the language, and everyone has to scramble to find the right way to use the terminology. For example, *Web site* or *e-mail* or *Internet* can be handled in a variety of ways; you may wonder if you should capitalize *Web site* and *Internet* or use a hyphen for *e-mail*. If you refer to a dictionary, the first reference (or spelling) is the preferred reference, but that doesn't mean everyone is on the same page. Your dictionary (if it even has the term) might say that the preferred spelling is to lowercase *web site,* whereas you notice that the copy on the Web site of the prospective company you're applying to uppercases the term. What are you supposed to do?

Follow the company's preference, so if the company capitalizes the *W* in *Web site,* then do the same. If the company lowercases *website* and considers it one word, then write *website.* (Be careful, however, not to use any of the company Web site's misspellings.) Granted, this is a small detail, but it points to a larger issue. A prospective employer wants to know if you are going to fit into the company's culture—that is, the way the company does things. Usually, your résumé and cover letter are the company's first glimpse of you, so put your best foot forward.

The good news is that you have a unique opportunity to discover whether you want to work at the new organization by visiting the company Web site. Thanks to the Internet, job applicants can now easily access all kinds of information about a prospective company. (Of course, for those of you who were preoccupied during the technology revolution, you can still do it the old-fashioned way—without the computer—but it's going to take you a lot longer.)

Another valuable tool is a stylebook. Although few nonprofessional writers are familiar with this handy resource, it is an invaluable addition. Stylebooks simplify the writing process by presenting in a straightforward manner the dos and don'ts of both style and grammar.

Which stylebooks are the best? It depends on your field, because writing styles vary from one profession to the next. For instance, those in the health professions use the *American Medical Association Manual of Style: A Guide for Authors and Editors;* those in science use *Council of Biology Editors Style Manual;* those in writing or academic professions use *The Chicago Manual of Style.* Find out if there is one stylebook that is used specifically in your field.

For those who need a more general—and usually simpler—stylebook, examine the following resources: *The Associated Press Stylebook and Libel Manual; The New York Times Manual of Style and Usage;* or, for business, *The Business Style Handbook: An A-to-Z Guide for Writing on the Job with Tips from Communications Experts at the Fortune 500.*

When you do get hired for the job, there's a good chance—in the digital age—that you're going to have to write an e-mail, memo, letter, or report, so having good resources (a current dictionary and stylebook) are an imperative.

THE STYLE AND VOCABULARY

Résumé writing is primarily about verbs: what action you performed while working. That's one of the reasons why almost every résumé book has a list of verbs to use in your résumé. To get into the writing mode, examine the verbs shown in the sidebar to see how they apply to what you did in your former positions and what you want to do.

Your particular profession probably has a few verbs of its own, so make sure you jot them down while doing your research. It's essential for prospective employers to think of you as a doer as well as an insider. One way to ensure an impression of doer is through the verbs you select to use.

Remember to use the correct *tense.* In your focus statement, use verbs in the present or future tense if you are describing what you can do for the prospective employer. In your professional experience section, use verbs in the present tense for your current position and the past tense for your earlier (past) experience, and try to remain consistent in your use of tense. Whenever possible, write in the simple present or past tense unless you are trying to convey a specific time sequence.

Personal pronouns *(I),* adjectives and articles *(a, the)* should take a back seat when writing a résumé.

- **Personal pronouns:** Although a common mistake, personal pronouns should not appear on your résumé. Instead of saying *I did this* or *I did that,* your

> ### **T** *u r n   i n t o   a* **D** *o e r*
>
> achieved, acquired, administered, allotted, analyzed, assisted, authored, automated, balanced, bought, branded, budgeted, calculated, completed, controlled, coordinated, conducted, converted, coordinated, created, decided, delivered, designed, developed, devised, discovered, divested, doubled, earned, economized, elected, eliminated, established, eradicated, exceeded, executed, expanded, figured, financed, gained, gave, grew, headed, helped, identified, implemented, increased, improved, invented, installed, instructed, introduced, initiated, led, limited, maintained, managed, minimized, motivated, operated, optimized, organized, originated, played, positioned, prepared, prioritized, projected, promoted, purchased, recovered, recruited, redesigned, reduced, relocated, researched, restructured, revamped, reviewed, revised, saved, scored, selected, served, streamlined, supervised, surpassed, tailored, taught, trained, verified, won, wrote

sentences have an implied subject. HR professionals know *you* managed the development staff, but to conform to résumé style, drop the *I* and write instead, *Managed the development staff.* And as Sherri Rest, a manager of staffing and solutions at Lucent Technologies, said, "Don't refer to yourself in the third person" either.

- *Adjectives:* Save these descriptive words for your thesis or future novel. The Fortune 500 participants stated, again and again, that they prefer résumés that are concise. Making every word count eliminates the temptation to hype or exaggerate. Sherry Rest goes on to say: "Don't try to be clever with your résumé. Just present the facts." And the facts won't be found in your adjectives; the facts are in your nouns and verbs.

- *Articles:* Space is limited on a résumé, so don't include all the possible articles. Write *worked in research department* instead of *worked in the research department.* Brevity is essential in résumés, even if your résumé sounds clipped. Kenneth Garrett of FMC Corporation advised keeping your résumé "crisp, uncluttered, and to the point."

UPPERCASE OR LOWERCASE?

You have probably noticed that the initial letters of job titles are lowercased throughout the text of this book. Follow a different style, however, for your résumés and cover letters. Job titles or descriptions are uppercased: Assistant Vice President, Customer Service Representative, Senior Analyst, Assistant Buyer,

Account Executive, Administrative Assistant. Company names are always upper-cased, but another deviation from mainstream style in résumés is that company departments—marketing, finance, sales, communications, accounting, human resources, editorial, and so on—are often uppercased as well. However you handle department names, remember to be consistent. (Make sure the spelling of company names is correct. Go to a company Web site for this information or go online to www.hoovers.com for the complete name as well as the address of larger companies.)

KNOW YOUR AUDIENCE

Effective writers know their audience. In the case of résumés, your audience will initially be human resources professionals and, ultimately, the head of the department where you want to work. Understand what your audience knows about the subject and the level of detail they will need to make an informed decision. You have 20 years' experience in systems, but your readers may have only a cursory knowledge.

Cut through the inessential and write so that everyone who comes in contact with your résumé can understand what you're saying. Time and again, the Fortune 500 participants emphasized that you need to be "clear." Complex technical detail may be absolutely clear to you, but will your audience understand? That's your challenge: to make them understand what you want and what you can do for them. John Tomerlin, a vice president in human resources at Enterprise, recommended in the survey that you should "be concise in your wording of your résumé."

One of the best tests for clarity is to show your résumé to another individual and ask for feedback. Whether it's a coworker, friend, spouse, or mother, ask if your descriptions are clear. In fact, ask several people and try not to be defensive when you get their feedback. Everyone needs an editor—*everyone*.

EMPHASIZING THE POSITIVE

Cecilia McKenney of Pepsi said you should be able to "sell yourself," but you won't be able to if you're stuck on all your shortcomings. Stop worrying about the gap in your work history or your lack of a graduate degree or your lackluster performance at your last job. Think instead of how you can turn a negative into a positive. Were you an active member of your library expansion board while you looked for work after a downsizing? Did you take continuing education courses to brush up on your computer skills? Did you learn a valuable lesson after your company went bankrupt? This is what employers want to hear about. If there's any one place where you should accentuate the positive, it's on your résumé.

VERIFIABLE HONESTY

Remember those Lincolnesque virtues of simplicity and humility referred to earlier. Another virtue that should be added to these is *honesty*. Part of a human resources professional's job description is to be able to detect exaggerated claims, hype, or downright lies on résumés. No matter what you think to the contrary, it is *not* all right to inflate your résumé. In the same *New York Times* essay where the Lincolnesque virtues were mentioned, David Brooks wrote: "Now things have calmed down. . . . [Instead, there's a] need to actually execute and finish your strategies, rather than just develop grand visions and capitalize in earth-shaking revolutions."

When surveyed, 50 percent of the Fortune 500 participants said they "always" verify information on résumés, but that doesn't mean the other 50 percent don't; they just do it at a later stage. Gary Moore, a recruiting director at Dollar General Corporation, verifies all information "prior to making an offer."

You may be wondering how you're supposed to "accentuate the positive" and "sell yourself" while still staying honest. Don't confuse a positive attitude with dishonesty—there *is* a difference. When you write your résumé, it's acceptable to say that you *plan* to increase sales by 20 percent, but it's not all right to say you did increase sales by 20 percent. It's perfectly acceptable to not mention your lack of a college degree, but don't say you have an MBA when you don't.

WHERE TO BEGIN?

Start with the information you put together earlier for your résumé: contact information, focus statement, professional experience, skills summary (if you do a functional résumé), and education. Let's start with the obvious: making sure that the key information is absolutely free of error.

Now take a look at your contact information again. Have you included your name, address, telephone number, cell number (if applicable), e-mail address, URL—and any other piece of information that's useful to a human resources professional? Is every letter and every digit correct?

This may sound mundane, but human resources professionals can attest to the fact that errors actually do crop up in the contact section of the résumé. Sherri Martin, a director of human resources at Deere & Company, said that the information on your résumé must be "100 percent error free" before it is even considered. Don't rush. Take two extra minutes to go over this information one more time.

ADDING FOCUS

An effective focus statement tells an employer what you are seeking and how you can help the company. This is the section of your résumé that you will tweak again and again, depending on the targeted position. You may call it by another name *(career objective, expertise, accomplishments, professional qualifications)*, but its aim is to zero in on a particular job and explain how you are the best match for that position.

Writing the focus statement shouldn't be difficult because you have already thought about who you are and what you want to do in your career—as well as how you can be of service to a prospective employer. Focus statements are your way of cutting through the superfluous: the ifs, ands, buts, and maybes of the job search. By the time you are ready to revise the earlier focus statement in your job search data file, you have narrowed your options and decided what it is you want from the employer. According to Janie Lopez, a human resources consultant at Tesoro Petroleum Corporation: "You must be specific on what you are looking for." A mere listing of your responsibilities at your former job won't hit the appropriate target in today's market.

When writing the focus statement, plan to write a few sentences that anticipate what the prospective employer needs as well as what you hope to accomplish at your future position. Your focus statement, according to the Office of Career Services at Ohio University, should "present evidence to the employer that you have the skills and knowledge necessary to perform the job."

If you're worried that your focus statement will limit your opportunities, especially if you haven't figured out exactly what it is you want to do, then you're right. To get a good job in today's economy, you have to examine your qualifications and experience to see how they will be used for a specific position. The Ohio University 2002 Career Services article continues: "A vague [focus statement] will be interpreted by employers as a lack of direction and self-knowledge."

Take, for example, this technology officer's focus statement:

Focus Statement: Senior information technology professional with more than 20 years' experience seeks management position in high-tech firm. Willing to relocate.

The above focus statement needs an overhaul for the following reasons:

- It lacks specificity.
- It undervalues the IT professional's skill and experience.
- It doesn't tell the hiring manager what the IT professional can do for the company.
- It lacks energy.
- If fails to utilize terminology from the IT profession.

So how do you improve the statement? Begin by describing yourself with your current job title (reflecting also the position you are seeking). Tell the employer what you know or what your personal strengths are—and how these skills can benefit the employer. Be specific about your background. Make sure your work history, which will be listed in your professional experience section, can back up these claims. Here's the new focus statement:

> **Focus Statement:** Senior information technology professional with extensive experience managing large-scale development projects. Personal strengths focus on understanding business objective, organizing teams, and delivering solutions. Highly developed skills in leadership, specifically in areas of staff and project management, organizational planning, budgeting and staff development, and development of best practices policies

Are focus statements required on every résumé? No, there are times when it is impossible to include one because of space limitations. In that case, you must show your focus in your cover letter. (Fortune 500 hiring professionals suggest all résumés be accompanied by a cover letter, especially if they don't have a focus statement.) What if the prospective employer asks you to skip the cover letter and send an e-mail version of your résumé and there's absolutely no room for a focus statement on it? Writing a focus statement is still a valuable exercise. Somewhere along the way in the hiring process, your future employer will want to know what you know and how that experience will help him or her. So take the time to write a focus statement—even if you believe you will never have a chance to put it on your résumé or cover letter.

You may have to continually tweak the focus statement while job seeking. Obviously, you have more skills and accomplishments than you are able to list in the statement. What skills and accomplishments you do highlight depends on the position you are seeking. In one focus statement you might highlight the marketing skills you acquired five years ago, and in another focus statement you might emphasize your ability to meet writing deadlines. Again, it depends on the job opening at the company.

When you look at a job posting or classified advertisement, pay close attention to the words and phrasing because you can use this language in your focus statement. Provided that you have the skills asked for and meet the other requirements, the words and phrasing are going to help you make the right match with an employer. If you're still at a loss for words, log on to Google for a job title and look at several job descriptions. Pick and choose phrasing and sentences that match your qualifications and then rework and paraphrase those sentences into a focus statement that resembles what you have to offer. Doing that can at least point you in the right direction.

TECHNICAL SUMMARY

If you're writing a functional or technical résumé, it's recommended that you include a technical summary. It's also a good idea to place it below your focus statement so that HR professionals don't have to search for it. (You can, however, place it wherever it looks best if you're certain a computer is scanning your résumé.) Writing a technical summary is easy because it's a straightforward account of your skills. The important thing to remember is that you spell everything correctly. (A computer scanner, for example, may miss your reference to *Xpediter* if you spell it *Expediter*.)

The Microsoft Careers newsletter of April 2003 advised that technology professionals should do this:

> Break the section into subcategories so the reader can quickly scan through your knowledge of programs and applications. Possible categories include technical certifications, hardware, operating systems, networking protocols, office productivity, programming languages, Web applications and database applications. Only list programs/applications that you could confidently discuss in an interview.

ADDING ZEST TO PROFESSIONAL EXPERIENCE

The section describing an applicant's professional experience is the heart of any résumé. It should back up every claim you make to a prospective employer. If you use a chronological format, it tells the employer where you worked and for how long. Make sure this information is accurate; you should include the name and address of past employers (street address is not necessary) along with your tenure there (month and year are sufficient). According to a 2002 Beta Research study featured in the *New York Times,* "Three years with a previous employer is the average length of time considered to indicate loyalty." If you have a short tenure at a few jobs, don't highlight your dates by putting them in first position or in boldface. Placement of this information will depend on the design you use, but the first line should contain the following information:

June 1980–May 1990   Whitney Communications   New York, NY

The next few lines should provide a little more detail. Let the employer know what results you had. (Numbers are always welcome.) If you were promoted, say so. If you streamlined the department, here's the place to tout it. If you never missed a deadline, that's remarkable as well. These accomplishments can be in a bulleted list or in paragraph form.

June 1980–May 1990 **Senior Editor** Whitney Communications, New York, NY
- Wrote monthly column that generated more feedback from readers than any other column.
- Established good relationships with writers and acquired news/articles for features.
- Proofed and copyedited (from manuscripts to blues) for 100-page magazine.
- Met tight deadlines.
- Promoted from assistant editor (1982) to associate editor (1984) to managing editor (1986) to senior editor (1990).

Just a reminder: Start this information with verbs (in the present tense if it describes a current position and the past tense if it describes past experience), and because the subject is implied, you end with a period after each bulleted item.

THE LEARNING CURVE

Whether you're a college graduate or not, list any information in this section that tells the employer you're a learner. In an ongoing series in *Investor's Business Daily* (January 10, 2003), fourth on the ten top secrets to success was "Never Stop Learning."

Your certifications and degrees should be positioned in the education section. If you graduated within the last five years and your work history is minimal or nonexistent, your education should get top billing on your résumé. A grade point average above 3.0 on a 4.0 scale should also be listed. If you are fluent in languages, this is the place to mention it. List any advanced classes, especially those that are relevant to the current position you are seeking.

The competition for a job is stiff, so make sure you've sharpened your key information. Even though more than 4 million people a day are looking for a job online, your key information is ready to hit its mark because you have thought long and hard about your career goals and you're ready to tell an employer just how you can be of service. You already know what you want and what you have to offer.

COVER LETTERS

*"The purpose of a cover letter is to summarize the person's relevant experience,
to express interest in the position, and to demonstrate writing ability."*

LISA WHITTINGTON
Director of Human Resources, Host Marriott Corporation

In the electronic job market, cover letters are nearly passé. Of the 50 Fortune 500 participants, only 11 said cover letters are attached to every résumé. It's too bad because applicants miss an opportunity to display their strengths—the accomplishments and abilities that never make it onto the résumé because of space limitations.

If it weren't for a cover letter, Martin Ward of Glen Rock, New Jersey, an IT manager at a major brokerage firm, might still be looking for a job. After his company downsized, laying off several hundred employees in the first quarter of 2001, Ward found himself without a job and stuck in the middle of "the longest job hiring slump since the Depression" (*New York Times,* June 15, 2003). He networked with friends, business associates, family, and headhunters. He e-mailed his résumé to a hundred openings and even sought the help of an Internet job search firm, which reminded him—for a $100 fee—that everyone was in pretty much the same leaky boat.

After following one false employment lead after another, Ward suddenly remembered a comment made in passing by a senior manager at his former brokerage firm: "If you ever need anything, give me a call," the IT manager said to Ward just before he left for his new job.

Ward, who is part of the growing phenomenon known as "boomerang employees" (those who return to work for a former employer), didn't pick up the telephone, but he did sit down and write a cover letter (with a résumé attached). He reminded the senior manager (who had now moved up in the firm) that they had worked on a project together—a project that had added value to the firm and whose success was still being felt today. The senior manager, who now had more than 40,000 people reporting to him, sent it down the hiring channel that had been previously closed to Ward. Ward's résumé got into the right hiring authority's hands, and he returned to the major brokerage firm several weeks later despite a "formal HR hiring freeze."

Without a cover letter, there's a chance that Ward's résumé would have spun around aimlessly in cyberspace's black hole. Granted, he did network, but it could have taken him twice as long to find his current position. In a way that a casual telephone call or an impromptu breakfast meeting couldn't, Ward's cover letter showed that he was indeed interested in returning to his former company. By committing to paper the value he added to the company while he was there, Ward convinced his old employer that he still had a lot to contribute.

THE FORMAT TO FOLLOW

Even though many Fortune 500 companies don't require it, cover letters *are* read. Jackie Coburn, a staffing manager at Federal-Mogul, said, "Only if I have an interest in the candidate do I read the cover letter," but 40 percent of the Fortune 500 participants said they "always" read the cover letter first. So what goes into a cover letter? Carol Eubank, a human resources manager at Aquila, Inc., said a cover letter should be a "quick summary of why you want the job and how your qualifications match the requirements."

Don't think that Eubank means you can dash off an e-mail in a heartbeat and be done with it. You have to put some effort and professionalism into a cover letter. In fact, 84 percent of the Fortune 500 participants said they expect applicants to adhere to the same standards they would if they were writing a formal letter (only two participants said e-mailed cover letters are more informal). One of those participants, Stacy Harshman of Albertson's, who maintains that e-mailed cover letters are more informal, said her expectation of an electronic cover letter is to "introduce the person and give an idea where the applicant received information about the company."

But what are the expectations of the other 84 percent of the Fortune 500 hiring professionals? Let's start with the format first. You can simplify your life by using block style for all your correspondence. (There's no indentation with block.) Here's the rudimentary arrangement: your address, the date, the employer's address, salutation, body, closing—all flush left.

A reminder about stationery: When searching for a job, you should invest in high-quality stationery. (Even if the application process takes place entirely online, you still need a résumé in hard copy for interviews—and also a few extra copies to carry around in your briefcase in case you run into an old colleague.) Make sure you have enough crisp, neutral paper for both the résumés and cover letters, and to further polish your professional image, it's a good idea to purchase matching envelopes. (If you have your contact information professionally printed on the stationery, don't put this information elsewhere in your cover letter.)

Examine the format and notice the placement of information: your address, date, the employer's address, the salutation, the body, the closing. Avoid short-cutting this style. Prospective employers want to see, at the very least, that you are familiar with the basics of business correspondence, so include all of this information, and—here's the difficult part—make sure it fits on one page. Time is in short supply these days, so no matter what, strive to be concise (try not to exceed 250 to 350 words). According to the participants, "neatness" also counts.

Let's look at some of the style features, beginning with the design. Remember there is nothing casual about the process of searching for a job. To be a consummate professional, all your communication must be formal, unless, of course, you are asking your best friend for a job.

The cover letter is in a block format, which means all information aligns along the left margin (no worry about indentation or tabs). It's centered on the page, with an equal amount of spacing on the top as well as the bottom. A line of spacing is used to separate paragraphs, except after your closing, which should get four lines to accommodate your signature (in black or blue pen).

Let's review some technicalities first. In the name and address section, include your courtesy title, which will either be Mr. or Ms. Instead of spelling out the state's name, use the postal service's two-letter (no periods) abbreviation; in the body of the text, spell out the state's name (Baltimore is one of the cities that can stand alone without a state name—check a style reference for stand-alone cities). In the employer's address, also include a courtesy title or professional title (Mr., Ms., Dr.). Using a department name will ensure that your letter gets to the appropriate hiring authority. Department names are capitalized in an address. Then use the full, legal name of the company. After the salutation, use a colon, not a comma. After your complimentary closing, use a comma.

Now let's look at the body of the letter. At its most basic, it should tell the employer where you heard about the position; it should tell the employer what position you are interested in; it should reinforce the idea that you are qualified for the job; and it should tell the employer how to contact you. Make sure your cover letter is written to a specific individual (never send a cover letter "To Whom It May Concern").

But there are a few more things a cover letter can accomplish, provided it's done well. Think of a cover letter as a means of furthering your cause beyond the résumé. So how does Carol Nadata's cover letter in Figure 5.1 do just that?

FIGURE 5.1 *Carol Nadata's Cover Letter*

Ms. Carol Nadata   **YOUR ADDRESS**
100 Grindall Street
Baltimore, MD 21100

May 1, 2004   **DATE**

Mr. Robert Leonard   **EMPLOYER'S ADDRESS**
Sales Department
Consolidated Finishing Corporation
100 Pennsylvania Avenue
Washington, DC 21100

Dear Mr. Leonard: **SALUTATION**

BODY   I recently read the *Baltimore Sun* profile of your company (April 28, 2004) and noticed
that you are expanding your business into the Baltimore area. I am sure you will need
accomplished account executives to increase your presence in this area, and I believe I am
perfectly suited to help you as I am already familiar with your company's innovative and
environmentally sound products.

The enclosed résumé outlines my skills and experience. I am adept at cultivating key
relationships with decision makers, so I believe I can grow your business significantly in
this area. As you can see from my résumé, I have innumerable contacts in the furniture
business—and I invest a good deal of my time through my community service and avid
golfing in strengthening my already healthy and profitable business relationships. I
believe this will carry over into your business at Consolidated Finishing, as well.

I am primarily interested in building your business in the Baltimore area, but I am willing
to relocate if necessary.

I will contact you next week to request an interview for current or future positions.
If you would like to contact me, I can be reached at my home telephone number at
410-539-1000 in the evenings or on my cell phone, anytime, at 410-556-1010.

Thank you for your time and consideration.

Cordially,   **CLOSING**

Carol Nadata

Enc.: Résumé

- It shows that she takes the initiative. Not only does she read up on industry news, but she acts on it too. She spotted a job opening before it even appeared.
- She tells the employer where she heard about the company.
- She anticipates the employer's need by informing the employer that "you will need accomplished account executives to increase your presence . . ."
- She adds information specific to this position, using language her employer understands—"cultivating key relationships with decision makers"—and thus reinforces the idea that she is qualified for the position.
- She includes information about her extracurricular activities, which is not listed on her résumé (notice that these activities are relevant to her sales career).
- She tells the employer that she is willing to relocate.
- She tells the employer she will contact him but provides enough information so that she can be contacted immediately.
- She thanks the employer.

Writing a good cover letter ensures that you will "stand out." Try to relish this opportunity to distinguish yourself but also know that employers are getting an added look at your communication skills, so the cover letter must be letter perfect, clear, and concise. Because businesspeople are inundated with information in the digital age, they want employees who know how to cut through the chaff and get down to the essentials. Your communication with your prospective employer must show you can do this. In addition, Amy Moers, a senior staffing manager at SYSCO Corporation, said the cover letter should "outline the interests and mobility of a candidate if they aren't in the city where the job is located."

ELECTRONIC COVER LETTERS

When Ken Dean, an assistant vice president of Bank of New York, reads a cover letter, he wants "to find out what position the candidate seeks" and expects that candidate to "add flavor to anything unusual on the résumé." That holds true for the electronic, or e-mail, cover letter as well, so don't bypass this chance to shine. One of the real advantages of an online application is that you have the time and resources to make the best of this opportunity. Yes, writing a cover letter is an opportunity.

Don't forget that before you even begin any online application process, you'll have your job search data file in front of you. You can pull the appropriate information out of your data file and—once you've tweaked it to the specific job opening—you can put the information into the e-mail message. In the predigital age, you probably would have completed the job application process by sitting in an office lobby struggling to think of something clever to say on your paper application (without the benefit of a dictionary or stylebook) and fighting a bad case of the jitters. You're in the driver's seat now, so prepare for this trip as you would for any other.

Stacey Webb, a human resources representative at Gannett, stated that the purpose of a cover letter is "to gain a general understanding of what an applicant seeks in a new position and to give information on background and qualifications." Leslie Humphries, a human resources specialist at State Farm, contended that candidates should "sell their interest" in the company. Look at the electronic cover letter in Figure 5.2 (placed in the body of an e-mail and not sent as an attachment) to see if it meets these requirements (notice that the text is plain, so features, such as em dashes or accents, are not present).

Even though e-mail was used initially as an informal tool of communication, it is quickly becoming the preferred form for business correspondence. According to Helen Cunningham, coauthor of *The Business Style Handbook:* "If you are using e-mail for formal correspondence, both within and outside your organization, apply the same standards you would to a letter."

As for the layout of an electronic cover letter, plan to follow the same block style, but this time there isn't any need to include your address, date, or employer's address as that information is being transmitted electronically. Instead, for an e-mail you need a *correct* e-mail address, the *correct* name of the hiring authority (if it's not a general "contact us" submittal), and a topic for the subject line (usually a job number or position title). Even though the job applicant could include an electronic signature, he doesn't, so there's no need to add spacing after his complimentary closing.

Beyond the design, let's take a look at some of the things the job applicant's electronic cover letter accomplishes.

- He uses a contact name in the first paragraph, a name he picked up when he submitted his résumé online.
- He tells the employer where he found the job opening (on the company Web site [notice he uses the company's preference for lowercasing the word *website*]).
- Even though he has had other jobs in his 20 years of experience (which are listed on his résumé), he highlights only two positions that demonstrate his leadership abilities.
- Each position he highlights is given a concise paragraph (no technical jargon here, but he does use language that is current and suggests he is an

FIGURE 5.2 *Michael Jones's Cover Letter*

To: bdephilips@siac.com   **RECIPIENT'S E-MAIL ADDRESS**

Subject: Systems Director Position   **POSITION YOU WANT**

Dear Mr. DePhilips: **SALUTATION**

BODY After reviewing the SIAC website, I noticed several opportunities in the development area (development director, technical director, and development project manager) and contacted Bill Smith, a colleague of yours in human resources, about these opportunities. He suggested I send my resume to you for your review.

As you can see by my resume, my experience includes more than 20 years of progressive leadership responsibilities in large technology environments.

At Chase Manhattan Bank I was actively involved in developing highly integrated, worldwide applications that supported all aspects of the business -- from sales and marketing through operations and finance. My role progressed from a programmer/ analyst to project leader, then project manager and finally to director.

At Winthrop Stimson I continued to focus on development but took on additional organizational responsibilities. Beyond leading teams developing mainframe, client/server, and Internet-based applications, I was responsible to a group of project managers for department planning and finances (workload of $40 million) and for department staffing and staff development (350 programmers). In this capacity, I was promoted to vice president.

Beyond these roles and responsibilities, my abilities to work with teams and get things done led to being selected for senior teams that drove reengineering and best practices. I have had successes with many different types of business units, and I believe I can bring experience and expertise to your highly regarded organization (I noticed on your website that SIAC was named "one of the 100 Best Places to Work in IT" by Computerworld magazine). I would like to help you strengthen your leadership team at an organization, group, or project level.

Thank you for reviewing my attached resume. I will contact you next week regarding this opportunity. If, in the meantime, you would like to contact me, please call my cell phone anytime at (973) 296-1000.

Sincerely,   **CLOSING**
Michael Jones

insider). He then limits the letter to 340 words (because he has written a rough draft of this cover letter in Word, he knows his word count is about one page before the electronic submittal).

- He uses numbers to substantiate his claims.
- He tells the employer that he is interested in working at this "highly regarded" organization and then backs up this statement with something he picked up when he was browsing through the company Web site.
- He tells the company how he can help it, emphasizing his progressive leadership abilities.
- He provides instant access (his cell phone number).
- He thanks the employer.

Notice, too, the style differences in the electronic cover letter. Because this is not a hard-copy Word document, Jones is limited to the characters on the keyboard, so he doesn't have access to such symbols as the em dash or the accent marks on résumé or the use of bullets. To be on the safe side, he doesn't italicize the name of the magazine, either, just in case the recipient's system can't translate this command. All text in an e-mail should be plain text so that it doesn't get garbled on the recipient's end.

More about this later, but it's always a good idea to e-mail the employer after you send a cover letter and résumé electronically whether it was received in readable form. Look at this as another opportunity to bring attention to your submission, so make sure you handle this professionally.

Even if you have to resend your documents five times because of a glitch on the other end, make sure you do so with grace. Paula Axelrod, a manager of staffing at BJ's Wholesale Club, said job candidates need to "be courteous to all [they] come in contact with."

Make the e-mail inquiry as brief as possible.

To: Mr. DePhilips

Re: Job inquiry/Recent submission

Dear Mr. DePhilips:

I just sent a cover letter and resume and am verifying whether you received them in readable form. If your system did not receive a readable copy, please let me know at your earliest convenience and I will resend the document according to your requirements. Thank you.

Sincerely,
Michael Jones

WHAT IF YOU HAVE NO QUALIFICATIONS?

The Fortune 500 participants stressed again and again that they want to know in your cover letter why you think you are qualified for the position. For newcomers to the job market or recent graduates, this topic may be a difficult one.

The question is how do you turn your experience at school or in your community into a marketable commodity? Let's look at the cover letter in Figure 5.3 from a job candidate seeking a summer internship at an advertising agency.

Internships are an excellent means for obtaining gainful employment once you graduate. You may even get college credit, provided you arrange for the internship with your school. Many company Web sites provide explicit directions to students about how to obtain a summer internship. Follow these directions precisely.

Chris Collier of Georgia-Pacific said he wants a cover letter to give an "overview of experience and value-added potential to his company. It should also express a high level of enthusiasm." With this advice in mind, look at the job candidate's cover letter in Figure 5.3 that was sent, as specified on the Web site, as hard copy.

Let's look at how this job candidate tailors her cover letter so that her lack of relevant experience doesn't work against her. She focuses on her education as well as how her past experience can be of value to the employer.

- She immediately tells the employer what she wants (a summer internship).
- She exhibits professional polish, even though she is still a student.
- She demonstrates in her writing that she is positive, upbeat, and enthusiastic.
- She tells where she read about the opportunity.
- She talks about her relevant coursework (accomplishing a 3.5 GPA).
- She zeros in on the position she had at the Career Center, where she demonstrated leadership abilities as well as sensitivity (steering students in the creation of résumés is not an easy task).
- She refers to some of her soft skills (patience and highly responsible character), which is acceptable as she has so little experience.
- She thanks the recipient and asserts that she will contact the employer. The applicant includes her cell phone number and e-mail address.

A FEW MORE TIPS FOR NEWCOMERS

David Murphy of McGraw-Hill said a cover letter should "grab my attention by the statement of one or two really salient facts that encourage me to read the full résumé." It's not always easy to anticipate what's going to grab someone's

FIGURE 5.3 *Marie Capelli's Cover Letter*

Ms. Marie Ann Capelli   **HER NAME AND ADDRESS**
10 Commonwealth Avenue, Apt. 100
Brighton, MA 02100

February 14, 2005   **DATE (winter application for summer)**

Ms. Suzann Roberts-Smith   **EMPLOYER'S NAME /ADDRESS**
Rogers & Cowan
100 Fifth Avenue
New York, NY 10010

Dear Ms. Roberts-Smith: **SALUTATION**

BODY I want to express my interest in a summer internship with Rogers & Cowan. I became aware of this opportunity with your company while investigating the InternshipExchange Website through my work at Boston College Career Center. I was attracted to your company because of its commitment to delivering outstanding service to its impressive collection of clients.

The highly regarded communication curriculum at Boston College provides a solid foundation in both public speaking as well as written communication. Besides intensive writing courses, I have completed an advertising and public relations course (with a GPA of 3.5).

As you can see in my résumé, my employment and activity record demonstrate my leadership abilities as well as my organizational skills. Working at Boston College Career Center as a peer adviser has given me the opportunity to lead and assist students in perfecting their résumés as well as their interview skills. In addition, working with children has taught me patience as well as the ability to use my organizational skill and creative flair in coordinating activities.

I am confident that my versatility and highly responsible character will be an asset to your summer program. I would like to be granted an interview so that we can discuss my qualifications further. I will contact you within the next week regarding this internship opportunity. If you would like to contact me, I can be reached immediately on my cell phone (201-236-1000) or through my e-mail address, which is marann@bcedu.com.

Thank you for your time and consideration.

Yours truly,   **CLOSING**

Marie Capelli
Enc.: Résumé   **ENCLOSURE**

attention, but telling a person something that he or she has never heard before usually is a good start. It falls within the suggestions of many Fortune 500 participants to "differentiate yourself." Hiring professionals at large companies see hundreds of résumés and cover letters, so telling them something new helps you stand out.

If a former part-time employer wrote an excellent reference for you, feel free to include it in your cover letter. Just make sure you use a substantial quotation: "Great kid" doesn't say much, but "I didn't get one complaint from customers about a missing section of the Sunday *New York Times* while Marie put together the paper at the store" does.

And always use language that is simple and direct. It may be tempting to finally throw around a few words that were hammered into you when you took your SAT prep class, but try to resist. Your writing should be a natural expression of who you are. Because the cover letter and résumé are your formal introduction to the company, don't use slang, colloquialisms, or clichés, but also don't be afraid to be yourself.

Even with minimal experience, it's important to demonstrate your professionalism—through your cover letter and résumé—and emphasizing that hiring you will be a good investment. A willingness to learn as well as a positive and enthusiastic attitude have a value not easily calculated but much in demand by employers.

6

ELECTRONIC SUBMISSIONS

"Follow the instructions on how to apply for the position."

STACY WILSON
Human Resources Administrator, United Parcel Service

The number of positions secured through company Web sites is growing daily. *All* of the 50 Fortune 500 companies surveyed for this book prefer electronic résumés, so job seekers must know the ins and outs of posting electronic résumés.

Of the 50 companies surveyed, 70 percent said most résumés at their companies are delivered via e-mail. Either your résumé is sent as a text-only document and is part of the body of the e-mail or it is sent as an attachment (usually a Microsoft Word document) in the e-mail. The second option is to fill out, at a company's request, the company's e-forms on its Web site, where the information is saved directly to the employer's database. (Of the Fortune 500 participants surveyed, 22 percent reported they use this method.) *All* of the 50 Fortune 500 companies surveyed use either of these methods to receive submissions—and you can be fairly certain that most companies will eventually follow suit.

GETTING PAST THE RESISTANCE

Remember when those electronic tags came along at the toll booths? In New Jersey, we call them E-ZPass. A lot of griping and grumbling ensued at first, but it didn't take long to catch on. After a few five-minute waits in the exact-change lanes, we started to get the picture and turned in our spare change for the electronic tags that sit on top of the dashboard. Zipping through the lanes was the enticement, so despite the initial resistance, E-ZPass became the way to go—simply because of its efficiency.

It's the same with the new electronic hiring environment. Once you figure out how to proceed, submitting electronic résumés is more efficient too. The key, however, is figuring out how to proceed. Based on the Fortune 500 survey, there are various methods for submitting a résumé. Your job is to find out what a particular company's preference is and then to follow those directions to the letter.

Because the 50 Fortune 500 hiring professionals surveyed prefer either submissions via e-mail or online e-forms, those two submission methods are the focus of this chapter. (For a more detailed and comprehensive overview of all types of electronic submissions—PDFs, Web-based résumés and portfolios, interactive Web pages—see either Meg Britton Whitcomb and Pat Kendall's *e Resumes* or Rebecca Smith's *Electronic Resumes & Online Networking* listed in the "Resources" section at the end of the book.)

GETTING READY TO CLICK AND SEND

To get all the necessary information, it's time to retrieve the job data file you created for your job hunt. In addition to your résumé, it should now contain your company research, several multipurpose cover letters, any names you picked up along the way, and various keywords relevant to the position you are seeking.

If you don't have access to the Internet, go to the local library or use a friend's Internet connection. If you use the library, it will now become your base for job searching; but find out if yours is one of the libraries that enforces a time limit for Internet use. For obvious reasons, you don't want to conduct your job search while you're at your current job. (Companies monitor e-mail usage, and seeking another job from your office may be interpreted by your boss as a conflict of interest!) If, however, you are asked to send a résumé immediately to a prospective employer—and there's no waiting until you get to your own computer—then use your own e-mail account, which you've created specifically for your job search, instead of your current company's account.

If you don't have an e-mail address, now is the time to create one. Cory Kleinschmidt, the Web master of Traffick.com, says the best e-mail portals are Hotmail and Yahoo!. Go to either one (www.hotmail.com or www.yahoo.com) and set up a new account. It's relatively simple: click on the new e-mail account button and fill in the profile. The directions are easy to follow and the service is free, but you will have to look at banner advertisements (not a bad tradeoff for a free address). Create an e-mail address devoted solely to your job search. Make a notation of your password and address in your data file (refrain from putting this information on an old receipt or piece of scrap paper). To simplify matters at a later point, use the same password when you go to company Web sites to fill out their e-forms and create a profile.

Don't forget that your e-mail address will be viewed (and possibly used) by your future employer, so choose a conservative address. You are likely to get a better response from an employer if your address is TXSmith@yahoo.com rather than honeybuns22@yahoo.com. If you already have an e-mail address on your home PC and it falls into the "honeybuns" category, create a new e-mail address for the job search. Don't let a silly e-mail address ruin that critical first impression.

A FEW INITIAL QUESTIONS

Before sending your résumé to a prospective employer, make sure you know exactly what the employer's preference is for receiving it. If the preference is unknown, then send an e-mail or call the recipient and ask. If you're unsure what to ask, consider these questions.

- Should I mail my résumé? Fax it? E-mail it? (If the employer tells you to mail it or fax it, you can skip this chapter.)
- Should I attach my résumé to an e-mail?
- What file formats do you prefer in attachments? MS Word (.doc) or Rich Text Format (.rtf)?
- Should my résumé be in the body of the e-mail (converted to plain text or ASCII, pronounced *askee,* as noted earlier)?
- Should I go to the company Web site and fill out the e-forms?

THE ATTACHED RÉSUMÉ

Companies use many different methods to recruit and hire their employees. Even though many still accept snail mail or faxed résumés, the preference is electronic. Whitcomb and Kendall, authors of *eResumes,* say that 80 percent of employers in 2001 recruited their employees online.

Many job seekers prefer to send their résumés and cover letters as attachments to their e-mails because it retains their formatting (bold, italics, underscore, bullets, etc.) as it's transmitted, and some employers request this method. If you are asked to send your résumé as an e-mail attachment, the process is fairly straightforward. Assuming you have Windows and Microsoft Word, here are the basics.

- Put the address (either an individual or department address) in the To line.

- Put the job number (if you have one) in the Subject line (or the name of the specific job (e.g., *Account Executive, Facilities Manager*) as well as your name *(Equity Sales Trader/John Smith)*.
- Write a cover letter in the body of your e-mail. (See Chapter 5 for details.)
- Attach the Word version of your résumé by clicking on the Attach icon in the e-mail menu.
- Scroll down and hit File, then select your résumé file. Once your résumé file is highlighted, hit Open, and the file now automatically attaches to the e-mail. (The attachment may cover the To line, but the address is still underneath.)
- Before you hit Send, double-check that the e-mail cover letter and attachment are in good order. Do not send the e-mail to an employer until you have tested it by sending it to your own and/or a friend's address.

PLAIN AND SIMPLE

In a study conducted for *The Business Style Handbook* in 1998, it was revealed that 90 percent of the Fortune 500 companies surveyed use Microsoft (MS) Word as their primary word-processing package. Because MS Word is probably even more ubiquitous today, it may be safe to assume that most large companies use this program. That doesn't mean, however, that you can create an MS Word résumé and count on it arriving at an employer's desk in the format in which you sent it. No matter what software you use to write your résumé and cover letter, compatibility problems can occur. That's why some companies are adverse to attachments. In addition, (1) attachments can contain viruses, and (2) they take a few seconds longer to download.

Don't be surprised if an employer requests an ASCII version for e-mail submissions. If the acronym ASCII *(askee)* makes you squirm, don't worry; it's just another term for plain text. ASCII means *American Standard Code of Information Interchange* and is the universal language of the Internet that can be read by any personal computer. It uses only characters that exist on the standard keyboard (no bullets or foreign currency symbols or em dashes). ASCII is mentioned here because if you are asked to send your résumé in ASCII form, it simply means the employer wants a plain-text version of your résumé instead of an MS Word document.

If you plan to send your résumé in the body of an e-mail, you may cut and paste the original Word version with all its elaborate formatting, but it may not end up on the employer's desktop looking the way you sent it (those bullets and em dashes may convert into questions marks). The best method to use for sending your résumé in an e-mail is as a plain text (or ASCII) document, which requires converting your original résumé. Your formatting disappears and your résumé, designwise, is no longer distinguishable from the next person's. This can be a blow to those who have spent days designing a unique résumé, but it's better to be universally recognized with your plain text résumé than to send a document that arrives on the employer's PC in an unreadable form.

Fortunately, it's not necessary to learn a whole new computer language to make a conversion. Your word processor does it automatically, but you will have to clean up the formatting in your text version afterward. Once you convert, the only design elements you can insert in your new plain text résumé must be picked up from the standard keyboard (for example, bullets must be replaced by asterisks and em dashes replaced by two hyphens). Follow these steps to convert your résumé to plain text (ASCII).

1. Once in your e-mail, retrieve your original résumé from Word. (Drop in all relevant *keywords* for the particular job you are applying for online.)
2. Go to File and hit Save As.
3. In the Save As window that pops up, rename your original resume document *P-text (your last name)*. HR will appreciate that your document includes your name. (In the text's résumé example, the document has been renamed *P-text-Bailey*.)
4. Underneath the File Name bar, go to Save As Type. Click on the arrow and then scroll down and highlight Text Only. Then hit Save.
5. When the warning pops up that your formatting will be lost, hit Yes. (Another option is using the Text Only with Line Breaks when you hit Save As. It's the same as Text Only, but it puts in hard returns, so the lines break where you intended.)
6. Complete the conversion by closing the document and then reopening it so you can readjust the margins and clean up any formatting.

Your formatting has disappeared and you can now go in to clean up any errant margins and add any elements that will help organize the material (asterisks, capital letters, readjusted spacing between lines). Fix the alignment, making sure it is flush left. For hard-copy résumés, it was recommended that the font size not be reduced to less than 11 points. A text-only version, however, converts to 10-point Courier that allows for about 65 characters per line, which most e-mail screens can accommodate. After cleaning up the formatting in the text version (keep it as simple as possible to ensure compatibility on the other end), save the document again.

With these few steps, you have created a universally recognizable résumé. Don't worry about that beautifully designed original. Because you renamed your résumé when converting, your original résumé is still fully intact (in a different file)—formatting and all.

"BEFORE" AND "AFTER" TEXT RÉSUMÉ

Examine the résumés shown in Figures 6.1 and 6.2. The one in Figure 6.1 is an MS Word document whose content is identical to that of Figure 6.2 except that the new text version doesn't have a continued line on the second page with the person's name as does the first. That's because the new text résumé will run continuously in the body of your e-mail (no second page, so remember to delete the continued line when reformatting the text). To separate a cover letter in an e-mail from the text résumé, use

- a hyphen line ——
- or asterisks ***

When sending the text résumé in an e-mail, set it up like this:

- Put the employer's e-mail address in the To line.
- Put the name of the position being applied for or the job number (along with your complete name) in the subject line. Be as specific as possible.
- The cover letter (as explained in Chapter 5) should be written in the body of your e-mail. It's best to have a name of the person you are sending it to, but if you don't, write *Dear Human Resources Manager.*
- Separate the cover letter from the text résumé with either a line of asterisks or a line of hyphens.
- Cut and paste the text version of the résumé into the body of the e-mail below the line of asterisks or hyphens.
- Double-check that everything aligns correctly and that all the formatting is stripped out of the text version (sometimes stray elements remain).
- Be sure your cover letter and résumé are in the same e-mail message. Do not send a cover letter in one e-mail and your résumé in another unless you are asked explicitly to do this.
- Do a test by sending it to your e-mail address or a friend's. Check once more that everything is correct. Send it to your own e-mail address—and look at it again.

Examine the original ("Before") and the plain text version ("After") of the same résumé in Figures 6.1 and 6.2. Before you transmit your résumé electronically to a prospective employer, experiment. The two versions of the same résumé should resemble the examples in Figures 6.1 and 6.2.

FIGURE 6.1 *William Bailey's Original ("Before") Résumé in MS Word*

William Bailey
1 Dogwood Lane, Greenbrier, TN 37100 (615) 643-1000 (H) E-mail: WB1234@hotmail.com

CAREER OBJECTIVE: **Safety Manager** in manufacturing, where expertise in ergonomics, OSHA compliance, workers' compensation and safety can significantly reduce injuries and decrease costs through preventative measures, employee accountability and educational programs

SUMMARY OF QUALIFICATIONS: Fourteen years' experience establishing safety programs and developing **safety cultures in manufacturing environments.** Adept at training and communicating with employees, supervisors and upper management. Extensive experience complemented by effective communication skills

AREAS OF EFFECTIVENESS:

Safety Programs
Develop written safety programs that provide overall facility safety.
Develop behavior-based safety programs for employee accountability.
Develop training programs to ensure compliance with OSHA standards.
Conduct air and noise testing to ensure exposure levels do not exceed recommended levels.
Perform ergonomic evaluations.
Conduct workplace audits to identify injury sources and identify corrective action.
Establish facility safety committees.
Involve employees, supervisors and management to develop safety culture.
Investigate accidents to determine root cause and develop corrective actions.
Educate supervisors and managers on maintaining injury-summary logs.
Analyze injuries to identify trends and develop corrective actions to reverse them.
Quantify safety purchases by showing injury-prevention savings.
Communicate plans and objectives with management to ensure support.
Identify morale issues that can lead to workplace injuries and develop solutions to improve.
Maintain loss records and cost-impact to report to management.
Oversee internal budgeting for loss-prevention staff.

Workers' Compensation
Develop transitional return-to-work programs.
Communicate with claims adjusters to ensure that physicians release injured employees.
Develop drug-free workplace programs.
Educate employees, supervisors, and management on workers' compensation laws.

TRAINING: Provide training of regulatory and nonregulatory topics to employees.
Provide train-the-trainer classes for supervisors.
Evaluate training to improve presentation and information covered.

FIGURE 6.1 *(continued)*

Bailey continued

WORK HISTORY:

Staff Leasing, Brentwood, Tennessee, 1998 to present
EBI Companies (Insurance), Nashville, Tennessee, 1995 to 1998
Travelers Insurance, Nashville, Tennessee, 1990 to 1995

<u>Accomplishments</u>
Selected as team coach.
Reduced injury-frequency rate by 52 percent, exceeding company goal.
Reduced injury-cost rate by 41 percent, exceeding company goal.

**MILITARY
EXPERIENCE:**

Kentucky Army National Guard, Fort Knox, Kentucky
1982 to present
First Sergeant / E-8, HHC First Sergeant

Plan and coordinate training and supplies.
Assign soldiers to provide support for five different companies.
Provide retention guidance for soldiers ready to extend.
Maintain Unit Duty Roster ensuring soldiers perform share of extra duty.
Counsel soldiers on ways to improve performance.
Provide annual performance evaluations of senior enlisted soldiers.
Provide development training for noncommissioned officers.
Effectively delegate responsibility to promote leadership growth of
subordinate soldiers.
Emphasize safety in every aspect of training.

<u>Accomplishments</u>
Developed and implemented an absenteeism policy that resulted in 19%
increase in soldiers present in first month.
Retention actions resulted in a 92% retention rate of eligible soldiers.
Provide body-strengthening instruction for leaders and soldiers, resulting
in 10% increase in strength in past three months.
Consistently receive ratings of "Superior" at leadership development
courses.
Consistently receive ratings of "Excellence" on annual performance
evaluations.
Recognized for excellent platoon safety record while a Platoon Sergeant.
Awarded Army Achievement Medal for training that resulted in 100%,
first-round, platoon gunnery qualification.
Awarded Kentucky Commendation for training, resulting in 100%, first-
time passing scores from external evaluators on platoon tactical tasks.
Selected as Outstanding Noncommissioned Officer

EDUCATION:

Murray State University, Murray, Kentucky, 1990
Bachelor of Science in Occupational Safety and Health

FIGURE 6.2 *William Bailey's "After" Résumé in Plain Text*

```
William Bailey
1 Dogwood Lane, Greenbrier, TN 37100
(615) 643-1000 (H) E-mail: WB1234@hotmail.com

CAREER
OBJECTIVE:

Safety Manager in manufacturing, where expertise in ergonomics,
OSHA compliance, workers' compensation and safety can significantly
reduce injuries and decrease costs through preventative measures,
employee accountability and educational programs

SUMMARY OF
QUALIFICATIONS:

Fourteen years' experience establishing safety programs and developing
safety cultures in manufacturing environments. Adept at training and
communicating with employees, supervisors and upper management.
Extensive experience complemented by effective communication skills

AREAS OF
EFFECTIVENESS:

Safety Programs

*Develop written safety programs that provide overall facility safety.
*Develop behavior-based safety programs for employee accountability.
*Develop training programs to ensure compliance with OSHA standards.
*Conduct air and noise testing to ensure exposure levels do not exceed
recommended levels.
*Perform ergonomic evaluations.
*Conduct workplace audits to identify injury sources and identify
corrective action.
*Establish facility safety committees.
*Involve employees, supervisors and management to develop safety culture.
*Investigate accidents to determine root cause and develop corrective actions.
*Educate supervisors and managers on maintaining injury-summary logs.
*Analyze injuries to identify trends and develop corrective actions to
reverse them.
*Quantify safety purchases by showing injury-prevention savings.
*Communicate plans and objectives with management to ensure support.
*Identify morale issues that can lead to workplace injuries and develop
solutions to improve.
*Maintain loss records and cost-impact to report to management.
*Oversee internal budgeting for loss-prevention staff.

Workers' Compensation

*Develop transitional return-to-work programs.
*Communicate with claims adjusters to ensure that physicians release
injured employees.
*Develop drug-free workplace programs.
*Educate employees, supervisors, and management on workers'
compensation laws.
```

FIGURE 6.2 *(continued)*

TRAINING:

*Provide training of regulatory and nonregulatory topics to employees.
*Provide train-the-trainer classes for supervisors.
*Evaluate training to improve presentation and information covered.

WORK HISTORY:

Staff Leasing, Brentwood, Tennessee, 1998 to present
EBI Companies (Insurance) Nashville, Tennessee, 1995 to 1998
Travelers Insurance, Nashville, Tennessee, 1990 to 1995

Accomplishments

*Selected as team coach.
*Reduced injury-frequency rate by 52 percent, exceeding company goal.
*Reduced injury-cost rate by 41 percent, exceeding company goal.

MILITARY
EXPERIENCE:

Kentucky Army National Guard, Fort Knox, Kentucky
1982 to present
First Sergeant / E-8, HHC First Sergeant

*Plan and coordinate training and supplies.
*Assign soldiers to provide support for five different companies.
*Provide retention guidance for soldiers ready to extend.
*Maintain Unit Duty Roster ensuring soldiers perform share of extra duty.
*Counsel soldiers on ways to improve performance.
*Provide annual performance evaluations of senior enlisted soldiers.
*Provide development training for noncommissioned officers.
*Effectively delegate responsibility to promote leadership growth of
subordinate soldiers.
*Emphasize safety in every aspect of training.

Accomplishments
*Developed and implemented an absenteeism policy that resulted in 19%
increase in soldiers present in first month.
*Retention actions resulted in a 92% retention rate of eligible soldiers.
*Provide body-strengthening instruction for leaders and soldiers,
resulting in 10% increase in strength in past three months.
*Consistently receive "Superior" ratings at leadership development courses.
*Consistently receive "Excellence" ratings on annual performance
evaluations.
*Recognized for excellent platoon safety record while a Platoon Sergeant.
*Awarded Army Achievement Medal for training that resulted in 100%,
first-round, platoon gunnery qualification.
*Awarded Kentucky Commendation for training, resulting in 100%, first-
time passing scores from external evaluators on platoon tactical tasks.
*Selected as Outstanding Noncommissioned Officer

EDUCATION: Murray State University, Murray, Kentucky, 1990
               Bachelor of Science in Occupational Safety and Health

A FEW DOS AND DON'TS

Because both the MS Word document and the plain text version were written for a safety manager position at a large company, they are identical. If the job applicant were to send the plain text résumé to another job opening, he would customize both his cover letter and plain text résumé to reflect the requirements of the new position. Often companies request that you use the text version of your résumé when you go to a company Web site and use its e-forms. The information on the text résumé is then cut and pasted into the e-forms.

As already mentioned, content is king, especially in today's electronic environment. The ASCII version of your résumé may not be pretty, but it is compatible. In today's digital environment, the primary purpose of design is to make your information more readable. You don't have a lot of options in plain text, so keep it simple: shoot for readability (and compatibility) rather than visual appeal.

If you are ever in doubt whether the employer wants your résumé as an attachment or as text, then opt for sending it as text. Some career experts suggest sending both an attachment and a plain text version in the body of the e-mail. A simple preliminary call or e-mail to clarify the employer's requirements, though, will eliminate this guesswork, so find out what the best submission method is *before* sending the résumé.

Many companies, especially the smaller ones, are still in the process of refining their electronic hiring practices, so there is no such thing as standard procedure. In fact, electronic hiring procedures at some companies can have a lifespan of about six months because they are still, literally, developing a process that works. Spend some time on the company Web site. Read the directions carefully. Then contact the company via e-mail to make sure you understand the procedure, before you send your résumé to the job that seems a good fit for you.

ELECTRONIC FORMS

At this point, it's a good idea that the data file contains the following: an original version of your résumé, any pertinent company research, sample cover letters (with a plain-text version of a multipurpose cover letter as well), the names of hiring authorities picked up along the way, a list of keywords, and, now, a plain-text (ASCII) résumé. Many companies prefer that you use the text version of the résumé to cut and paste into the electronic forms (e-forms) on company Web sites or job boards.

Think of an e-form as an online version of those paper job application forms you used to fill out in the employer's lobby. The paper forms usually required more than the basic information already included on your résumé (maybe a list of references or an essay on your particular strengths). It's the same with e-forms, or what some sites refer to as *résumé builders.*

Before you do a log-in and submit a résumé or complete an e-form, you will most likely have to create a new account with your e-mail address and password. In addition to including a résumé, e-forms often require you to answer specific questions relating to the position you are applying for. The good news about e-forms is that you can complete them at your own workstation—and with the help of a dictionary and stylebook. (Whatever you do, refrain from rushing through this process.)

Another advantage to using e-forms is elimination of the guesswork about what to include. With e-forms, the employer tells you exactly what information to provide (some sites even specify the character count of the résumé). Depending on the particular company Web site—*and there are a lot of variations from one site to the next*—be prepared to answer all kinds of questions. Some of the fields in the e-forms are small, so you have to type in the information. Other fields are large, so you can cut and paste from your plain-text résumé. In addition to the contact information and a request to cut and paste the résumé (some forms refer to the résumé as a CV, *curriculum vitae*), an e-form may ask:

- Whether you are willing to relocate
- What your GPA was at the highest level of education
- What your salary range is
- Whether you are willing to travel
- Where you heard about the position

Be prepared by having the answers to all of these questions. Having a figure for a salary range, or a list of your technical skills, or a brief description of how your education relates to the position cuts down the chances of error or inaccuracy. Even though most of these e-forms allow you to review and edit the material before submitting it, the more prepared you are, the less likely you will stumble over the details. And there are plenty of details. You may want to experiment with résumé builders on job boards before actually completing a company's e-form.

If you use the e-forms at company Web sites, you'll discover that the process varies from one Web site to the next. Some allow you to cut and paste the entire plain text résumé into a data field (which generally ranges between 16,000 to 18,000 characters and which means your résumé could be approximately seven or eight pages. Fortunately, you've already cut it down to two or three pages so you won't need that much space.) Other e-forms ask for bits and pieces to be dropped into data fields regarding work history, technical skills, interpersonal skills, and so on. Some e-forms even allow you to paste your Word résumé into the appropriate space. Take a look at the generic e-form in Figure 6.3, which should give you a general idea of what to expect when visiting an employer's site.

FIGURE 6.3 *A Sample Generic E-Form*

* = Required

Name   *First [   ]   Middle [   ]   *Last [   ]

*e-mail access?   Yes ○   No ○

*If Yes, Enter e-mail Address   [   ]
(Required if you have e-mail access)   (mxsmith@yahoo.com)

*Home Address   [   ]
     [   ]
     [   ]

*City   [   ]

*State or Province   [▼]

*Country   [United States ▼]

*Zip/Postal Code   [   ]

Country Phone Code   [001]

(*)Home Phone   Area Code ([ ]) [ ] – [ ]

Work Phone   Area Code ([ ]) [ ] – [ ]   Ext. [ ]

Mobile Phone   Area Code ([ ]) [ ] – [ ]

School Phone   Area Code ([ ]) [ ] – [ ]

(*)Non-U.S. Phone   [   ]

*How should we contact you?   [▼]

Best days/times to contact you by phone   [   ]

What is your salary range?   [   ]

What position are you applying for?   [   ]

List your technical skills here (do not exceed 600 characters):

[   ]

List your nontechnical skills here (do not exceed 600 characters):

[   ]

Attach your resume here (do not exceed 16,000 characters):

[   ]

If you are asked to cut and paste your entire résumé, follow these six steps (for MS Word):

1. Retrieve the plain-text version of the résumé.
2. Highlight the *entire* résumé.
3. Go to Edit and scroll down. Click on copy.
4. Go to the e-form and then to the appropriate field or button. Right click on the mouse and paste the résumé into the appropriate field.
5. Fix the indentation (and anything else that may have gone awry in the transmission) right in the e-form.
6. Take the extra time to proof and edit, then submit the résumé or, if necessary, continue completing the rest of the fields.

If the e-form requires just bits and pieces of the résumé, then follow the preceding steps, but in Step 2 highlight only the pertinent information instead of the entire résumé (for instance, the career objective or just the work history).

THE PARTICULARS OF E-FORMS

Some electronic forms are better than others—ranging from explicit to vague. On the ALLTEL site, potential candidates are given a comprehensive overview of the hiring process in four steps. The first step covers online applications.

"Go here [a hot link] to search our open positions and submit your résumé. We recommend you first search for a position that interests you. Search often—our postings update daily. Then, build your candidate profile and submit it directly to that position by simply cutting and pasting your résumé and completing our online application. Make a note of your login and password, as you will need these for future access to our system. You will be able to apply for additional jobs using your existing profile.

In another sample, this one from UPS, job candidates are given the choice of whether to use just the e-form or simply submit a résumé.

As the first step in becoming eligible to be considered for employment opportunities at UPS, we ask you to complete the following online resume/CV. You can either cut and paste your existing resume/CV here [a hot link], or complete the [e-] form below. When you enter a valid e-mail address, you will receive an automated acknowledgment of receipt of your online resume/CV. If you do not have an e-mail address, you may sign up for free at http://mail.yahoo.com. The e-mail field is a required field to complete.

Keep your job data file in front of you with all the appropriate information, and then follow directions. After completing a few e-forms, you'll get the hang of it. But, as already mentioned, not all sites are explicit. Some company Web sites make it difficult even to find the career link (often, if it's not on the home page, then look in the About the Company link or the Contact Us link).

When you first start working with e-forms, there is a margin of error. If any aspect of the e-form procedure is still unclear after contacting an HR representative at a particular company or asking your IT friend, then you may be better off applying for the dream job you discovered on the Web by more traditional methods—fax or snail mail—because it's important that you follow the e-form steps precisely in order to be considered.

SPECIFIC KEYWORDS

When filling out e-forms and submitting electronic résumés, keywords take on a whole new meaning because you are applying for a specific job. Read the job description carefully. See what words apply to your qualifications and then use them in your application.

Take a look at the following job description for a Network Security Researcher. The keywords are italicized:

Candidate should have a *Ph.D.* with expertise in *network security*. Candidates must be willing and able to obtain a *Government Security clearance*. Candidates should have a broad knowledge of *IP (4&6) networking* plus a record of accomplishment (e.g. publications in *peer-reviewed journals*) in some of the following technology areas: *Architecture* and *design* of *secure data communications networks*, both *conventional* and *wireless, mobile IP, IP multicast, network security*, especially *security* of the *Internet* and *WWW*; security strengths and weaknesses of *protocols* at the *network, transport*, and *application layers; intrusion detection systems; information security systems; firewalls; antivirus systems, honeypots; virtual private networks; footprinting, scanning* and *hacking* techniques, etc. In particular, we are interested in people who have experience developing *prototype applications* involving such technology and in performing research in the underlying *algorithms* and *computer science*. Candidates should be creative, innovative thinkers capable of identifying and proposing new research projects.

Chances are your online application won't make it past the first round unless keywords are a part of it. In a weak job market, employers look for perfect matches, so the more keywords the better. Approximately 20 to 30 keywords in the preceding job description should be included on the application—provided, of course, that the candidate has these qualifications.

In the push to include keywords, many applicants randomly include qualifications that don't necessarily apply to their expertise, a problem especially rampant in the technology field. Charles Greene, a managing director at SIAC, said, "Many applicants include all kinds of keywords on their résumés, but once they get to the interview, they are incapable of supporting these claims. It's fairly evident after ten minutes who is qualified and who is not. Still, it's a waste of time to include keywords that don't apply to your skills and qualifications. Sooner or later, the truth is revealed."

In addition to the two methods covered in this chapter, other methods are used to hire employees.

THE JOB BOARDS

If you opt to bypass company Web sites and use job boards exclusively, the wait to receive a response may be long or indefinite. Two of the biggest job boards, Monster and HotJobs, get millions of hits each month from applicants. In September 2002, Monster.com had 13.3 million visitors and HotJobs had

---

Southern Edison Offers Some Suggestions on Keywords:

- Use enough keywords to define your skills, experience, education, professional affiliations, etc.
- Describe your experience with concrete words rather than vague descriptions.
- Be concise and truthful.
- Use more than one page if necessary. The computer can easily handle multiple-page résumés.
- Increase your list of keywords by including specifics.
- Use common headings, such as: Objectives, Experience, Employment, Work History, Skills, Affiliations, etc.
- If room allows, describe your interpersonal traits and attitude.
- Use jargon and acronyms specific to your industry (spell out the acronyms).

4.4 million, so posting an online résumé can be impersonal, to say the least, at these sites.

Such sites are helpful, though, as career management tools because they offer plenty of advice about the hiring process and may be a good place to work out the kinks of your electronic submissions. You may have more success at the specialized job boards (in the writing, engineering, IT fields, etc.); the match rate for the mainstream job boards is about 2 percent, whereas the match rate in the specialized job boards is approximately 15 percent (*New York Times,* October 29, 2002). The only job board mentioned by the Fortune 500 participants in the survey was DirectEmployers.com. Dan Bankey, of Mutual of Omaha, comments: "We love DirectEmployers.com as a leading edge Internet sourcing tool."

Many employers reportedly use software that scans the most recent entries in a job board's database, so it's important that you "renew" or "refresh" your résumé as often as possible. Sometimes a fee is charged to keep a résumé among the most recent listings; at other sites this option is free. Another issue in posting your résumé online is privacy: Be careful how much information you release; check each job board's privacy clause, and err on the side of caution.

In an article, "The New Rules of Web Hiring," in *Time* magazine (November 24, 2003), Barbara Kiviat wrote that "shotgunning" your résumé indiscriminately out to job boards can be dangerous: "Keep tabs on where your résumé is going. The nonprofit World Privacy Forum last week published a study documenting instances of personal information sold, even identities stolen, from job search sites."

SCANNABLE RÉSUMÉS

Some large companies scan hard-copy résumés into their databases, which takes between 15 to 60 seconds for each résumé. If a prospective employer scans résumés and you are uncertain how to proceed, follow these steps as a guideline (posted on the Southern Edison Careers page).

1. Use white or light-colored 8½ by 11 inch paper.
2. Provide a laser-quality original if possible.
3. Do not fold or staple your résumé.
4. Use standard fonts, such as Times or Courier.
5. Use a font size of 10 to 14 points.
6. Place your name at the top of the page on its own line.
7. Use standard address format below your name.
8. Use boldface and/or all capital letter for headings.

9. Avoid fancy treatments, such as italics and shadows.

10. Avoid vertical and horizontal lines, graphics, and boxes.

11. Avoid two-column formats.

12. Don't condense spacing between letters.

Your online résumé must convince the employer that you can move right in and get the job done, so try to create a résumé that reflects this. A survey on Job-web conducted by the National Association of Colleges and Employers lists the top ten qualities that employers seek in a new hire:

1. Communications skills (verbal and written)
2. Honesty and integrity
3. Teamwork skills (work well with others)
4. Interpersonal skills (relate well with others)
5. Motivation and initiative
6. Strong work ethic
7. Analytical skills
8. Flexibility and adaptability
9. Computer skills
10. Self-confidence

Depicting these traits in a cover letter and résumé or e-form can be a challenge, as many of these "soft skills" don't translate well into an application and is why it's important to focus on your qualifications. According to Sherry Rest of Lucent, "qualifications are what we look for first." Make sure most of your effort is spent honing your application so that it portrays your qualifications and skills in the best light. You will, after all, have an opportunity to reveal those top ten traits eventually—in your interview.

NETWORKING

*"Make a contact with someone at the company who is willing to give
you background about the company—its culture, the type of jobs
available, and business."*

BILL G. VLCEK
Manager, Strategic Staffing, International Truck & Engine Corporation

"**N**etwork, network, network" is the advice Cecilia McKenney of Pepsi Bottling Group gave job applicants. Eleven other Fortune 500 survey participants made it a point to advise job seekers to network as well. Career experts and counselors agree that networking is a vital element in your job search. So how do you do it? And where do you begin?

Start with bringing out that focus statement. By the time you're ready to network, you should know—by heart—what type of job you are looking for and what you can do for an employer. Your aim improves tenfold when you are specific and clear, because it's essential you know what you want to do and how you can be of service before you start networking. Calling up an acquaintance to say you are looking for a job won't hit the mark; in fact, don't even ask for a job. Instead, tell your contact you are looking for a particular type of job in a particular industry and then ask for help—any kind of help he or she can provide.

That help may arrive in many different forms—at any given time. The best kind of help, of course, is to be given the name of a hiring manager, but most networking initiatives begin in a more roundabout way. The majority of people need time to gather their resources. They may have to examine their Rolodex. Or they may have to take note of the job postings in the cafeteria. Or they may have to spread the word among department heads. Or they may have to make a few phone calls. Or, because of budget constraints, they may only be able to provide background information. Call everyone you know to tell them what you need, and then be receptive to any kind of input you can get.

PROFESSIONAL AFFILIATIONS

Don't limit yourself to professional contacts within a certain company. Sherri Martin, a director of human resources at Deere & Company, offered this advice: "Network with others through trade and professional organizations." Because industry insiders know what's happening in their fields, let them steer you toward the companies that are hiring and/or expanding.

Nearly every occupation has a professional affiliation. Simply do a Google search on your profession, and pages of listings appear—whether you're a copyeditor (American Copy Editor's Society) or a structural engineer (Structural Engineers Association). If you haven't done so already, you should become a member of the appropriate professional organization. Not only will it help you keep abreast of the latest developments in your field (usually via electronic newsletters), but many organizations also offer low-cost learning opportunities and career guidance as well as insider information on job opportunities. A union-affiliated organization that trains 110,000 people per year, the Consortium for Worker Education, actually provides its members free computer and skills-training classes to both unionized and nonunion workers (Greenhouse, *New York Times*, August 10, 2003).

Building a professional network takes time. Ideally, you have kept in touch with your direct contacts and your Rolodex is up-to-date. If you have lost contact with former colleagues, then start to build another network. Attend job fairs and conferences related to your field. Ask for business cards and share information you have about the industry. Don't wait until you are unemployed to nurture these contacts.

If you are employed but concerned you may be swept away in an imminent layoff six months from now, don't hesitate to get the word out as soon as possible. Tell your professional contacts you are considering a move to another company. According to a *Wall Street Journal* article (Tejada, December 24, 2002), many companies prefer to "poach" the still-employed from other companies. Even though the economy is soft, companies are skittish about anyone who has floundered too long in the pool of the unemployed. That may be one reason why many companies prefer to review only the most recent résumé postings on the big job boards.

FROM THE GENERAL TO THE SPECIFIC

Your networking strategies will work best when they begin as general fact-finding missions. Call people—ex-colleagues, former managers, mentors, friends, and acquaintances—to ask them what they know about certain companies. It is highly unusual to get to a hiring source directly or immediately. Count on a few degrees of separation: Your friend knows a sales manager at XYZ company who knows someone in the finance department who is a good friend of the HR director. It takes some time, but follow every lead.

Alumni associations are also excellent resources when job hunting, so look into the alumni association at your college or university. The University of Pittsburgh Alumni Association partnered with its Career Services to create AlumNet, "a career-networking program designed to help Pitt students and alumni connect with alumni who can help them advance their careers and explore job opportunities." Rutgers University has a similar network, an online "service that provides a mechanism for alumni to give advice, conduct informational interviews, and provide other career assistance," and it even has an Alumni Networking Club. Many of these associations, such as the one at the University of Indiana, ask that you become a member first, but again it's simply a matter of signing up and providing an e-mail address. Whether you're in the job market or not, it's a good idea to make these groups a part of your network. Because networks are reciprocal by nature, you'll be expected to share information and expertise when you are in the position to do so, but it's a small price to pay for having a viable network. In the end, you get what you give.

As with all other research, keep the name of every person you contact in your job data file, especially as you'll want to thank them at a later date for their assistance—whether you get the job they steered you toward or not. If your direct contact puts you in touch with someone who can help you, ask permission to use his or her name when you initiate contact.

Some people find it difficult to ask for help, but if you're one of them, try to get past this resistance. Even though networking contacts may not be able to secure a job for you, most people welcome the opportunity to be helpful. And remember that once you are gainfully employed, you will have the opportunity to help someone else. Paula Axelrod, a manager of staffing at BJ's Wholesale Club, said, "Don't be afraid to network and use referrals." That's how many positions are filled at major corporations.

And for good reason. James Manktelow, editor of *Mind Tools* and an experienced recruiter has this to say: "Recruiters love networking. After internal promotion, it is often seen as the most reliable and cost-effective strategy for hiring." Manktelow lists the following reasons:

1. You come personally recommended by someone the recruiter knows and trusts.
2. The recruiter can see you quickly and without waiting for intermediaries to act.

3. The recruiter avoids the high costs of agency fees and advertising costs.

4. The recruiter can see you and make a decision without the need for performing tedious work or writing a job specification and preparing and placing an advertisement.

THE JOBS NOT ADVERTISED

Networking helps you tap into the hidden job market—the jobs that never make it into the classified advertisements and estimated to be between 50 and 75 percent of all jobs. It makes sense then to *develop* personal and business contacts who can help you identify these openings, especially in a tight job market. The networking list you create should be composed of as many individuals as you can think of at various levels in a corporation. What you want is information and advice, not necessarily the offer of a specific job.

Once you have created a networking list, ask certain contacts about arranging an informational interview, taking no more than 10 or 15 minutes of their time. According to Janet Shlaes in "Beyond the Basics: Career Strategies That Work" (JVS Career Development Website), you should narrow the topics you want to cover in these informational interviews. Stick to one topic, such as career advice, industry information, names of key contacts, information concerning planned expansions, the skills necessary to perform a certain job, or how to start out at his or her company.

Always follow up these informational interviews with a thank you note that provides some detail about your progress to date.

Another reason for relying on networking as a primary tool in the job hunt is that your chances of success increase dramatically. In fact, surveys have shown that you have an 86 percent chance of securing a job through networking compared with a 7 percent chance through a classified ad. So why pursue any other method?

The problem with networking is that it takes time, and most people who find themselves suddenly unemployed feel a pressing need to make things happen right away. That's why it's important to build your network before you ever need it—networking should be an ongoing process. If you hear about a company that intrigues you, create a data file before you ever consider applying there. Learn about the company; pay attention to what goes on there. E. Humpal, a manager of employment services at J.C. Penney Corporation, suggests that you "network with current employees" at the targeted company. Or, as Stephen Heckert of JDS Uniphase, said, "If you don't have any contacts, try to make some."

When many people hear the word *networking*, the first image that pops into their minds is a dark, cavernous conference hall where everyone is running around with big smiles on their faces, introducing themselves, and exchanging business cards with the hope of landing some six-figure job. It all seems a little self-serving. Even though this avenue may be part of the process for some, it's not the whole picture. *Networking is about building relationships.* This includes touching base with former employers, as Martin Ward, the IT professional mentioned in Chapter 5, did. That's an example of networking too.

Chances are you won't be working for the same company (let alone in the same industry) your entire life, so if you haven't done so already, make sure you develop professional contacts along the way. The best way to do that is to show up and work hard, treat people fairly and courteously, be generous, and help others. You'll have a professional network without the need to ever pass out a single business card.

MAKING THE CONNECTION

An unpredictable economy may waylay your best plans: Your industry is hit with massive layoffs, and your networking skills, which have gotten rusty while you steadily climbed the corporate ladder, have all but disappeared. Or you may be a recent graduate, whose primary goal is to move away from home rather than build working relationships. Or you may have reared a few children and, as a returnee to the job market, were preoccupied while everyone else was making those valuable working connections. Or you may have been more of a maverick than a team player during your working life and never felt the need to nurture any professional contacts.

According to John P. Kotter, author of *A Force for Change: How Leadership Differs from Management,* you're not unusual. "All too often these networks are either very thin—some people are well connected but most are not—or they are highly fragmented . . ." So how do you start to build a network when you've either neglected it or have never even begun to build one?

Step-by-step. Talk to people—whether they are friends, members of your church or community organization, professional affiliations, or industry experts— if you're fortunate enough to run into them at a professional conference, job fair, or the dry cleaners. Ask for suggestions or advice. If the conversation goes well, you may get a lead. If the conversation goes extremely well, someone may ask you to send your résumé. Again, though, don't expect immediate results. These things take time, and you'll have a few setbacks along the way. But look at these as opportunities for growth rather than a confirmation of failure. As Trang Gulian, a manager of staffing at Fannie Mae, put it: "Keep trying and keep a positive outlook."

REAL RESULTS

Networking is about building relationships. Sometimes you can initiate a relationship with a telephone call; sometimes it may take a few letters or inquiries. Whatever you do, make sure you take the time to do some homework about your industry or the company you want to work for. The more you know, the easier your entry into the desired field or position.

Also remember that many people you speak with as you travel down your career path have been in their profession for years, so be respectful. They know what they're talking about. Listen to them. The art of listening should extend beyond networking. Sherri Martin, of Deere & Company, said this: "If a retain search firm offers you counsel or advice relating to a position it is working on, listen . . . and follow the counsel. [These firms] know what works at the companies they work with."

For some, the thought of striking up a conversation with a stranger ranks right up there with jumping into Lake Michigan in January or . . . writing your résumé. Try to overcome this dread. Take a course on public speaking, or perhaps you could take an interim job and become a telemarketer or a customer service representative to sharpen your people skills. If the ability to talk to people doesn't come naturally, then ask yourself what you need to do to develop it. It's a valuable skill to have on all fronts. The ability to articulate what you need and want in a direct and clear manner will bear fruit in other areas of your life as well. For those who simply refuse to strike up a conversation, an emerging form of networking is currently taking place online. According to Barbara Kiviat, "broader business networking sites, such as Linkedin.com and Ryze.com," are becoming increasingly popular, and "Monster plans to roll out its own networking service" early next year (*Time*, November 24, 2003).

In "10 Secrets to Success," a series *Investor's Business Daily* conducted (January 10, 2003), the editors found that one of the top ten traits (ranking fourth) of leaders and other successful people in all walks of life was their predisposition to "Never Stop Learning." The article suggests that you "[g]o back to school or read books. Get training and acquire skills."

In Greek mythology, Athena jumps out of the head of Zeus, fully armed and ready to do battle, thus becoming Zeus's favorite daughter. Unfortunately, we rarely jump out of anywhere fully formed, armed, and ready because . . . we're human.

All your energies during college may have been consumed by a demanding major in physics; or by several children who refused to give you a minute's peace; or by dreaming up cutting-edge applications for the Internet. As a result, your people skills may be a little rusty. Many companies are eager, especially during chastening economies, to hire employees who know how to turn a negative into a positive. One of the surest ways to do this is to become teachable . . . yet again. Be open toward expanding your arsenal of job skills.

MAKING FORMAL INROADS

If a face-to-face encounter with unfamiliar people is not the best way for you to network (and there certainly are instances where you may not be able to have any personal contact) and online networking leaves you cold, then consider writing letters of inquiry to the company that has captured your interest. Do everything in your power, though, to have the name of a person. As Stacy Wilson of UPS said, "If someone from the company calls you, make sure you have [that person's] full, [correct] name." Sending a résumé or cover letter or letter of inquiry to Sir or Madam is too vague—especially for letters of inquiry. Take the time to find the name of the appropriate person to receive your correspondence.

Although a letter of inquiry may resemble a cover letter, its purpose is different. You are still on a fact-finding mission when networking and requesting information or expressing interest. You are not asking for a job yet. You can cover all kinds of topics in a letter of inquiry, especially if you have recently read about a particular company in either the industry news or the general news media. Topics include these:

- Explain your interest in the company and ask where you can send a résumé in the event an opening occurs.
- Request an informational interview with a particular person you read about.
- Ask what skills are required to work at the company.
- Ask if the person knows anyone in particular—in finance, accounting, editorial, IT, engineering, marketing, or sales—who may be interested in seeing your résumé. If the person says yes, ask to use his or her name when introducing yourself in your inquiry letter to the suggested person.

As is the case with cover letters, keep these inquiry letters brief (no more than one page) and concise. In the example in Figure 7.1, a recent graduate expresses his interest in the emerging field of depolymerization, a new technological process that turns waste products into oil, gas, and minerals.

FIGURE 7.1 *An Example of an Inquiry Letter*

Mr. Myles Williams
10 Huntington Street
New Brunswick, NJ 08100

August 20, 2003

Mr. William Lange
Director of Engineering
Changing World Technologies, Inc.
100 Hempstead Avenue
West Hempstead, NY 11100

Dear Mr. Lange:

Recently I read Brad Lemley's compelling article "Anything into Oil" in *Discover* magazine. The article leads me to believe your company, Changing World Technologies, Inc., may be on the brink of advancing one of the most inventive technological discoveries of this century.

I am intrigued by the depolymerization process—and the possibility of transforming carbon-based waste into environmentally safe oil, gas, and minerals. Turning "600 million tons of turkey guts and other waste" into "4 billion barrels of light Texas crude each year" is an innovation bound to have a major impact on both the environment and global affairs.

Thermal depolymerization is particularly interesting to me because of my background in chemical engineering. I am a recent graduate of Rutgers' engineering program and I would like to learn more about your company's conversion process. Your Website indicates that touring the Philadelphia plant is not feasible. Perhaps you could direct me to an individual at your Naval Business Center in Philadelphia who can speak with me about the skills needed to pursue a career in this field.

I would welcome this opportunity. I will contact you in the coming week to follow up on this request. Alternatively, I can be contacted via e-mail at mxwill@hotmail.com or on my cell phone at 973-296-6000.

Thank you.

Sincerely,

Myles Williams

The letter in Figure 7.1 is an example of how to express an interest in a company. In fact, no overt request for a job is ever made; it is simply an example of initiating contact. If a response is received, then the writer has another opportunity to build the relationship. Notice that the style of the first inquiry letter is formal. Provided you get a response that is friendly and familiar, then you can adopt a less formal (but professional) style in your next letter.

For those who are wondering what you are accomplishing by taking this approach, here is a breakdown.

- Contact with a particular individual at a specific company is made.
- Candidate expresses an interest in the company's business.
- Candidate demonstrates that he or she follows industry news and events in the field.
- Candidate shows familiarity with company's Web site.
- Candidate exhibits initiative.
- Candidate asks for a session to gather additional information.

The candidate may pursue this relationship through additional inquiry letters or through subsequent telephone calls or even a brief meeting or two. It all depends, however, on the prospective employer. Eventually, you want the opportunity to send your cover letter and résumé to an individual with whom you have a relationship. This networking strategy works best when it is developed in a deliberate, informed, and respectful manner. Make sure all of your communication with a prospective employer is professional and purposeful. Don't waste people's time by being unclear about what you want and what you have to offer.

PUTTING IT ALL TOGETHER

Kenneth Garrett, a vice president of human resources at FMC Corporation, advises that whatever you do, "spend time networking." You may be tempted to spend 90 percent of your time tweaking your almost-perfect résumé. This is a mistake. Your résumé needs to be in excellent shape, but here are ways to further your cause tenfold.

- Attend job fairs or industry conferences to get a chance to get out there and make contact with industry insiders.
- Get on the telephone and spend the morning tracking down the people who can steer you to the job vacancies that are a good fit.
- Write letters of inquiry to individuals at companies you want to work for.

- Talk to professionals who are part of your network at home or in the community or even on the golf course or tennis court.
- Follow leads, but don't "stalk" a job. Be patient and know when to back away gracefully.

When you network, what you want are job leads. You can't get leads if you're not prepared to put yourself out on the line and ask. If you don't have a network in place, start by cold calling your way into one. It takes initiative and courage, but it's all good practice for a rewarding career.

8

THE INTERVIEW

*"Do not delay in decision making. If an offer is made, either accept it or reject it.
A company does not like to have its offer of employment leveraged against
your current employer."*

ROCCO MANGIARANO
Director of Human Resources, Engelhard

You have been asked to come in for an interview—your chance to show a prospective employer that you are competent and a perfect fit for the position. A lot is riding on this brief encounter. From the survey "What Matters in Hiring Decisions" (NYTimes.com, February 5, 2002): "More than two-thirds (68 percent) of hiring managers say that an interview is the most effective way of determining whether they will hire a candidate."

You usually get one shot to make a favorable impression, so it's necessary to convince the employer—usually in less time than it takes to actually transport yourself to the company—that you are the perfect candidate for the job. Plan to be confident, persuasive, and positive from the time you extend your steady hand till the minute you thank the interviewer for his or her time. Cecilia McKenney of Pepsi Bottling Group sums it up by advising you to "sell yourself and be prepared for your interview."

PREPARATION IS KEY

Gearing up for the interview is a physical, emotional, and mental process, so make sure you cover all these bases, because interviews don't materialize without a good deal of hard work and preparation. Your meeting with the employer should showcase your talents and accomplishments. If you look at it as a challenge and opportunity, you'll arrive for your interview in the right frame of mind, provided you have done all your homework beforehand.

Precisely what type of preparation do you have to do before an interview?

A polished professional image is important at this stage, and your interview uniform depends primarily on the type of industry in which you work. For the corporate world, begin by investing in a good suit—the more conservative, the better. In the article "New Interview Uniform: Gray Means Business" in the *New York Times* (January 19, 2003), Francine Parnes wrote this comment: "As the unemployment rate continues to rise in an economy that remains stubbornly sluggish, ultraconservative is becoming the norm, and gray the color of choice." But adapt your style to your industry—a three-piece button-down gray suit may not work as well in entertainment, manufacturing, or the arts.

Even though the suit may be the big-ticket item, other details can add credence to—or detract from—your presentation. Think neat and professional, avoiding wearing anything outlandish. Whatever you can do to add polish to your image (fresh haircut) will increase your odds of getting an offer. Shoes should be shined and your briefcase (if you bring one to the interview) should contain extra copies of your résumé as well as letters of reference. Make sure it's organized, too, and that papers and pens don't come spilling out when you open it up to hand the interviewer your résumé or references.

Three letters of reference or three names of former employers (or professional associates) are usually the norm. If you haven't already provided these references to the prospective employer, it's a good idea to have them ready when you arrive for the interview. The letters may have been written by you and signed by your contacts, or they may have been written by the professional contacts themselves. Make sure you have made copies of these letters. If you are merely providing the names of your references, then type up a neat list that includes each name, the person's profession, address, telephone number, and the length of time each has known you. It's a good idea to give these people a heads-up that they may be receiving a telephone call from your prospective employer.

If you're feeling ill and can't conceal it, you may be better off rescheduling the interview. The stories of interviews gone sour are legion. A friend said she had the flu when she went to an interview at a large investment bank on the 58th floor of a building in Lower Manhattan, but because she had been in the job market for a while, she felt it was critical to show up. By the time she made it downtown and up the elevators, she was feeling faint and perspiring profusely. As the interview progressed, it became increasingly difficult for her to focus. She felt woozy, handed the interviewer her résumé, and lost her balance. When the interviewer asked her if she felt OK, she wouldn't admit having the flu and instead said she had vertigo and that the view from the window was making her dizzy.

When the interviewer asked her if working in the company's 58th-floor office would be a problem, she realized she didn't get the job.

Getting a good night's sleep before an interview will ease jangled nerves and help you present yourself in the best light. Try not to allow anything to get in the way between you and the interviewer. Your personal hygiene will be a factor (these people have to work with you if you are hired), so don't overwhelm the interviewer with your perfume or cologne. If your interview is after lunch, invest in some mints and check to make sure there is no spinach between your teeth. You want the focus of the interview to be on your skills and qualifications—not on some distracting quirk that shouts to the interviewer that you won't fit in.

ARRIVING ON TIME

Lateness is a red signal, so arrive approximately five minutes before the scheduled appointment. Arriving too early may be a nuisance. In an article on the art of the interview, "How Not to Succeed in Business" (*Fortune*, December 30, 2002), Stanley Bing wrote as follows: "So when my assistant knocks on my door half an hour before I'm supposed to see you and says, 'Betty Roover is here. I put her in the small conference room,' I have to think about you before I intended to do so, and that peeves me."

If you arrive earlier than planned, eat a croissant at a nearby deli (go easy on the coffee). Or you could listen to a CD or tape in the car (perhaps a Sedona Method tape that gives listeners a quick self-esteem boost). Or you could practice visualization (see yourself being offered the job). Check your directions the night before and give yourself plenty of time to get to your destination because *you do not want to be late.*

Prepping yourself for the interview is not unlike getting ready for a big game. Your frame of mind matters, so try not to have a heated dialogue about a curfew before you walk out your front door. You want to project a quiet energy in the interview. If you seem frazzled or unsettled, the employer may be reluctant to consider you for that deadline-heavy position. Don't worry, though, if you are slightly nervous. It's one of the hazards of the interview, and most prospective employers understand that. Overfocusing on your jitters, however, will just make them worse. Know that everyone in the world gets a bit tense when meeting someone for the first time. The best exercise for interview jitters is to stop worrying about being interesting and be interested in the job instead.

ONCE YOU'RE IN THE DOOR

Your general appearance and the time of your arrival register as soon as you walk into the office, but you can do a few more simple things to get off on the right start.

- Smile.
- Shake hands firmly (but don't break any bones).
- Take a seat after you are asked to—and then sit up straight.
- Make eye contact throughout the interview.
- Listen carefully.
- Don't complain about the weather or your old boss—or anything else for that matter.

The style of most interviews is conversational. The interviewer wants to know if you are qualified for the job and whether you will fit in well at the company. Usually the interviewer will restrict inquiries to these topics, though occasionally he or she may ask more specific or, in some cases, probing questions. All the research you have done about the company prior to this meeting will bolster your answers. Remember that you must sell your interest to the company, but you can't do this if you haven't already done your research. Hiring managers want to know if you can do the job. They are rarely interested in your personal life or your political opinions, so focus on the new job. Stick to the topic.

Patrick Dunn, a director of workforce planning at Unisys Corporation, said that "lack of related experience" usually disqualifies a candidate for a position at his company—and this can be easily revealed in the interview. Chances are you won't get to the point of interviewing without the necessary qualifications. But if the company's hiring manager does call you, and the new job is something of a stretch for you, then be prepared to convince the hiring manager that you are a quick learner and eager to tackle this new challenge.

WHAT WILL THEY ASK?

The first round of questioning is usually general (querying you on the specifics, such as your knowledge of computer languages, may be posed at a later point in the interview or further down the line at another interview with a department head). Speak clearly and authoritatively when answering questions and know exactly what is listed on your résumé. Here are a few questions an interviewer may ask you that you should think about ahead of time so as to be prepared with good answers before you go into the interview:

- What was your role at your previous job?
- What are your strengths and talents?
- What are your weaknesses?
- What impact did you have at your last job?
- What would you like to be doing in 5 years? 10 years? 15 years?
- How have you demonstrated your leadership abilities in previous employment?
- Are you willing to relocate?
- What is the most positive thing that a past employer has said about you?
- What is your salary range?
- Why do you want this job?
- How have you changed throughout your career?
- What was your most important career lesson?

Think about these questions, but don't memorize a script. You want to be as natural and relaxed as possible. Highlight your career accomplishments in your head, and then be prepared to talk about them. You might want to review the following items:

- Your past relationships with your boss as well as your coworkers
- Your values and personal ethics and respect for the values of others
- Your credibility with customers, managers, and peers
- Your ability to meet deadlines
- Your ability to rally support for a project
- Your value-oriented approach to problem solving
- Your efficient use of time
- Your ability to multitask, especially in cross-functional aspects of a project
- Your initiative
- Your ability to address all the details but see the bigger picture
- Your commitment to continual learning
- Your ability to communicate effectively
- Your thorough knowledge of your industry
- Your ability to adapt to your surroundings as well as to the personalities of those with whom you work
- Your ability to remove obstacles—such as legal or financial delays, deliverables or data from other groups, authorization for a proposal—from the work path of others

• Your commitment to integrating independent functions and keeping management briefed on all aspects of a project

Be prepared to back up all of your claims with examples of how you accomplished these capabilities in your previous employment. If you feel insecure and don't know what the right answers are to these types of questions, you may want to look at *The Perfect Interview: How to Get the Job You Really Want,* by John D. Drake (AMACOM, 2 ed., June 2002).

BEYOND THE USUAL

You probably didn't list your outside interests on your résumé, but sometimes interviewers will ask you about them during your meeting to differentiate you from the competition. Use this opportunity to speak about those interests in a way relevant to the job. According to Sherry Rest, of Lucent: "Outside interests are considered when weighing the candidate against other candidates with similar qualifications and work experience." Play down your love of poker, but feel free to mention your membership on the library's fundraising board. Don't offer any personal information, though, unless you're asked. On the Lehman Brothers company Web site, an article on the careers page, "Interviewing Tips," included this advice: "Your personal life is your own business. If it doesn't affect your ability to do the job, don't discuss it."

Always accentuate the positive. You've already passed the first test of getting in the door. Here's a comment in the study mentioned at the beginning of this chapter, "What Matters in Hiring Decisions": "Most (85 percent) hiring managers say that personality is a 'very' or 'extremely' important factor in their hiring decisions." Companies want solution-oriented individuals, not problem-ridden employees. If, by nature, you are dark and pessimistic, don't wear it on your sleeve.

You want to build a rapport with the person who is interviewing you, so don't send signals that you are bored, uncomfortable, or untruthful. Be direct and clear and use language your interviewer understands, even if you are an engineer or computer analyst. In *10 Insider Secrets to Job Hunting Success!* (Chicago: 10 Step Publications, 2002) Todd Bermont had this to say: "If interviewers see some of their qualities in you, they will be much more receptive to what you have to say." Bermont suggests further that you take note of the cues interviewers are sending: nodding and smiling are good; crossing the arms and looking out the window are not. If you notice that you are losing the interviewer's attention, ask what aspect of your background would he or she like you to focus on. A question, at this moment, may save the interview. Do not ask questions, however, that you should already know the answer to from looking at the Web site. You want to appear as informed as possible. If you feel stumped by the prospect of asking the interviewer questions, you may want to review a book by John Kador, *201 Best Questions to Ask on Your Interview* (McGraw-Hill Trade, February 2002).

By the time the interview is over, you will have volunteered a lot of information about your experience and background, asked a few relevant questions, and thanked the interviewer for his or her time. According to the article "Preparing for 'Tell Us About Yourself'" (*New York Times,* July 27, 2003), Anthony DePalma commented that "[i]nterviewers rarely give applicants an honest assessment of their performance," so you shouldn't quit your job until you get a solid offer.

You still have a few things to do before you celebrate. One of them is to send a thank you note immediately after the interview. It is acceptable to write—instead of type—this note on quality note paper so long as it is brief. If you want to add anything that you may have overlooked in the interview, and it requires more than a few sentences, then type the letter to make it more readable. But, again, use your best stationery.

A sample of what you should write in your short thank-you note is shown in Figure 8.1.

FIGURE 8.1 *A Sample Thank-You Note to an Interviewer*

January 29, 2003

Dear Ms. Gaines:

I enjoyed meeting you on Wednesday to learn more about the position with NAME OF COMPANY. I am excited by the prospect of working for your company and I believe my credentials are a good match for the NAME OF POSITION. If you need any additional information, please don't hesitate to contact me. Thank you for your time and I look forward to hearing from you.

Sincerely,
(Your signature)
Adam Smith

IF AN OFFER IS MADE

It is unlikely that an offer will be made at your first interview, although it does happen. For that reason, it's a good idea to know what salary is acceptable to you. If you have no clue what to ask for (or whether you should reject what is being offered), then check to see what the range is for people in similar positions in the same industry. Salary data are available on many Web sites, but for information on more than 150 professions, go to http://www.business2.com and look at "Who's Making What" (March 2003 issue). Engelhard's Rocco Mangiarano said that you should "know what you want to do, and what you would expect to be paid for doing it. Be flexible, and have a good understanding of what your minimally acceptable offer is. Too much procrastination and negotiation will get the offer taken off the table."

Another reason to be familiar with the company Web site is that it often posts the salary range for a particular job, which is a real advantage. Don't always expect top dollar, though. According to Dan Bankey of Mutual of Omaha: "We post the complete salary range with each job but would rarely ever hire at the top of the range. So we often use our online application question format to identify the specific target salary we have budgeted and then ask candidates to respond whether they will consider the job at that wage."

WHAT EMPLOYERS WANT

The *New York Times* hiring managers' survey already mentioned lists seven skills as "extremely" or "very" important: multitasking, the ability to learn new skills, leadership, analytical skills, writing, presentation, and project management. Nearly everyone has a few of these skills, so focus during the interview on what you do best. Don't get caught in the trap of interviewing the interviewer.

Take note of a few things you *shouldn't do* during an interview presented in Stanley Bing's December 30, 2002, *Fortune* article "How Not to Succeed in Business," which sums up his experience interviewing a candidate.

Ah, my friend! How different this could have been! You could have been right on time and researched the job and known what I was seeking and looked me in the eye and told me how you might be able to help me, because I need help, I really do. You could have made me feel that being with you for a couple of years would be fun. You could have made me like you. I wanted to!

GETTING A JOB
WITHOUT A RÉSUMÉ

"In the past we would work hard to fit a square peg into a round hole,
but today, with so many well-qualified candidates in the job market,
we no longer have to do this."

DAN BANKEY
Manager of Strategic Staffing, Mutual of Omaha

Just as technology has dramatically changed the applicant's process of looking for a job, so too has it changed the employer's process of making new hires. Today, a growing number of companies are pushing technology in new directions, leveraging their Web sites with software that gives them more control over the hiring process and a whole new level of efficiency.

If this trend represents the future of recruiting, it will spell the end of the résumé as we know it—and has significant implications for anyone in the job market.

CHANGE OF FOCUS

In today's recruiting environment, every position posted on a corporate Web site or Internet job site engenders a flood of résumés, which someone in human resources wades through manually to identify candidates. This process usually includes keyword searches to hone in on particular skills, knowledge, and credentials. Generally, the first review of résumés is surprisingly quick. In fact, survey results indicate that most of the Fortune 500 participants spend an average of one to two minutes per résumé.

Both companies and applicants would no doubt agree that a rapid pass through a pile of résumés is a rather haphazard way to identify the top candidates. Even so, this prescreening part of the hiring cycle is time consuming for companies, especially now that the Internet makes it so easy for job seekers to apply online (combined with a job market in which the supply of applicants frequently exceeds demand).

To make the prescreening process more methodical and efficient, a growing number of companies are using recruiting software.

ONE COMPANY'S EXPERIENCE

Technology has literally redefined Mutual of Omaha's recruiting practices, according to Dan Bankey, manager of strategic staffing, who has primary responsibility for hiring. The company uses an "electronic applicant management system" called Recruitsoft. "It has caused us to really reexamine how we do business," Bankey said. "We believe we stand on the edge of a major shift in how we connect with people interested in job opportunities."

In the past, Mutual of Omaha relied on résumés to prescreen candidates. "The old model for hiring was really driven by the résumé," Bankey continued. While noting that résumés can run the gamut from horrible to outstanding, he added that all of them have one thing in common: "Résumés seek to provide information to the prospective employer as the job candidate wants to present it."

In other words, résumés put the applicant in the driver's seat, with the leeway to decide which information to include, which to emphasize, and which to leave out. Even though this may seem to give the job seeker an advantage, that is not necessarily so, because applicants almost never have a complete understanding of what the company is looking for, what it values in employees, and what resonates with human resources.

Mutual of Omaha has turned the résumé-driven approach upside down via its recruiting software. "Now we obtain information the way we want to see it," said Bankey. "We elicit specific information from applicants that we can easily process and manipulate."

For the company, the advantages of this shift are plentiful. The software does the following:

- Makes data easier to sort and retrieve.
- Filters candidates by matching data against the job requirements.
- Enables the company to ask job-specific questions regarding experience, skills, and interests for each position that is posted.
- Ranks candidates.
- Improves and accelerates communication with applicants.

Looking at the bigger picture, Bankey agrees this new model is helping Mutual of Omaha achieve its goal of hiring top-quality talent at a reduced cost.

HOW IT WORKS

Mutual of Omaha advertises job openings online on its corporate Web site and on other job Web sites, including DirectEmployers.com. Candidates interested in a specific position apply online, answering the types of personal information questions that appear on standard paper applications.

The system also asks candidates job-specific questions, which are designed to ensure the company receives both the information and the focus it wants, according to Bankey. These questions typically explore areas that may not show up in standard applications and résumés, and job seekers are frequently asked to quantify their accomplishments. For example, a sales manager position might include questions on the types of products that applicants have experience with; the size of the geographic areas they covered; the amount of revenue they produced; and their areas of sales management (e.g., recruiting, training, line manager).

To assess skills for a technology position, the questionnaire might ask candidates to list the applications and software they know and to define their level of proficiency. It might also inquire whether they are interested in using those applications or tools again—a query that wouldn't usually come up until the interview.

Mutual of Omaha often takes the opportunity to ask behaviorally based questions as well. For example, the questionnaire for a customer service position might ask how the applicant would handle an irate customer and what the applicant learned from a difficult experience.

If visitors to the Mutual of Omaha site are not interested in specific positions, they have the option to complete Job Finder, a form on which they can list skills, experience, and interests. The company also refers people who send unsolicited résumés or other communications expressing interest in employment to Job Finder. As with the job-specific applications, Job Finder requests information in a format that is easily searchable. The information then resides in the company's database as a source of potential future candidates.

Each time a new job opens, Mutual of Omaha "mines" the database containing job-specific applicants as well as the Job Finder database, explained Bankey. If a close match surfaces from either one, the company invites candidates to consider applying for that specific job.

Bankey stressed that in screening candidates, the company focuses on the information it requested, even though candidates have the option to include résumés and specific comments about themselves. "We're moving away from résumés, but getting applicants away from résumés is the biggest challenge," he said, adding that it's only a matter of time. "We're going to take résumés out of the system altogether at some point."

WHAT RECRUITING SOFTWARE MEANS FOR THE APPLICANT

From the applicant's point of view, a good way to think about recruiting software is that it makes the individual, rather than the résumé, the key driver in the hiring process. Moreover, the fact that software helps companies streamline their process can also make job-hunting more efficient for applicants. Indeed, Bankey noted that Mutual of Omaha has actually seen a slight increase in the number of applications it receives.

To utilize these recruiting software systems, applicants will ideally have an Internet connection and enough expertise to use a PC. But for those who don't, some companies offer a work-around. Bankey, for instance, noted that Mutual of Omaha established an 800 number, giving people the option to enter information over the telephone, although he expects to eventually phase out this feature as it is used by only a small percentage of applicants.

Most important, applicants need to focus on completing the prescreening questionnaires, investing the time to tailor their responses to the company's requirements. "Job candidates really need to think about how to market themselves," said Bankey. "They need to clearly and concisely relate their background to the opportunities we're trying to fill." Examples of recruiting software from Mutual of Omaha's Career Section are displayed in Figures 9.1 and 9.2.

For applicants who are serious about a particular job, methodology such as Mutual of Omaha's presents an opportunity to put their best foot forward with thorough and thoughtful responses, giving the prospective employer a broader picture of skills and personality than a résumé and cover letter can convey. Although some job seekers may feel shortchanged because they would rather meet someone from human resources in person to discuss their skills and career goals, human resources professionals may take a different view. According to Bankey, "Face-to-face doesn't have to happen this soon."

Another advantage of recruiting software is quicker response time. "We want to recruit the most qualified candidates, and the faster we can get to them, the better chance we have of hiring them," said Bankey. This desire by the company to push the process forward also accelerates the hiring cycle for applicants.

Anyone who makes the first cut at Mutual of Omaha finds out quickly—and has the knowledge that they've cleared a fairly rigorous prescreening process. Likewise, if individuals are not qualified, the company lets them know immediately, thus allowing all parties to avoid wasting time with communications that won't lead to job offers. "The system takes much of the lag time out of the hiring process," noted Bankey.

Yet another plus of recruiting software is that candidates remain in databases, up to three years in the case of Mutual of Omaha—according to Bankey's research, this is well above the average of 6 to 12 months at most large companies—and means that even if your application is not suited for a specific job, your information remains on file for other positions or future openings. "Before, it was one job, one look at a résumé," said Bankey. "Now we can remine candidates for other jobs." As an example, he explained how Mutual of Omaha receives thousands of letters of interest from interns. "In one day, we used the system to find four interns who were a perfect match."

In sum, recruiting software is just another extension of the technology that can make job-hunting both easier and more demanding, and it's probably here to stay. "I believe this is the way of the future—and not the too-far-off future," concludes Bankey.

FIGURE 9.1 *Sample Recruiting Software from Mutual of Omaha Describing District Sales Manager Position*

Exit

District Sales Manager (Houston, Texas) – 008492

Job Description

(Apply Online)

Description
Plan, staff and direct a unit of independent contracted agents; develop market and territory strategies to effectively meet the long-term objectives of the division office.

Work with the Recruiting Specialist to build a pool of high potential candidates and ensure selection processes are appropriately administered.

Oversee the formal training programs provided for the agents in all sales, marketing and product areas.

Conduct field training for agents assigned to the unit. Join the agent when making client calls, assisting them as needed to introduce the product, answer client questions and close the sale. Provide constructive feedback to the agent to aid in career development.

Manage the day-to-day performance of agents assigned to Sales Units. Establish performance guidelines including call volumes, product mix, persistency levels, loss ratios, etc. to provide agents with attainable sales targets.

Monitor agent performance, provide feedback for encouragement and evaluate sales results, measuring achievement against planned objectives. Discuss any agent performance issues with the General Manager to seek concurrence for appropriate corrective action.

Manage the environment and activities of the Unit to ensure agents maintain a professional and ethical relationship with each other, Company associates and clients; communicate clear expectations for them as representatives of Mutual of Omaha.

Support the General Manager in the total management of the division office; remain focused on long-term objectives, make sound business decisions in support of Company goals, and comply with all Company policies, Federal regulations and industry guidelines.

Qualifications
Proven sales management skills.

Current licensure or ability to become licensed with Mutual, United and any required Affiliate Company in the state(s) required for the agency.

Successful career as an insurance agent.

Complete understanding and knowledge of insurance products, policies, and coverages, and related guidelines.

Good communication, human relations and motivational skills.

Strong planning and leadership skills; sound judgment and problem-solving skills.

Profile
Job Field Sales/Marketing
Locations TX-Houston
Schedule Full-time
Shift Day Job

Compensation and Benefits
Pay Basis Yearly

Flex Time Available? Yes

Send This Job To A Friend   (Apply Online)

FIGURE 9.2 *Sample Recruiting Software for Applicants Seeking Position of District Sales Manager at Mutual of Omaha*

Exit | Help

District Sales Manager (Houston, Texas) – 008492

Hold down the **Ctrl** key to make multiple selections or to deselect items.
Required fields are marked with an asterisk (*).

☐ Accept invitations by email on career opportunities matching this profile.

Personal Information
**Please do not include punctuation such as commas or periods in your name and address.
Include name suffix (ex: Jr) following your last name. Please keep your email address current.**

First Name*   Last Name*   Initial
[   ]   [   ]   [   ]

Street Address (Line 1)*   Street Address (Line 2)
[   ]   [   ]

City*   Zip/Postal Code*
[   ]   [   ]

Country*   County*
[————Not Specified———— ▾]   [   ]
State/Province*
[————Not Specified——— ▾]
Closest Metropolitan Area*
[————Not Specified——— ▾]
Home Phone   Work Phone
Include area codes in your phone numbers. *
[   ]   [   ]

Email Address*
[   ]

If referred to Mutual of Omaha by an employee, please indicate their name here.
[   ]

Are you at least 18 years of age?*   If not, are you at least 16 years of age?
[————Not Specified———— ▾]   [————Not Specified———— ▾]

Are you related to anyone in our employ?*
[————Not Specified——— ▾]

If yes, who?   Relationship
[   ]   [   ]

Were you ever employed or contracted by Mutual of Omaha?*
[————Not Specified——— ▾]

When? (Month, Year) Where?
[mm ▾] [yyyy ▾]   [   ]

If your name differed from your present name during your education
or while employed for any position noted, please indicate former name:
[⌃]
[   ]
[⌄]

FIGURE 9.2 *(continued)*

Are you currently employed by an affiliate company?*   If yes:

————————Not Specified————————   ⌄   ————————Not Specified————————   ⌄

Please list the counties and states you have resided
at for the last 7 years:*

Are you one of the following?   If no, what is your immigration status?
U.S. Citizen
Permanent Resident
Asylee or refugee
Temporary resident under on the 1986 amnesty programs*

————————Not Specified————————   ⌄

Have you ever been convicted of any felonies (for any reason) or
misdemeanors involving dishonesty, moral turpitude, harm to an
individual, breach of trust, misappropriation of funds, fraud, or forgery?*

————————Not Specified————————   ⌄

If yes, please explain:

May we contact your current employer?*

————————Not Specified————————   ⌄

Questionnaire
Please answer the following questions.

1. **Do you have prior insurance sales experience?***
   ⚪ Yes
   ⚪ No

2. **What was your personal annualized 1st year commission sales results and what year did this occur? (If not applicable, indicate none.)***

3. **What percentage of these results was from life insurance sales? (If not applicable, indicate none.)***

FIGURE 9.2 (continued)

4. **Do you have a current life and health insurance license?***

○ Yes

○ No

5. **If yes, please indicate the states in which you are currently licensed: (If not applicable, indicate none.)**
*

6. **Which licenses do you currently hold? (Select all that apply.)***

☐ Series 6

☐ Series 7

☐ Series 24

☐ Series 26

☐ Series 63

☐ I do not have any of these licenses, but I am willing to complete the requirements to obtain these licenses.

☐ I do not have any of these licenses and I am not interested in obtaining them.

7. **Have you managed a career agency sales office?***

○ Yes

○ No

8. **If yes, how many agents were you managing? (If no, indicate none.)***

9. **If yes, what was the last year you were active as the manager of this operation?***

○ 2000-Present

○ 1996-1999

○ Prior to 1996

○ Not applicable

10. **If yes, what were the annualized 1st year commission sales results of your office? (If no, indicate none.)***

FIGURE 9.2 *(continued)*

11. How many new career agents were recruited by you in the last year you were there? (If not applicable, indicate none.)*

12. Are you currently involved in any personal or professional development programs?*
- ◯ Yes
- ◯ No

13. If yes, describe the programs you are involved in.*

14. Indicate current professional certifications:*

15. Indicate the responsibilities in which you have proven experience:*
- ☐ Recruitment
- ☐ Interviewing/Selection
- ☐ Planning Projects
- ☐ Mentoring/Career Counseling
- ☐ Coaching and Joint Field Work
- ☐ Retention Strategies
- ☐ Affirmative Action Plans
- ☐ None of the above

16. Indicate the Financial Service Products in which you have a thorough knowledge:*
- ☐ Life Insurance
- ☐ Disability Income
- ☐ Long-term Care
- ☐ Annuities
- ☐ Critical Ilness
- ☐ Variable Products
- ☐ None of the above

FIGURE 9.2 *(continued)*

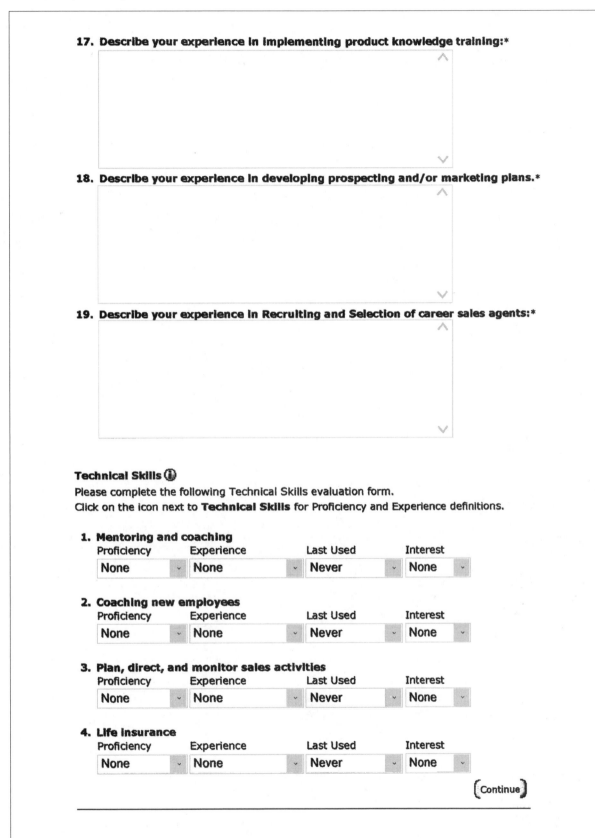

17. Describe your experience in implementing product knowledge training:*

18. Describe your experience in developing prospecting and/or marketing plans.*

19. Describe your experience in Recruiting and Selection of career sales agents:*

Technical Skills ⓘ

Please complete the following Technical Skills evaluation form.

Click on the icon next to **Technical Skills** for Proficiency and Experience definitions.

1. Mentoring and coaching

Proficiency	Experience	Last Used	Interest
None	None	Never	None

2. Coaching new employees

Proficiency	Experience	Last Used	Interest
None	None	Never	None

3. Plan, direct, and monitor sales activities

Proficiency	Experience	Last Used	Interest
None	None	Never	None

4. Life insurance

Proficiency	Experience	Last Used	Interest
None	None	Never	None

(Continue)

10

THREE FORTUNE 500 HIRING PROFESSIONALS CRITIQUE ONE RÉSUMÉ

"At least 50 percent of résumés contain errors. With my previous background, those errors tend to jump out at me."

DAN BANKEY
Manager of Strategic Staffing, Mutual of Omaha

Even with the best qualifications and skills, job applicants need to know how to tailor their résumés so that hiring managers pull them out of the pile and onto their desk or into their database. That often means recasting your skills and accomplishments to fit a specific job description.

I asked three Fortune 500 hiring professionals to critique one résumé—see Figure 10.1. Host Marriott's Lisa Whittington (23,000 employees), Kindred Healthcare's Donna Campbell (53,400 employees), and Jabil Circuit's Heather McBride (20,000 employees) offer their comments and suggestions for improvement.

To summarize their recommendations: Accomplishments—with verifiable numbers—speak volumes as does progressive responsibility. Many job seekers can stay in the same job for ten years, but hiring managers are practiced at recognizing the ones who steadily progress throughout their careers. Those are the job applicants who catch their attention.

Make sure your résumé reflects your true accomplishments and job progress. If you do that, you increase your chances of not floating around in the unemployed pool for too long. Before reading the comments from the Fortune 500 hiring professionals, review the same résumé they did and see if you can spot the areas that need improvement.

FIGURE 10.1 *Theresa Smith's Original Résumé*

THERESA SMITH
100 East 10th Street, #10E, New York, NY 10000
(212) 674-1000

EXPERIENCE

1999-present   **Alexandria International Finance Corporation,** New York, NY
                   Director, Corporate Communications
- Work with senior management to develop and implement communications strategies and programs to support the company's business objectives.
- Serve as editor of monthly internal publication, managing content development, writing, editing, design and production.
- Write speeches, memos and other communications for senior executives.

1992-99   **Shearman & Sterling,** New York, NY
                   Marketing Manager
- Planned, wrote, edited, and oversaw design for firm's first annual review, working with partners in offices around the world.
- Developed strategies and materials for presentations and proposals to multinational corporations, investment banks and governments.
- Developed new materials for firm practices and regions including Latin America and Asia.
- Served as editor of the internal newsletter, managing content development, writing and editing.

                   Media and Communications Specialist
- Worked with partners to write articles for business press.
- Assisted director in developing and implementing communications plan.
- Wrote and edited press releases and fielded calls from the media.

1991-92   **United Nations Development Programme** and **The Economist Group**
- Consultant for Latin American projects

1990-91   **Senie Kerschner International Housing Ltd.,** Moscow, USSR
                   Deputy General Director, Joint Venture Rosinka
- Served as first Moscow-based representative for Western partner in U.S.-Soviet joint venture in construction sector.
- Conducted meetings with Soviet partner, international and Russian banks, international construction companies and potential clients in the business and diplomatic community.
- Participated in negotiations with Soviet government officials.

1988-90   **Philip Morris International,** New York, NY
                   Business Communications Specialist, International Planning Department
- Wrote/edited presentations for senior management. Projects included president's five-year business plan for board of directors and vice chairman's presentation for securities analysts.
- Summarized international business for president's monthly written report to board of directors.

1984-88   **Business International Corporation/The Economist Group,** New York, NY
                   Editor, Business Latin America and *Senior Analyst/Latin America*
- Analyzed the impact of economic, political, regulatory and financial changes in Latin America.
- Planned and edited *Business Latin America,* a weekly newsletter.
- Traveled to region on fact-finding missions, conducting interviews with government officials, economists, executives and bankers.

1981-84   **Whitney Communications Corporation,** New York, NY
                   Managing Editor; Senior Editor; Editorial Assistant
1980-81   **Marsans International,** New York, NY. *Administrative Assistant*
1978-80   **Inlingua Idiomas,** Barcelona, Spain. *Language Instructor*

EDUCATION: New York University, Master of Arts, Latin American Studies. **McGill University,** Bachelor of Arts, English. **LANGUAGES:** Fluent Spanish; proficient French; rudimentary Russian **CITIZENSHIP:** United States, Ireland

GENERAL FEEDBACK

Many times, job seekers spend too much time with formatting the résumé and less time with the actual content. You want the résumé to look clean, but you should spend the most amount of time figuring out how to market your experience in a way that recruiters and hiring managers see how it relates to the job he or she is trying to fill. I have many versions of my résumé. I always start with the job posting that I am applying for and then I adjust my résumé to draw attention to the requirements that the company is looking for.

POSITIVE FEEDBACK

- Theresa has chosen to highlight her professional experience by placing it first. Because she has had a great deal of professional experience, this is the ideal place for it. Had she been a recent graduate, placing her education first would be more desirable.
- Theresa was also able to keep her résumé to one page. This is desirable—as long as she is able to emphasize why her experience qualifies her for the job to which she is applying.

AREAS FOR IMPROVEMENT

- Always place your e-mail address on your résumé. Recruiters like myself find it is sometimes easier to make contact with candidates via e-mail rather than playing phone tag.
- Think about placing a list of accomplishments or professional achievements inside your résumé. Your résumé is simply an advertisement about you, a quick list of why you are better than your competitors is a classic marketing ploy. For example, if Theresa had been able to increase sales by 10 percent by creating a marketing plan at Shearman & Sterling, she should definitely place that in her résumé. If the communication strategy she developed at her present employer resulted in winning a $100 million contact, that is also something she wants to mention. Numbers always talk; if you can relate your accomplishments to dollars, your résumé will get more attention from recruiters.
- Computer skills: In the electronic era, almost all positions require knowledge of Microsoft products. SAP, Peoplesoft, and other operating systems are also very desirable. Without that information on your résumé, you might be overlooked by someone who has a little less experience but lists experience in the operating system the company uses.

Heather McBride
Sr. HR Generalist/Recruiting Manager
Jabil Circuit

GENERAL FEEDBACK

It would be a little easier to give constructive comments if I had an actual job with a description to which this candidate was responding. Of course, this isn't the case, so I will give more general feedback.

POSITIVE FEEDBACK

- I liked the candidate's use of past tense when referring to past positions and present tense when referring to her current job.
- Overall, a good résumé.

AREAS FOR IMPROVEMENT

- Résumé, in this case, should have been expanded to two pages. This would have made it appear less "bunched up" and would have allowed the bullets under each position to be indented, giving a more readable overall look. It would have also enabled the candidate to add some useful information, such as:
  - ✓ An objective, which gives the screener an idea of the candidate's purpose in applying.
  - ✓ A line stating nature of the business for each employer (really important).
  - ✓ A section listing technical familiarity/capabilities.
- The heading could have been expanded to include an e-mail address and alternate phone numbers, if applicable.
- Candidate should have shown the dates of the two positions held at Shearman & Sterling.
- The position at United Nations Development Programme should have been better explained. What kind of projects?
- Perhaps the two earliest positions (Administrative Assistant and Language Instructor) could have been omitted, as they are quite dated and don't tie in to recent experience.

Donna Campbell
Manager of Recruiting Services
Kindred Healthcare

POSITIVE FEEDBACK:

- I like that the résumé is on one page—easy and quick to review.

AREAS FOR IMPROVEMENT:

- I like to know what phone number is listed—work or home—so I know if I need to be discreet when I call.
- I like it when a résumé has an objective listed first; that way I know what the person is looking for and whether it matches our objective.
- I would probably remove the earlier work history as it's really not relevant to her current experience, and the assignments have short tenure.
- I would remove the citizenship information if the applicant is applying in the United States, unless the employer is requiring it be included for security purposes, for example.
- I would recommend moving the employment dates to the right side of the résumé, especially if there is a short tenure with some employers, so they aren't the first thing the person reviewing the résumé sees.
- For some specialized positions, it helps to include the type of business that the former employer conducted, especially if the names aren't easily recognizable.
- My last recommendation would be to always include a cover letter that tells the prospective employer why you are looking for work and why you are the best person for the position for which you are applying. I often have multiple openings and don't know which position people are applying for if they just send their résumé without a letter.

Lisa A. Whittington, CEBS, PHR
Director, Human Resources
Host Marriott Corporation

THE REVISION

Lisa Whittington and Heather McBride both liked that the résumé is on one page but then asked for additional information, including an "objective" or list of "accomplishments" and technical skills, so the revised résumé (see Figure 10.2) will be expanded to two pages to accommodate the additional information.

First, the type size (10.5) is bumped up to 12 points. If it's necessary to reduce the size to squeeze in more information at a later point, then it's better to start at 12 than to start at 10.5. Next, it's important to add more white space—to give the

FIGURE 10.2 *Sample of Theresa Smith's Revised Résumé Incorporating Three Critiques*

THERESA SMITH
100 East 10th Street, #10E
New York, NY 10000
(212) 674-1000 (H)
TS100@worldnet.att.net

PROFESSIONAL OBJECTIVE

Senior Corporate Communications position with an international organization that will benefit from my executive and employee communications experience, knowledge of international business and finance and leadership skills

EXPERIENCE

Alexandria International Finance Corporation, New York, NY   1999-present

Director, Corporate Communications

- Work with senior management to develop and implement communications strategies and programs to support business objectives of financial services organization with offices in 25 countries.
- Write speeches, memos and other communications for senior executives, including Chairman, CEO, CFO, COO and CIO.
- Work with senior executives on presentations and memos to the Board.
- Write, edit and oversee production of 20-page monthly internal publication, working with executives to provide coverage of all subsidiaries' business initiatives, internal programs, such as Six Sigma; and major industry developments.
- Write sections of annual report and edit entire document.
- Oversaw redesign of internal newsletter, improving quality of content, graphics and design while reducing costs; conducted readership survey that indicated 94 percent of employees find it a valuable tool for staying abreast of business.

Shearman & Sterling, New York, NY   1992-1999

Marketing Manager, Corporate Communications   1994-1999

- Planned, wrote, edited and oversaw design for international law firm's first annual review, working with law partners in offices around world.
- Developed strategies and materials for presentations and proposals to win business from multinational corporations, investment banks and governments.
- Developed marketing materials for firm's areas of practice (such as securities, law, mergers and acquisitions) and regions, including Latin America and Asia.
- Served as editor of monthly internal newsletter, writing, editing and producing publication and working with partners in all offices to develop ideas.

Media and Communications Specialist   1992-1994

- Worked with law partners to write articles for placement in business publications, including the *Wall Street Journal* and the *New York Times*.
- Assisted director in developing and implementing communications plan.
- Wrote and edited press releases and fielded media inquiries.
- Served as editor of monthly internal newsletter, writing, editing and producing the publication, and working with partners in all offices to develop ideas.
- Recruited to join the firm's newly created Marketing Department after two years and promoted to Marketing Manager.

FIGURE 10.2 *(continued)*

United Nations Development Programme and **The Economist Group**   1991-1992

- Wrote a brochure on procurement best practices for division of United Nations.
- Wrote articles for *Business Latin America;* edited a Latin American research report; helped organize Latin American finance seminar for The Economist Group, a provider of business information and analysis on international business and world affairs (and a former employer).

Senie Kerschner International Housing Ltd., Moscow, USSR   1990-1991

Deputy General Director, Joint Venture Rosinka

- Served as first Moscow-based representative for Western partner in U.S.-Soviet joint venture in construction sector.
- Conducted meetings with Soviet partner, international and Russian banks, construction companies and potential clients in business and diplomatic community.
- Participated in negotiations with Soviet government officials.

Philip Morris International, New York, NY   1988-1990

Business Communications Specialist, International Planning Department

- Wrote/edited presentations for senior management at Fortune 500 company. Projects included President's five-year business plan for Board of Directors and Vice Chairman's presentation for securities analysts.
- Summarized international business for President's monthly written report to Board.

Business International Corporation/The Economist Group, New York, NY   1984-1988

Editor, Business Latin America and *Senior Analyst/Latin America*

- Analyzed impact of political, regulatory and financial changes in Latin America.
- Planned and edited *Business Latin America,* a weekly newsletter.
- Traveled to region on fact-finding missions, conducting interviews with government officials, economists, executives and bankers.
- Promoted to Editor and Senior Analyst after two years.

Whitney Communications Corporation, New York, NY   1981-1984

Managing Editor

- Promoted after one year to Managing Editor for monthly consumer magazine.
- Promoted after two years to Senior Editor.
- Edited, proofread, researched and handled administrative work for Editor in Chief.

EDUCATION
New York University, Master of Arts, Latin American Studies
McGill University, Bachelor of Arts, English

LANGUAGES
- Fluent Spanish (worked as Language Instructor at Inlingua Idiomas, Barcelona, Spain)
- Proficient French; rudimentary Russian

CITIZENSHIP   **COMPUTER SKILLS**
United States, Ireland   Word, Excel, Lotus Notes

text a less "bunched-up" look. At this point, you can see what you have to work with to add the other features that the Fortune 500 hiring professionals requested.

It's essential today that an e-mail address be part of your contact information, so, as suggested, this has been included in the contact section.

All three Fortune 500 hiring professionals did request a focus statement so that they understand precisely which position the candidate is qualified for. The professional objective that begins this résumé now binds the key information together.

The most recent position in a résumé usually is the most important one, which is why the job description for the first job listed was expanded. The candidate also adds *results,* something emphasized again and again by most of the Fortune 500 participants.

Moving the employment dates to the right is a useful suggestion provided by Lisa Whittington for those who have short tenure at jobs. The dates were further de-emphasized by putting them in roman typeface rather than bold.

Experience dating back more than 15 years is often considered irrelevant by *many* (but not all) hiring professionals, especially if it is unrelated to the position you are currently seeking. The suggestion to remove the last two positions is taken, but because the new professional objective now emphasizes the international focus, the candidate's experience in Spain is reconfigured in the language section. Removing the last two positions also provides the candidate an opportunity to highlight the progressive responsibility at Whitney Communications.

A description of the type of business is given in each position held. If you struggle for the language to describe your business, go to the company's Web site to find the wording you need to briefly describe what your company does. If your former employer is a smaller company, make sure you mention somewhere what type of business it is. For larger, well-known companies, it isn't necessary to mention the type of business, as those employers need no description. That's one of the rewards for working for a large corporation. In fact, Carol F. Nelson, second vice president of staffing and relocation services at TIAA-CREF, said that candidates who have worked for "large or nationally recognized employers" usually catch her attention.

Finally, promotions were highlighted. Companies want to see your career progress. The suggestion by Donna Campbell to provide a date for the first position at Sherman & Sterling is taken, but the promotions are also reemphasized in the bulleted material. One- and two-page résumés cannot fully do justice to your contributions, so listing your promotion(s) allows hiring professionals to see in a nutshell that your former employers valued you as an employee.

It's essential that the hiring professional doesn't have to work too hard when reading your résumé. Overall, the new résumé is more results oriented and precise, and it highlights the candidate's qualifications and strengths in a more readable format. Once you have the basic information on a résumé, revisions are not time consuming, so take another look at your résumé and make sure it does justice to your skills and accomplishments.

THE MANY FACES OF YOUR RÉSUMÉ

It can be daunting to think of revising a résumé every time you apply for a job, but don't be discouraged. Now that you know what hiring professionals expect to see in a résumé, the revision doesn't have to be extensive and is relatively painless to perform. The revision in Figure 10.2, based on the feedback from the three Fortune 500 hiring professionals, is now full of specifics and detail about career progression. It's a much stronger résumé as a result—and the original took only an hour to revise.

The two versions in Figures 10.3 and 10.4 illustrate how one résumé can be tweaked in such a way that the emphasis slightly shifts according to the particular job being applied for. The first sample (Figure 10.3) focuses on the job candidate's marketing *sales* experience (with an accompanying plain text version); the second sample (Figure 10.4) focuses on the job candidate's marketing *communications* experience (accompanied by a plain text version).

TIME TO EXPERIMENT

Now that you know the importance of having an e-mail-friendly plain text résumé as well as an original version with all its embellishment and elaborate formatting, plan to experiment a little by tweaking your own résumé so that it fits an array of job descriptions. Look at the samples in Figures 10.3, 10.4, 10.5, and 10.6. The first revision (Figure 10.2) didn't take long, but the job candidate said the second revision was the deciding factor in getting the interview for the position of Marketing Director in Internet Media.

FIGURE 10.3 *Sample Résumé Emphasizing Sales Experience*

Megan Kearon
100 Sunnyside Avenue * Mill Valley * CA 94941 * 415.388.1000 * Mbyrn@hotmail.com

PROFILE: Marketing communications professional with both international and domestic sales, public relations and account management experience with a focus on high technology and Internet media properties

International
- Built European sales-operations teams for Excite Europe in London, England.
- Recognized more than $10 million in annual revenue for Excite UK and Excite Europe.
- Worked in various sales-related roles, with more than four years' experience in sales, account management and sales operations for Internet companies.
- Increased in-territory sales by more than 50% within one-year period.
- Managed Excite Key Accounts that accounted for more than $12 million in annual revenue.

Management
- Managed four sales-operations groups across ten European Web sites.
- Managed group budgeting, development (organizational and employee), hiring and training.
- Chosen to train in LeadSmart Leadership Workshop and Sales Management Training.

Public Relations
- Handled publicity, international and domestic, for *Star Wars: Episode II Attack of the Clones.*
- Managed international and domestic public relations for CNET: The Computer Company (Internet and television shows).
- Provided PR for Lotus Development Corp., LBMS, and Tivoli Systems.
- Enrolled in related coursework: Writing for Public Relations, Public Relations for Managers.

Work Experience

Lucasfilm Ltd., Nicasio, CA
PUBLICITY PROJECT COORDINATOR (January - June 2002)
- Assisted Lucasfilm domestic and international publicity teams on the launch of *Star Wars: Episode II Attack of the Clones.*
- Worked with domestic and international press to secure interviews with *Star Wars* cast and crew members; provided movie images; and fact-checked final articles.
- Assisted with development and execution of the *Star Wars: Episode II* Press Junket, which hosted more than 400 press people.

Excite@Home, Redwood City, CA
SENIOR MANAGER, INTERNATIONAL BUSINESS DEVELOPMENT (Nov. 2000 - August 2001)
- Led international negotiations to secure distribution and content deals with Apple, Microsoft, The Weather Channel, etc.

FIGURE 10.3 *(continued)*

- Coordinated International Business Development and U.S. Business Development team.
- Leveraged U.S. content deals internationally, such as Muze, MapBlast and MusicMatch.
- Resolved conflict on deals that were no longer viewed as beneficial to Excite.

Excite Europe, London
DIRECTOR, ACCOUNT MANAGEMENT EUROPE (May 1999 - November 2000)
- Hired, trained and managed staff of 20 people, which consisted of four teams (Partner Services, Sales Finance, Advertising Development and Ad Technologies).
- Negotiated Pan-European business contracts, global and Pan-European distribution and sponsorship deals, such as DoubleClick, Real Media, Matchlogic, Microsoft, Hewlett-Packard, Netscape, Egg and Travelocity.
- Generated more than $10 million in annual sponsorship revenue.
- Developed business processes that impacted Excite Europe's day-to-day business practices.

Excite, Redwood City, CA
ACCOUNT MANAGER, SPONSORSHIP AND PROMOTION (January 1998 - May 1999)
- Generated more than $30 million in sponsorship revenue.
- Consulted with clients to identify, establish and measure online business objectives.
- Optimized and maximized partner deals by pinpointing key e-commerce opportunities.
- Developed and successfully maintained relationships, both internal and external, to Excite.
- Executed coordination and implementation of multimillion-dollar integrated advertising.

CNET: The Computer Network, San Francisco, CA
ACCOUNT EXECUTIVE, ADVERTISING SALES (August 1996 - December 1997)
- Identified/prospected/pursued/closed accounts across northern/southern California.
- Managed $3 million territory, increasing territory sales by more than 50% over one year.
PUBLIC RELATIONS MANAGER (February 1996 - July 1997)
- Wrote corporate press releases, executive biographies and collateral material.
- Managed speaking opportunities and awards programs.
- Managed trade and international press relations.

Professional Training

LeadSmart: (May 2000) Attendees nominated by company executives to attend three-day leadership workshop. **Sales Management Training:** (August 2000) four-day seminar for Sales Managers

Education

University of California/Berkeley Extension, San Francisco, CA
- Creative Writing; Intro to Microcomputers; Photographic Screenprinting, Art of Film
Harvard University, Cambridge, MA
- Graduate courses in Leadership; Writing for Public Relations; Public Relations for Managers; and Financial Management for Nonprofits
University of Massachusetts, Amherst, MA
- Bachelor of Science, Marketing

FIGURE 10.4 *Plain Text Sample Résumé Emphasizing Sales Experience*

```
Megan Kearon
100 Sunnyside Ave. * Mill Valley * CA 94941 * 415.388.1000 *
Mbyrn@hotmail.com

PROFILE: Marketing communications professional with both international and
domestic sales, public relations and account management experience with a
focus on high technology and Internet media properties

International
* Built European sales-operations teams for Excite Europe in London.
* Recognized more than $10 million in annual revenue for Excite UK and
Excite Europe.
* Worked in various sales-related roles, with more than four years'
experience in sales, account management and sales operations for Internet
companies.
* Increased in-territory sales by more than 50% within one-year sales period.
* Managed Excite key accounts generating more than $12 million annual
revenue.

Management
* Managed four sales-operations groups across ten European Web sites.
* Managed group budgeting, development (organizational and employee), hiring
and training.
* Chosen to train in LeadSmart Leadership Workshop and Sales Management
Training.

Public Relations
* Handled publicity, international and domestic, for Star Wars: Episode II
Attack of the Clones.
* Managed international and domestic public relations for CNET: The Computer
Company (Internet and television shows).
* Provided public relations for Lotus Development Corp., LBMS, and Tivoli
Systems.
* Enrolled in related coursework: Writing for Public Relations, Public
Relations for Managers.

Work Experience

Lucasfilm Ltd., Nicasio, CA
PUBLICITY PROJECT COORDINATOR (January - June 2002)
* Assisted Lucasfilm domestic and international publicity teams on the launch
of Star Wars: Episode II Attack of the Clones.
* Worked with domestic and international press to secure interviews with Star
Wars cast and crew members; provided movie images; fact-checked final
articles.
* Assisted with development and execution of Star Wars: Episode II Press
Junket, which hosted more than 400 press people.

Excite@Home, Redwood City, CA
SENIOR MANAGER, INTERNATIONAL BUSINESS DEVELOPMENT (Nov. 2000 - August 2001)
* Led international negotiations to secure distribution and content deals
with Apple, Microsoft, The Weather Channel, etc.
* Coordinated International Business Development/U.S. Business Development
team.
* Leveraged U.S. content deals internationally, such as Muze, MapBlast and
MusicMatch.
```

FIGURE 10.4 *(continued)*

* Resolved conflict on deals that were no longer viewed as beneficial to Excite.

Excite Europe, London
DIRECTOR, ACCOUNT MANAGEMENT EUROPE (May 1999 - November 2000)
* Hired, trained and managed staff of 20 people, which consisted of four teams (Partner Services, Sales Finance, Advertising Development and Ad Technologies).
* Negotiated Pan-European business contracts, global and Pan-European distribution and sponsorship deals, such as DoubleClick, Real Media, Matchlogic, Microsoft, Hewlett-Packard, Netscape, Egg and Travelocity.
* Generated more than $10 million in annual sponsorship revenue.
* Developed business processes that impacted Excite Europe's day-to-day business practices.

Excite, Redwood City, CA
ACCOUNT MANAGER, SPONSORSHIP AND PROMOTION (January 1998 - May 1999)
* Generated more than $30 million in sponsorship revenue.
* Consulted with clients to identify, establish and measure online business objectives.
* Optimized and maximized partner deals by pinpointing key e-commerce opportunities.
* Developed and successfully maintained relationships, both internal and external, to Excite.
* Executed coordination and implementation of multimillion-dollar integrated advertising.

CNET: The Computer Network, San Francisco, CA
ACCOUNT EXECUTIVE, ADVERTISING SALES (August 1996 - December 1997)
* Identified/prospected/pursued/closed accounts across northern/southern California.
* Managed $3 million territory, increasing territory sales by more than 50% over one year.
PUBLIC RELATIONS MANAGER (February 1996 - July 1997)
* Wrote corporate press releases, executive biographies and collateral material.
* Managed speaking opportunities and awards programs.
* Managed trade and international press relations.

Professional Training

LeadSmart: (May 2000) Attendees nominated by company executives to attend three-day leadership workshop. Sales Management Training: (August 2000) four-day seminar for Sales Managers

Education

University of California/Berkeley Extension, San Francisco, CA
* Creative Writing; Intro to Microcomputers; Photographic Screenprinting, Art of Film
Harvard University, Cambridge, MA
* Graduate courses in Leadership; Writing for Public Relations; Public Relations for Managers; and Financial Management for Nonprofits
University of Massachusetts, Amherst, MA
* Bachelor of Science, Marketing

FIGURE 10.5 *Sample Résumé Emphasizing Marketing Skills*

Megan Kearon
100 Sunnyside Avenue * Mill Valley * CA 94100 * 415.388.1000 * mbyrn@hotmail.com

Profile: Marketing communications professional with both international and domestic sales, public relations and account management experience with focus on entertainment and Internet media properties

Public Relations
- International and domestic publicity for *Star Wars:* **Episode II** *Attack of the Clones*
- International and domestic publicity for CNET: The Computer Company (Internet and television shows)
- Public relations for Lotus Development Corp., LBMS, and Tivoli Systems
- Related courses: Writing for Public Relations and Public Relations for Managers

International
- Coordinated Filmmaker's Hospitality for Mill Valley International Film Festival.
- Built European sales operations teams for Excite Europe, based in London.
- Recognized more than $10 million in annual revenue for Excite UK and Excite Europe.

Management
- Managed four sales-operations groups across ten European Web sites.
- Managed group budgeting, development (organizational and employee), hiring and training.
- Chosen for related training: LeadSmart Leadership Workshop and Sales Management Training.

WORK EXPERIENCE

Lucasfilm Ltd., Nicasio, CA
PUBLICITY PROJECT COORDINATOR (January - June 2002)
- Assisted Lucasfilm, domestic and international, publicity teams on launch of *Star Wars:* **Episode II** *Attack of the Clones.*
- Worked with domestic and international press to secure interviews with *Star Wars* cast and crew members; provided movie images; and fact-checked final articles.
- Assisted with development and execution of the *Star Wars:* **Episode II** Press Junket that hosted more than 400 press people.

Film Institute of Northern California, Mill Valley, CA
HOSPITALITY COORDINATOR, MILL VALLEY FILM FESTIVAL (September 2001 - October 2001)
- Secured donations for Filmmakers Hospitality Suite.
- Created Mill Valley Film Festival Pocket Guide for Festival Guests.
- Trained and managed volunteer staff of 32 for Filmmakers Hospitality Suite.
- Developed and assembled Guest Packets for distribution to Filmmakers.
- Assisted Filmmakers Liaison with travel arrangements and accommodations for guests.

FIGURE 10.5 *(continued)*

Excite@Home, Redwood City, CA and London
SENIOR MANAGER, INTERNATIONAL BUSINESS DEVELOPMENT (Nov. 2000 - August 2001)
DIRECTOR, ACCOUNT MANAGEMENT EUROPE (May 1999 - November 2000)
ACCOUNT MANAGER, SPONSORSHIP AND PROMOTION (January 1998 - May 1999)
- Hired, trained and managed 20 people, who were divided into four sales-operations teams (Account Management, Sales Finance, Advertising Development and Ad Technologies)
- Led negotiations and secured Pan-European and global distribution, content and sponsorship deals, such as DoubleClick, Real Media, Matchlogic, Microsoft, Hewlett-Packard, Netscape, Egg, Travelocity, Apple, Microsoft and The Weather Channel.
- Generated more than $30 million domestic/$10 million international annual sponsorship revenue.

CNET: The Computer Network, San Francisco, CA
ACCOUNT EXECUTIVE, ADVERTISING SALES (August 1996 - December 1997)
- Identified/prospected/pursued/closed accounts across northern/southern California.
- Managed a $3MM territory and increased territory sales by more than 50% over one year.
PUBLIC RELATIONS MANAGER (February 1996 - July 1997)
- Wrote corporate press releases, executive biographies and collateral material.
- Managed speaking opportunities and awards programs.
- Managed trade and international press relations.

Louis Paul & Partners, Foster City, CA, and Lexington, MA
ACCOUNT EXECUTIVE (September 1995 - February 1996) Foster City, CA
ASSOCIATE ACCOUNT EXECUTIVE (September 1994 - August 1995) Foster City, CA
ACCOUNT COORDINATOR (August 1993 - August 1994) Lexington, MA
- Wrote corporate press releases, executive biographies and collateral material.
- Developed, managed, pitched and secured speaking opportunities.
Clients: Lotus cc: Mail, Lotus Approach, LBMS and Tivoli Systems

PROFESSIONAL TRAINING

LeadSmart: (May 2000) Attendees nominated by company executives to attend a three-day leadership workshop
Sales Management Training: (August 2000) Four-day seminar for Sales Managers

EDUCATION

University of California/Berkley Extension, San Francisco, CA
- Creative Writing; Intro to Microcomputers; Photographic Screenprinting, Art of Film
Harvard University, Cambridge, MA
- Graduate courses in Leadership; Writing for Public Relations; Public Relations for Managers; and Financial Management for Non-Profit Organizations
University of Massachusetts, Amherst, MA
- **Bachelor of Science,** Marketing

FIGURE 10.6 *Plain Text Version of Marketing Résumé*

Megan Kearon
100 Sunnyside Avenue * Mill Valley * CA 94100 * 415.388.1000 *
mbyrn@hotmail.com

Profile: Marketing communications professional with both international
and domestic sales, public relations and account management experience
with focus on entertainment and Internet media properties

Public Relations

* International and domestic publicity for Star Wars: Episode II Attack
of the Clones
* International and domestic publicity for CNET: The Computer Company
(Internet and television shows)
* Public relations for Lotus Development Corp., LBMS, and Tivoli Systems
* Related courses: Writing for Public Relations and Public Relations for
Managers

International

* Coordinated Filmmakers Hospitality for Mill Valley International Film
Festival.
* Built European sales operations teams for Excite Europe, based in
London.
* Recognized more than $10 million in annual revenue for Excite UK and
Excite Europe.

Management

* Managed four sales-operations groups across ten European Web sites.
* Managed group budgeting, development (organizational and employee),
hiring and training.
* Chosen for related training: LeadSmart Leadership Workshop and Sales
Management Training.

WORK EXPERIENCE

Lucasfilm Ltd., Nicasio, CA
PUBLICITY PROJECT COORDINATOR (January - June 2002)
* Assisted Lucasfilm, domestic and international, publicity teams on
launch of Star Wars: Episode II Attack of the Clones.
* Worked with domestic and international press to secure interviews with
Star Wars cast and crew members; provided movie images; fact-checked
final articles.
* Assisted with development and execution of the Star Wars: Episode II
Press Junket that hosted more than 400 press people.

Film Institute of Northern California, Mill Valley, CA
HOSPITALITY COORDINATOR, MILL VALLEY FILM FESTIVAL (Sept. 2001- October
2001)
* Secured donations for Filmmakers Hospitality Suite.
* Created Mill Valley Film Festival Pocket Guide for Festival Guests.
* Trained and managed volunteer staff of 32 for Filmmakers Hospitality
Suite.
* Developed and assembled Guest Packets for distribution to Filmmakers.
* Assisted Filmmakers Liaison with travel arrangements and accommodations
for Festival guests.

FIGURE 10.6 *(continued)*

Excite@Home, Redwood City, CA and London
SENIOR MANAGER, INTERNATIONAL BUSINESS DEVELOPMENT (Nov. 2000 - August 2001)
DIRECTOR, ACCOUNT MANAGEMENT EUROPE (May 1999 - November 2000)
ACCOUNT MANAGER, SPONSORSHIP AND PROMOTION (January 1998 - May 1999)
* Hired, trained and managed 20 people, who were divided into four sales-operations teams (Account Management, Sales Finance, Advertising Development and Ad Technologies).
* Led negotiations and secured Pan-European and global distribution, content and sponsorship deals, such as DoubleClick, Real Media, Matchlogic, Microsoft, Hewlett-Packard, Netscape, Egg, Travelocity, Apple, Microsoft and The Weather Channel.
* Generated more than $30 million domestic/$10 million international annual sponsorship revenue.

CNET: The Computer Network, San Francisco, CA
ACCOUNT EXECUTIVE, ADVERTISING SALES (August 1996 - December 1997)
* Identified/prospected/pursued/closed accounts across northern/southern California.
* Managed a $3MM territory and increased territory sales by more than 50% over one year.
PUBLIC RELATIONS MANAGER (February 1996 - July 1997)
* Wrote corporate press releases, executive biographies and collateral material.
* Managed speaking opportunities and awards programs.
* Managed trade and international press relations.

Louis Paul & Partners, Foster City, CA, and Lexington, MA
ACCOUNT EXECUTIVE (September 1995 - February 1996) Foster City, CA
ASSOCIATE ACCOUNT EXECUTIVE (September 1994 - August 1995) Foster City, CA
ACCOUNT COORDINATOR (August 1993 - August 1994) Lexington, MA
* Wrote corporate press releases, executive biographies and collateral material.
* Developed, managed, pitched and secured speaking opportunities.
Clients: Lotus cc: Mail, Lotus Approach, LBMS and Tivoli Systems

PROFESSIONAL TRAINING

LeadSmart: (May 2000) Attendees nominated by company executives to attend a three-day leadership workshop
Sales Management Training: (August 2000) Four-day seminar for Sales Managers

EDUCATION

University of California/Berkley Extension, San Francisco, CA
* Creative Writing; Intro to Microcomputers; Photographic Screenprinting, Art of Film
Harvard University, Cambridge, MA
* Graduate courses in Leadership; Writing for Public Relations; Public Relations for Managers; and Financial Management for Non-Profit Organizations
University of Massachusetts, Amherst, MA
 * Bachelor of Science, Marketing

LOOKING AT THE SAMPLES

The changes in the résumé were minor, but the rearrangement of information helped the job applicant to highlight the skills that she thought were most relevant to two different employers. Don't neglect to go through this step-by-step process of creating your own résumé by thinking about what you want in your next job and what you have to offer an employer. Such a process strengthens how you choose to display your qualifications and improves your chances of hitting your target. It also helps you to forge a career path that is more thoughtful, profitable, and meaningful.

ESSENTIAL ELEMENTS

Established rules for writing a good résumé don't exist, but there are a few constants that you should adhere to when creating yours. These constants are consistency, balance, format, and content.

Consistency is a good indicator of a logical mind and HR professionals are practiced at noticing inconsistent patterns in the layout of your résumé, so spend a few extra minutes taking note of the following:

- *Spacing:* Be consistent in the amount of spacing between lines or between words or between headings.
- *Spelled-out versus abbreviation:* If you spell out September in one line, don't use the numerical alternative in the other line. Or if you use the abbreviated version of a state name in one line, don't spell it out in the next. Because of space limitations, however, there will always be exceptions. For instance, to avoid creating another line, you may have to abbreviate November to Nov. Remember, use your best judgement. These are guidelines, not rules to die by.
- *Typeface:* If you use boldface for your job title in one reference, make sure you use boldface for it in the next. Or if your headings are 14 points on one page, make sure they are 14 points on the next.
- *Indents:* Tabs have a way of playing tricks on you, so make sure everything is aligned correctly.
- *Verb tense:* If you use past tense in one bulleted item, use the past tense in the next bulleted item. Of course, tense must be used to indicate the correct time sequence, but try to establish a pattern to make it easier on readers.

- *Periods:* End complete sentences with periods (even when the subject is implied), but note that periods are not necessary when your design (white space) indicates the obvious. Decide exactly where periods are necessary (always between a series of sentences) and be consistent.
- *Punctuation:* Consistency is important in punctuation as well. Avoid the serial comma (the comma before the *and*), but if you're committed to this comma, make sure you use it correctly and consistently. The same is true for dashes: If you are committed to the en dash, make sure you are consistent in its usage. For instance, if you use an en dash between years (1999–2000), then don't use a hyphen (2000-2004) in the next reference.

Balance is visually pleasing. Fortune 500 professionals strongly recommend that you confine your résumé to one or two pages (there are always exceptions, three of which are included in this book), but it's a good design choice to write a *full* page or a *full* two pages. Adherence to this suggestion is not always feasible, but remember that it's better to rigorously edit your two-page résumé to get it down to one page than to have two lines flop over to the second page. Also aim for *symmetry.* An even distribution of lines to break up the text always works well. Finally, don't squeeze too much information on one page, as that's hard to read. Using white space to break up the page is a better alternative—and will be appreciated by the HR professional who is reading Résumé #75 that day.

Format—whether chronological, functional, or a combination of the two—may vary depending on how you want to display your information, but all résumés must contain *key information.*

Content is the essence of a good résumé. Focus on the content of your résumé instead of spending hours, or even days, on the layout (a simple design works well, especially because so many résumés today have to be converted into plain text—e-mail-friendly versions in which all formatting and embellishments are lost). It's more important to provide the information employers want. And, according to the Fortune 500 participants, employers prefer the following:

- *Hard skills* ("Proficiency in AutoCAD LT") rather than soft skills ("Excellent computer and people skills")
- *Verifiable accomplishments* ("Increased sales by 30 percent in the Northeast) rather than unsubstantiated claims ("The best salesman in the Northeast").
- *Extensive experience* at profitable companies ("13 years' experience at a Fortune 500 company") rather than short-time stints at flighty businesses ("two years' experience at Hair Today, Here to Stay" [your brother-in-law's entrepreneurial venture in hair replacement therapy]).

- *Hard-core results* ("Streamlined processes to increase turnaround by three months) rather than a listing of responsibilities ("Responsible for billing").
- *Progressive* promotions or responsibilities rather than clinging to the same responsibilities for the past ten years.

Most people have experience that can be put into these positive terms. You just may not be trained to think in this language, so make an effort to revamp your mind-set while working on your résumé. Instead of resorting to tired clichés to describe your work experience, think hard about what you've done and accomplished—and then make sure your résumé reflects this. The payoff could be substantial.

Tom DiDonato, a human resources vice president, said good résumés should be "concise" and "match requirements." He also likes the candidate to have a "work history with strong companies."

STYLE CONSIDERATIONS

Base your writing style on your audience. When you write a résumé, you should write in the style that hiring professionals are familiar with, even if you are a stickler for formal prose. One of the problems you will encounter when you write your résumé is space—or the lack of it. Distilling eight years' of experience into four sentences can be a challenge. For that reason, don't rely solely on your ear to determine which words to choose. Style shortcuts are used—and accepted—in résumés (but not necessarily in the annual report); for example, clipped sentences and familiar abbreviations are typical in résumés. You have to get a lot of essential information into a small space, so you can't afford to wax long-winded. In fact, that would be counterproductive, even if it sounds "correct" to you. Stay away from those empty adjectives—and remember that nouns are good, but verbs are better (you want to convey yourself as a doer).

After you have looked at a few samples, you will probably begin to detect a style unique to the résumés in this book. Note the many variations of style for presenting your career accomplishments in a readable format. Because no one style is absolutely correct, you must decide what will work best for you and your industry. To review some style guidelines for the preparation of your résumé, though, I have included a checklist of style points that were used for the résumés in this book. Some style preferences are unique to résumés; some are standard style guidelines.

- List town and state for all companies (not street address); two-letter postal abbreviations (rather than the standard state abbreviation) were used consistently throughout this book.

- Use either hyphens (1990-1999) or en dashes (1990–1999) for dates. Newer computer operating systems automatically insert the en dash, but the older systems do not, so make a decision and then be consistent.

- Use present tense verbs to describe current jobs, past tense verbs to describe jobs held in the past.

- Use sentences with implied subjects (avoid using *I*), and put a period in a bulleted item with an implied subject; for example, *Managed 20-person sales staff* (period).

- Dispense with periods in stand-alone sentences or lists (where white space separates one line from the next), unless period is necessary for clarity.

- Use periods for incomplete sentences when they are followed by another sentence.

- Use full company names in the first reference but shortened forms thereafter (e.g., Pepsi Bottling Group, then just Pepsi in the second or third reference).

- Use the same typeface for the punctuation after boldface, italics, and so on (**Systems Analyst,** Microsoft Corporation [note the bold comma]).

- Accompany résumés lacking specific career objectives with a cover letter so the hiring professional knows what job you are applying for, where you noticed the opening, and what you have to offer the employer.

- Describe the business, *if it's not obvious,* of the companies you worked for. A word or even a brief description after the company name or in the body of your duties/accomplishments will do.

- Spell out degrees, such as Bachelor of Science or Master of Arts. If space is limited, you may use these abbreviations: BA, BS, MA, MS, MBA, PhD. If you prefer to use periods, be consistent.

- Dispense with a comma between the month and year (January 2000, not January, 2000).

- Use either the percent sign (%) or write 50 percent; do not write fifty percent.

- Capitalize job titles (Account Executive, Media Planner, IT Director) and the names of departments (Human Resources, Accounting) within companies (notice this style was not used in the text of this book; used only in the résumés).

- Only use ampersands (&) if they are part of the company's name.

- Use American spellings, unless a word is part of the company's or organization's name, such as United Nations Development Programme.

ORIGIN OF RÉSUMÉ SAMPLES

Most of the samples in this book are actual résumés used by actual people who work in actual jobs. The samples are models that should generate ideas about design and language and how to best display your information.

Those who provided sample résumés are gainfully employed and not seeking employment, but some adjustments were made to reflect the input of the Fortune 500 hiring professionals. For the most part, though, only the names, addresses, and telephone numbers have changed significantly. Company names, employment histories, and tenures are virtually the same.

The résumés are divided into two sections: those with focus statements and those without. As recommended by the Fortune 500 participants, résumés should have cover letters (especially if they do not have a focus statement) so the HR representative knows what position you are applying for and what your qualifications are for that position.

In addition, most of the sample résumés are suited for the corporate world, but a few fall outside the boundaries of the office (teacher, social worker, physical therapist, nurse). These résumés were included because the input offered by the 50 Fortune 500 hiring professionals (some receive more than 500 résumés a day) is invaluable—whether you work in an office, a classroom, or an emergency room.

Doreen O'Dea

123 Bergen Avenue
Jersey City, NJ 07100

Phone: (201) 333-1000
Facsimile: (201) 333-1000
email: DDgallery@aol.com
www.ddgallery.com

GRANT WRITER

KEY FEATURES: *Recent Transaction:* $2.5 million. **Largest Transaction:** $20 million.
Project Manager for Jersey City (a wayfinding signage program). Public/private partnership
between nonprofit organizations and city of Jersey City. Wrote additional grants:

- $1.3 million grant writing. Jersey City (Bergen Avenue local lead application)
- $319,000 grant writing. Jersey City (pedestrian safety application)
- $1.5 million grant writing. Long Hill Township (ecotourism)
- $849,000 grant writing. Long Hill Township (transportation enhancement)
- $150,000 grant writing. Long Hill Township (pedestrian safety)
- $250,000 grant writing. Long Hill Township (municipal aid)
- Eligibility Research and Writing: National Register of Historic Places (for designation and subsequent tax credits for private developer)
- $342,000 grant writing. Consultant to S3x Associates (bikeway program for municipality)
- $20 million grant writing. Consultant to S3x Associates (variety of funding for private developer)
- $304,000 grant writing. Essex County Division of Cultural & Historic Affairs (NJSCA application)
- $40,000 grant writing. Essex County Division of Cultural & Historic Affairs (Staffing initiative: NJSCA)

Experience:

1982-2002   *Kearon-Hempenstall Gallery*

Owner. Fine art, custom framing and art appraisal business
- Marketing, sales, finance for art business
- Public relations, advertising
- Corporate and residential art collection management
- Appraisal of fine and decorative art
- Exhibition management for gallery and corporate locations (locations provided on request)
- Consultant — Artistic event planning: auctions, corporate sponsorship, arts marketing
- Consultant — Nonprofit management: fundraising, grant writing, 501(c)3 Incorporation, planning

2000-Present   *City of Jersey City and Liberty Science Center*
Consultant — Project Manager — Destination: Jersey City
Wayfinding Signage Program for Jersey City
- Write grant applications.
- Facilitate and coordinate communications, meetings, committee resources.
- Act as liaison to government agencies and nonprofit organizations.
- Present materials to business community and general public meetings.
- Oversee Public Relations firm.
- Manage $2.5M budget.

1998-Present   *Essex County Division of Cultural & Historic Affairs*
Consultant — Long-Range Planning
- Create, design, write agency long-range plan.
- Develop steering committee, design and lead workshops; create public surveys.
- Analyze data.

Essex County Division of Cultural & Historic Affairs
Consultant — Grant Writing
- Created Essex County Block Grant Application for FY 2000.
- Developed and led workshops for applicants FY2000.
- Wrote FY2000 and FY2003 NJSCA: Grant for Essex County $848,000 budget.
- Grant Panel Evaluator

Jersey City Economic Development Corporation
Consultant — Brownfields
- Developed plan for land reuse (brownfields).

Jersey City Episcopal Community Development Corporation
Consultant — Business Planning
- Created business plan and grant to federal government for non-profit agency to develop for-profit business, enabling low-income residents to gain full employment.
- Created business plan for Dress for Success license: Hudson County.

1998   *Union County Division of Cultural & Heritage Affairs*
Consultant – Grant Administration
- Essex County Block Grant Coordinator administered through Union County FY99

1992-1995   *Hudson County Cultural & Heritage Affairs*
Coordinator of federal and state aid for county government agency for promotion of arts and heritage

- Reviewed incoming grants. Wrote grant proposals.
- Administered grant budget.
- Coordinated and implemented Arts-in-Education Programs (60 programs).
- Designed nonprofit development institute for 501c3 organizations (skills for administration of nonprofits).
- Co-Chair American Heritage Festival Committee (Festival won the NJ Tourism Award: major sponsor, Bell Atlantic).
- Coordinated Arts Fair Day with local corporate businesses (introduction of arts to corporate community).
- Researched and wrote Hudson County Artists Directory.
- Coordinated and implemented Hudson County St. Patrick's Day event televised by Fox 5 WNEW.

1985-1989   *New York City Board of Education*
Teacher. High School English Teacher at Curtis HS and Townsend Harris HS.

- SAT Prep, social studies, journalism, English literature, careers
- Designed curriculum for and implemented Photography Enrichment program.
- Designed Writing through Word Processing Program.

Education:

1994   New York University. Art Appraisal Program
1986   Queen's College, CUNY. (M.S.Ed. in progress)
         (Research Assistant to Dr. Phillip Anderson for Poetry Pilot in schools)
1980   Jersey City State College (now NJCU). Bachelor of Arts (Philosophy)

Professional Associations:

Commissioner, Jersey City Historical District Commission, 1994-2001
Co-Chair, Hudson County Chamber of Commerce Special Event Committee, 1999-2002
Founding Board Member - Hudson County Dress for Success
Board of Trustees, Educational Arts Team 1994-2000, President of Board 2001, 2002
Board of Trustees, Lincoln Association, 1999-2002
Media Advisory Board, Hudson County Schools of Technology, 1997-2000
March of Dimes Hudson County Chair, 1994, 1995; Jail and Bail Fundraising Committee; FDR Award, 1995; County Committee, 1994-1999; Promotional Chair, 1997-1999
Associate Member, American Association of Appraisers
Adjudicator: Hudson County Senior Citizen Art Show; Jersey City Board of Education Permanent Student Art Collection; Congressional Art Competition for HS Students

Lorna Steinberg
100 East 100th Street, Apt. 1C
Home: (212) 410-1000 / Office: (212) 582-1000

E-mail: STB10@worldnet.att.net

SUMMARY OF QUALIFICATIONS

Multilingual Senior Executive with 15 years' experience selling high-end products worldwide. Skilled at problem-solving, financial analysis and intercultural communications. Decision maker who can troubleshoot and has proven track record in opening and emerging markets

---

EXPERIENCE

Stuart Weitzman, Inc., New York, 1989-present
Account Executive
- Develop financial and marketing strategies for customers to increase sales and gross margins (open-to-buy budgets, sell-through analysis, special promotions design, trunk shows).
- Spearhead international expansion, increasing overseas market presence to 53 countries in 2002 from 12 in 1989; new markets include China, Australia, Spain, South Africa, Mexico.
- Team with other senior executives to manage major accounts, including Saks Fifth Avenue, Browns (Canada) and Russell & Bromley (United Kingdom).
- Play key role in diversification of the Stuart Weitzman product line, introducing new products to existing clients.
- Market new brands for third parties, such as Vera Wang, growing shoe sales for this line by 80% since November 2001 launch.
- Sell product line at trade shows in Milan, Düsseldorf, New York and Las Vegas, counseling international customers on the logistics and requirements for importing.
- Train and manage sales force and customer representatives in the United States and abroad.
- Ensure timely production and delivery, working with overseas factories.

Key Accomplishments

- Increased sales tenfold in one of the three largest accounts since 1990.
- Increased sales by an average 20% per year over the past five years.
- Improved efficiency of day-to-day operations by establishing new data management systems.

Dianne B. Corporation, New York, 1987-88
Vice President Operations/Acting Chief Executive Officer
- Managed three high-end retail stores and a wholesale operation.
- Responsible for financial planning, including sales/costs forecasting, short-term financial strategy, accounting and banking relations and product pricing
- Managed Hong Kong private label import business.
- Contributed to long-term strategic planning, including dealing with venture capitalists to finance expansion and identifying new store locations.
- Managed staff of 25 at three locations.

Chose Classique/Mishaan Innovations Inc., New York, 1985-87
Chief Operating Officer
- Planned and executed financial budget of a wholesale contemporary sportswear operation.
- Coordinated trade shows.
- Established and managed Hong Kong import division.

Sonia Rykiel, New York, 1984
Assistant Manager
- Managed and ran day-to-day business of Madison Avenue store.

Holmes Protection, Inc., New York, 1981-83
Executive Assistant to the Chairman
- Responsible for the chairman's personal finances.
- Planned, budgeted and maintained real estate holdings in the United States and abroad, including supervision of construction and contracting personnel.
- Assisted in the reorganization and automation of the company's accounting department, including training of new personnel.

De la Ronda, S.A., Bogotá, Colombia, 1978-81
Assistant Manager
- Contributed to start-up of wholesale operation for designing, manufacturing and selling swimsuit/leotard line.
- Conducted market research and analysis to launch expansion into new active wear and sportswear lines.
- Oversaw De la Ronda manufacturing operation.

EDUCATION
- **Monterey Institute for International Studies, Monterey, CA**
  Master of Arts, International Management
  Certificate in translation and interpretation (Spanish/English/French)
- **Vassar College, Poughkeepsie, NY**
  Bachelor of Arts, Anthropology

LANGUAGES
- Fluent French, Spanish, English; proficient Italian and German

Tara Paine

100 Medford Lane
New Canaan, CT 06100
Home Telephone: 203-555-1000
Work Telephone: 203-565-1000
Cell Phone: 203-554-1000
E-mail: APA100@yahoo.com

CAREER PROFILE

Fortune 500 Financial Adviser with 18 years of finance and general management experience working at IBM, Philip Morris, General Motors and as a management consultant with KPMG Peat Marwick. Bachelor's degree in Finance with expertise in:

- *Financial planning and analysis, financial modeling*
- *Cash management, strategic planning and business development*
- *Project management*

PROFESSIONAL EXPERIENCE

IBM CORPORATION. White Plains, NY   **11/99 - Present**

Principal Financial Adviser — Small and Medium Business Sector

Coordinate 2003 Global Revenue Plan for largest Sales and Distribution sector, committing $20B of revenue to IBM.
Build business cases by quickly understanding issues and translating them into business opportunities. Develop profitable strategy to capture this opportunity.

Program Manager — Integrated Product Development   **12/98 - 10/99**

Architected financial models built by deconstructing complex business issues, determining probability of occurrence and using Monte Carlo simulation tools to assign investment-level risk.
Developed Web-based Content Management Programs to leverage information across IBM organization to reduce development costs and reduce key "time to profit" metric.

C. S. BROOKS. New York, NY
(consumer products company, retails home products)   **10/97 - 11/98**

Treasurer — Corporate Officer

Maximized cash flow by monitoring and managing worldwide cash position.
Reduced cost by managing risk though interest rate and currency hedging strategies.
Drove profitability by tightening control over cash receipts and disbursements.

IBM CORPORATION. Armonk, NY   **09/95 - 10/97**

Senior Consultant, Internal Consulting Practice

Led multimillion-dollar business transformation consulting project in PC group as Executive Relationship Manager, Project Engagement Manager and financial strategy subject matter expert.

AMERICAN BUREAU OF SHIPPING. New York, NY   **12/92 - 09/95**

Manager Cash Management and Assistant Treasurer

Reduced costs by rationalizing more than 160 bank accounts in 120 countries, establishing payments netting center and centralizing invoicing process.
Reduced cash flow variability by establishing more disciplined cash-management approach allowing for optimization of both cash flow requirements and tax considerations.
Increased the performance of $250 million pension portfolio by rigorously analyzing past performance and uncovering opportunities.

KPMG PEAT MARWICK. New York, NY   **11/89 - 12/92**

Manager, Corporate Finance Consulting

Developed Corporate Finance Strategy for Fortune 200 clients that included interest rate and currency hedging strategy, treasury management and optimal capital structure.

PHILIP MORRIS CORPORATION. New York, NY   **09/88 - 11/89**

Senior Planning Analyst

Corporate financial planning liaison between Chairman's office and Asia Pacific Tobacco organization

GENERAL MOTORS CORPORATION / E.D.S.
Canada and Brazil   **09/84 - 09/88**

Treasury Analyst

Managed foreign exchange exposure working in Canada and Sao Paulo, Brazil.

EDUCATION

1984   Series 7 Qualification
1984   Bachelor of Arts, Finance, University of Western Ontario, Canada

THOMAS DEPHILLIPS
100 E. 31th St., Apt. 10
New York, NY 10000
Thomas.dephillips@gs.com
Work Phone: 212-357-1000
Mobile Phone: 917-685-1000
Home Phone: 212-684-1000

PROFESSIONAL PROFILE: *Fortune 500 **Equity Sales Trader** researched, designed, negotiated and leveraged highly favorable market share opportunities*

WORK

EXPERIENCE

Goldman, Sachs & Company — Equity Sales Trading
New York, NY
July 2002 - present
• Bridge execution focus with knowledge of the research product by identifying catalyst-driven trading ideas for accounts.
• Cover accounts for both the Listed and OTC markets as a member of sales trading team.
• Understand liquidity and supply/demand in determining appropriate price levels for capital commitment transactions.
• Monitor and interpret intraday news flow for potential market impact.

Goldman, Sachs — Technology Research Sales
New York, NY
July 2000 - July 2002
• Leveraged Goldman, Sachs Technology Research franchise as a member of specialized sales team focused on technology-sector investing.
• Co-covered mid-Atlantic and New York–based accounts, including both mutual funds and hedge funds.
• Designed and marketed presentation for generalist portfolio managers, detailing tech-sector investment themes and opportunities — as well as food-chain overview.
• Developed internal database system to better identify market-share opportunities and to assist in creation of goals for all domestic tech-sales members.
• Involved with recruiting and development of post-undergraduate positions at firm; selected in the summer of 2001 as mentor for new financial analysts.

INTERNSHIP

EXPERIENCE

Goldman, Sachs — Equities Division
New York, NY
Summer 1999
• Participated in summer program consisting of presentations/classes, rotations and desk assignment.
• Shadowed employees from all areas of Equities Division, including Institutional Sales, U.S. and International Trading and Private Client Services.
• Created a "how-to" manual for Securities Lending Operations desk.
• Assigned to desk at Global Securities Lending; focused on daily management of short-sale contracts.

Lexington Management Corporation
Saddle Brook, NJ
Summer 1998
• Teamed with the domestic equities group.
• Attended analyst conferences and IPO road shows.
• Researched competitive mutual funds, developed comparison reports for Lexington Growth & Income Fund.
• Prepared research reports for senior analysts regarding stocks to be added to Growth & Income Fund.

Fowler, Rosenau & Geary, LLC
New York, NY
Summers 1996, 1997
• Worked on floor of NYSE alongside specialists.

ENTREPRENEUR

EXPERIENCE

Eagle Alliance, LLC
1997 - 2000
Co-Chairman
Eagle Alliance, LLC, was student-operated investment company licensed in Delaware.
• Goals of organization included capital appreciation for investors and education of student shareholders about financial marketplace.

EDUCATION

Chartered Financial Analyst
• Level 2 Candidate
Boston College, Carroll School of Management
Bachelor of Science — Finance. Graduated: May 2000. GPA: 3.6 / 4.0. Major GPA: 3.7 / 4.0. **Honors:** Magna cum Laude, Dean's List, Peer Leadership Program, Golden Key National Honor Society

DAVID FELDMAN
100 Grand Street, #1-W, Croton-on-Hudson, New York 10100
(914) 271-0001 • E-mail: dfelsen@msn.com

QUALIFICATIONS SUMMARY

Qualified for a Business - Legal Counsel / Manager function including: corporate governance, compliance department start-up, regulatory agency liaison. Served as corporate accountant for more than 5 years. Developed training manuals / seminars. Scope of experience:

- cost and general accounting
- asset management / disposition
- accounts payable / receivable, capital budgets
- internal controls, job costing
- cost avoidance, debt financing, equity financing
- credit and collections
- financial statement analysis
- audit controls / management
- financial reporting, regulatory compliance
- profit / loss analysis

Provided more than 14 years of Human Resources support: Grievances, arbitration, policy and development. Attorney proficient in: NLRA, ERISA, FLSA, EEO, TITLE VII, ADA, FLMA, ICRA, ADR. Accomplished writer, researcher and speaker. Scope of experience:

- labor and employment relations law
- contract review / administration
- grievance and arbitration proceedings, mediation
- union negotiations and mediation
- Unemployment and Workers' Compensation hearings
- collective bargaining agreements
- litigation, discrimination claims, labor hearings
- HR policy and design

Personal Contributions: Extensive volunteerism to business and civic organizations. Served in United States Naval Reserve for six years.

PROFESSIONAL EXPERIENCE

ATTORNEY, OF COUNSEL
Law Offices of Robert J. Hilpert
Croton-on-Hudson, New York (2001-present)
Areas of practice: Commercial and Employment litigation; general labor advice

ATTORNEY, PRIVATE PRACTICE
Law Office of David Feldman
Ossining, Peekskill and Wappingers Falls, New York (1996-2001)

Areas of practice: All areas of Labor and Employment Relations Law, litigations including commercial litigation, arbitrations, mediations, labor hearings, policy manual development, contract reviews, negotiations, legal research and general labor counsel. Also served as in-house counsel to a consumer credit and collections firm.

LEGAL ASSISTANT / LAW CLERK
Parker Chapin Flattau & Klimpi, LLP
New York, New York (1988-1996)

Areas of practice: Litigation support in Labor and Employment Relations Law. Personally performed extensive legal research and writing on labor relations issues, including: NLRA, ERISA, FLSA, EEO, TITLE VII, ADA, FLMA, ICRA, ADR.

PRIOR TO 1988

- Legal Assistant: Bronx District Attorney, Bronx, New York
- Accountant: KingAlarm Distributors, Inc., Elmsford, New York
- Assistant to Controller: General Manufacturing Inc., Fort Lauderdale

EDUCATION

- Pace University School of Law
- Bachelor of Science – Business Administration (Economics and Accounting) University of Florida

ADMISSIONS

- New York State Bar; United States District Courts for the Southern, Eastern and Northern Districts of New York, and Second Circuit Court of Appeals

| SHEILA NADIA | CELL (914) 555-1000 | E-MAIL: aK11@netzero.com |

PROFESSIONAL OBJECTIVE
To meld nine years' diverse creative and administrative expertise at top-notch companies into Marketing Manager position in Entertainment industry

PROFESSIONAL EXPERIENCE

Gentlemen's Quarterly   *Sales Assistant*   2003
- Coordinate meetings and prepare sales collateral for luxury fashion and accessory clients.
- Track and process insertion orders and advertising positioning statements.
- Develop meeting calendars for fashion shows and presentations.
- Support directors, including answering phone calls, preparation of expense reports, filing, faxing, photocopying and other general administrative tasks.

Lazard-Freres & Co.   *Travel and Meeting Planner*   2001-2003
- Coordinated executive meetings; scheduled flight, lodging and limousine services.
- Recorded, processed and filed billing invoices/expenses.
- Originated calling lists and maintained department files and databases.
- Researched and compiled marketing materials for public-information booklets.

Wall Street Interactive Television   *Communications Manager*   2001-2002
- Created corporate communication materials, including company history and investment-relations content.
- Facilitated marketing outreach efforts to promote programming and public affairs segments.
- Produced online financial news, lifestyle, and entertainment sound bites.
- Coordinated and launched a September 11th benefit gala and downtown revitalization PSA campaign.
- Tracked market trends to create corporate profiles and establish contacts.
- Assisted sales team in preparing sponsor/partnership proposal and collateral.
- Generated sales leads through research of financial trade publications.
- Edited and placed job placement copy; recruited, interviewed and staffed consultants and interns.

a21 Group   *Freelance Copywriter*   2001-2002
- Composed online promotional copy and press releases for photographic agency.
- Wrote and edited online corporate communications; created corporate style guide for online and print collateral.
- Recorded marketing minutes and agenda topics for distribution to board members and partners.
- Coordinated graphics layout and site architecture.

NBC Internet   *Associate Manager of Client Marketing*   1999-2000
- Conceived and implemented integrated radio, television, online and print advertising campaigns.
- Conceptualized new programs, promotions and special events for NBCi advertisers.
- Collaborated with channel producers and marketing department on optimal advertising placements, internally reporting project status.

- Created pitch material and ad copy; produced content; designed sweepstakes, contests and raffles.
- Trained sales team to pitch multimedia campaigns to prospective clients.
- Supported East Coast advertising and sales team.

NBC, Inc.   *Marketing Specialist, NBC.com*   **1994-1999**

- Promoted "Must See TV" contests, series premieres, cliffhangers and talent appearances on newsgroup and fan sites.
- Coordinated design and development of Website marketing and affiliate programs, and "The More You Know" PSAs.
- Consulted design and advertising teams on revisions/approvals of broadcast, online and print materials.
- Co-wrote promotional commercial for "Passions," a daytime soap opera.
- Proofread corporate communication press releases and business proposals.
- Edited and reviewed Web site content for MSNBC.com re-launch.
- Collaborated and produced departmental style guideline and staff handbook.
- Supervised marketing interns.

RELATED MARKETING EXPERIENCE

Carnevale di Venezia Art Exhibit   *Events Coordinator*   **2003**

- Compiled guest list, facilitated invitation and press announcements to arts editors and buyers of Italian-American art.
- Managed event-opening reception, with net proceeds of $4,000 on the first evening.

8minutedating   *Marketing Events Associate*   **2002-2003**

- Assisted marketing outreach efforts to promote singles events.
- Registered participants and facilitated social activities.

NBC 2002 Winter Olympics   *Online Content Writer*   **2002**

- Researched and developed sports content for Olympics Web site.
- Collaborated with video producers and sports experts on accuracy and style.
- Incorporated IOC and NBC style guidelines.

Ballantine Books/Random House   *Proofreader*   **1995-1999**

- Proofread mass-market /trade fiction and nonfiction manuscripts.

AFFILIATIONS & ASSOCIATIONS

Dining by Design Industries Foundation Fighting AIDS, *Volunteer.* Heart*Share*, *Volunteer*
Make-A-Wish Foundation, *Volunteer.* Ryze Networking Group, *Member.* The Joyce Theatre, *Volunteer.*

EDUCATION

1996   New York University, Book Publishing Certificate, Copyediting & Proofreading
1993   Marist College, Bachelor of Arts, English: Creative Writing // Minor, Photography

SKILLS

Project management, event coordination, copyediting, copywriting and proofreading
Proficiency in Macintosh and Windows platforms
Proficiency in Microsoft Office and Lotus Notes 1-2-3
Familiarity with Microsoft Publisher, Adobe Photoshop and QuarkXPress

M A R I E   E L E N A   R A M O S
1 0 0   V A R I C K   S T R E E T • J E R S E Y   C I T Y • N J   0 7 1 0 0
P H O N E   (2 0 1) 4 3 2 – 1 0 0 0 • F A X (2 0 1) 4 3 2 – 1 0 0 0
E - M A I L: mariram@comcast.net

OBJECTIVE: Development Associate

*Strategic writer with eight years' experience fundraising more than $2 million and developing —
from start to finish — successful, long-term nonprofit, government and corporate projects*

WORK HISTORY:
1999-Present
> *Consultant/Freelance Writer*

• Create, assist and implement strategies for clients in nonprofit organizations with special events, fundraising publications for cultivation and solicitation of foundation and corporate prospects and membership base.

1997-1999   Jersey City Episcopal Community Development Corporation, Inc. Jersey City, NJ
> *Social Services Coordinator*

• Collaborated with development team to procure more than $2.1M grants for start-up and administration of social service programs in Jersey City.
• Created and spearheaded innovative cultural and recreational center for seniors.
• Obtained grants and designed enrichment program for two after-school programs and program start-up of third after-school program.
• Collaborated with other nonprofits to provide social service educational conferences, town hall meetings and seminars. Advocacy to address urban issues affecting women and children.
• Commended by the executive director and board of directors for expertise, hard work and dedication "as critical components in helping us grow from a small start-up organization to a multipurpose social service and housing agency."
• Identified and implemented solutions impacting 160 units of low-income housing by organizing two active tenant councils. Skilled advocate effective in stressful environment requiring personal diplomacy mediation.
• Wrote newsletter with other staff members and publication's contributor.

1995-1997   Learning Community Charter School, Jersey City, NJ
> *Founding Family*

• Developed, with core group of community activists, the first progressive Bank Street model public elementary school in Hudson County.
• Grant writing committee yielded $335K in Community Development Block Grants and foundation grants. Grass roots fundraising yielded $60K.

1995-1997   Garden Preschool Cooperative, Inc., Jersey City, NJ
> *Founder and Director*

• Launched first progressive nonprofit cooperative preschool in Jersey City. Procured 55K in municipal, state and foundation grants.
• Developed award-winning community garden plan, curriculum and philosophy.

- Instituted active scholarship fund.
- Hired consultants, staff and directed 80+ volunteers.

1988-1994   *The Village Voice,* New York, NY
              Assistant Production Manager
- Supervised pre-press operations for weekly national newspaper. Managed fast-paced, tight deadline office, with concurrent projects.
- Acted as liaison to multiple departments for final sign-off.
- Promoted from typesetting department to production staff. Knowledge of design, typography, Atex ad composition, type processing.

EDUCATON:

University of South Carolina: Bachelor of Arts, English, 1993. Dean's List: 1991, 1992, 1993
Recipient of Quarto Prize for Outstanding Literary Achievement

FELLOWSHIPS AND TRAINING:

2001 - Present   Jersey City Museum

Currently being trained on **Raiser's Edge fundraising software** to provide assistance to the Manager of Marketing, Membership and Special Events.

1997-1998   Pew Charitable Trust
Charlottesville, VA

Fellow. Pew Civic Entrepreneur Initiative. Selected for national/local leadership training program.

1997   Center for Non-Profit Corporations

Participated in grant-writing workshops.

1997   La Leche League International

Accredited as *Breastfeeding Peer Counselor Program Administrator,* a program designed to decrease infant mortality and morbidity by increasing the rate and duration of breastfeeding.

1993   Accredited by La Leche League International as a *Leader* serving Hudson County.

ADMINISTRATIVE AND COMPUTER SKILLS:

Proficient in Internet research skills; skilled at Microsoft Word; familiarity with MS Office and Atex software. Currently in training for **Raiser's Edge** fundraising software program. Portfolio and writing samples available on request.

VOLUNTEER:

2003   Currently serve on boards of two nonprofit organizations; volunteer on newsletter staff of community development corporation.

Matthew Daly   **Telephone 516-558-1000(H)**
100 America Avenue   **Cell Phone 516-557-1000**
West Babylon, NY 11100   **E-mail DetMD@yahoo.com**

EXPERTISE————————————————————

Extensive supervisory experience in criminal investigations in New York City Police
Department

OBJECTIVE————————————————————

To utilize more than 18 years' experience as **Commanding Officer** to provide protection
and security to targeted industries from terrorists

PROFESSIONAL HIGHLIGHTS————————————

- Varied background in managing and conducting criminal investigations
- Demonstrated proficiency in administration, management and training
- Proven ability to analyze, plan and reorganize
- Results-oriented — with numerous citations for excellence

EXPERIENCE HIGHLIGHTS———————————————

46th Precinct Detective Squad • Commanding Officer
- Managed Detective Squad and addressed all administrative and operational
needs in timely, efficient and results-oriented manner.
- Supervised investigations of more serious crime incidents.
- Recognized for excellence. The 46th Precinct Detective Squad amassed
highest case load as well as the Bronx's highest homicide clearance rate during tenure.
- Supervised and reviewed all case closings.

NYPD Detective Bureau Training Unit • Commanding Officer
- Administered and managed Detective Bureau Training Unit.
- Reorganized and enlarged Unit in addition to overseeing acquisition of
permanent classroom, office facilities and updated training aids for Unit.
- Analyzed training needs on continual basis for Detective Bureau.
- Managed preparation and presentation of lessons/courses for training 3,400
Detectives and Supervisors during semi-annual training cycles. Also addressed orientation
training for all supervisors and detectives transferred into Detective Bureau by administering,
preparing and presenting various courses involving specialized detective bureau issues.
- Initiated and edited monthly "Detective Bureau Training Bulletin," which was
distributed to all Detective Bureau personnel.
- Edited and wrote "Detective Squad Supervisors Handbook," NYPD Bureau
Manual, Number 764.
- Recognized for excellence. The Detective Bureau Training Unit was recipient
of NYPD Unit Citation in recognition of excellence in performance.

Bronx Robbery Squad • Commanding Officer

- Administered and managed operational needs of borough-wide Bronx robbery squad and oversaw managerial, administrative and investigative responsibilities of seven local precinct Robbery Investigative Units.
- Managed and supervised investigations involving more serious incidents of robbery as determined by Detective Borough Commander and borough-wide and inter-borough pattern robberies.
- Provided staff and operational assistance to all Bronx precinct detective squads involved in robbery investigations.
- Expanded investigative responsibility of the Bronx Robbery Squad to include robbery incidents in which firearms were discharged by perpetrators during robbery.
- Managed administration and operational functions of the Bronx Borough Criminal Intelligence Unit.

Manhattan Sex Crimes Squad • Commanding Officer

- Managed Manhattan Sex Crimes Squad.
- Acted as Preliminary Operational Supervisor for all serious sex crime investigations.
- Managed and supervised all serious sex crimes to detect borough-wide patterns of sex crimes.
- Investigated incidents involving physical and sexual abuse of special-category children within Manhattan.

34th Precinct Robbery Identification Program • Commanding Officer

- Managed 34th Precinct Robbery Identification Program Unit.
- Managed and supervised all robbery investigations with 34th Precinct.
- Identified and investigated all patterns of robbery with precinct.

Patrol Duties

- Integrity Control Officer and Desk Officer, 50th Precinct.
- Patrol Sergeant in 25th and 26th Patrol Precincts.
- Detective Anti-Crime, 30th Precinct, Police Officer, 30th and 32nd Precincts.

EDUCATION/RANKS/MILITARY————————————————

- Currently enrolled in John Jay College of Criminal Justice, NY. Coursework in International Terrorism and Crime. Projected graduation: 2006
- Associate of Applied Science, Criminal Justice, Rockland Community College, NY: Graduated cum laude
- U.S. Marine Corps, Honorable Discharge
- Progressive promotions from Police Officer to Detective (Grade 3) to Sergeant to Lieutenant to Lieutenant Commander (Detective Squad)
- Proficient in Microsoft Word, PowerPoint, knowledge of Macintosh.

Scott Peterson
1000 Canon Avenue
Oakland, CA 94602
Sco1000@yahoo.com
h. 510-336-1000 c. 510-335-1000

CAREER OBJECTIVE: Energetic and committed media planner
(and gamer) blends multimedia production and marketing
experience at company in interactive entertainment industry

Education
Tufts University, Medford, MA
1990-1994
Bachelor of Arts: English, Film

RELATED WORK EXPERIENCE

Media Planner
Foote, Cone & Belding
San Francisco, CA
2000-Present

• Design and implement media marketing initiatives for
national brands, including Compaq, Blue Shield of
California, LucasArts and MoMA (SF).
• Work in all mediums (TV, print, radio, out of
home, guerilla marketing) with an emphasis on
interactive, online and new technologies.
• Entrepreneurial endeavor within agency was conception,
design and creation of a new media lab: part education
center, part brainstorming space, part hands-on technology
produced with the intention of introducing the
agency and our clients to new media (interactive
television, wireless, instant messaging, broadband, gaming)

Director/Producer
"Land Without Blood"
Boulder, CO
1999-2000

• Wrote and submitted grant to Boulder Arts Commission.
• Made digital video documentary about Tony Perniciaro,
an 85-year-old illiterate Sicilian ghetto bricklayer from
Williamsburg, Brooklyn, who, at age 55, altered his life's
course to become a poet/primitive artist. Produced,

directed, wrote and edited the film. Piece premiered at Puffin Room (SoHo, NYC) for one month as supplement to exhibit showcasing Tony's artwork.

Grant Writer/Office Manager
New York, NY
1996-1997

• Researched and wrote grants for nonprofit organizations, including P.E.N.C.I.L. (Public Education Needs Civic Involvement In Learning) and P.O.V. (PBS's documentary showcase).
• Managed office for grant writer, independent film producer and theater set designer.
• Post-production office coordinator credits on two films: D.A. Pennebaker's documentary "Moon Over Broadway" and Tim Blake Nelson's first feature "Eye of God." Duties included: accounting, day-to-day office management, interaction with diverse groups of people.

Other Work Experience

Sous Chef
15 Degrees
Boulder, CO
1998-1999

• Butcher, baker, and chef (pastry, pantry and line) for gourmet restaurant. Duties included: cooking, designing specials, inventory, customer satisfaction.

Prep Cook
Daily Bread Café
Boulder, CO
1997-1998

• Worked as sandwich maker at independently owned bakery/café. The alternative to Starbucks and other chains, Daily Bread's cornerstone was high-end, gourmet customer service. Duties included: inventory, preparation of food, menu, specials creation and customer service.

World Traveler
Lived/worked in Thailand, Ireland, Nepal, Prague. Traveled extensively within U.S.

CHARLES JONES Telephone: 212-456-1000 (H)
100 Christopher Street Cell phone: 212-456-1010
New York, NY 10010 E-mail: hjhj@yahoo.com

Experienced Reporter capable of breaking news stories under real-time deadlines and with proven ability to translate financial terminology into plain but vibrant language.

PROFESSIONAL HIGHLIGHTS

Freelance Financial Reporter
2001-Present
- Write and cover foreign, emerging and domestic equity markets, industry sectors and mutual funds.
- Articles have appeared in *Wall Street Journal* and *New York Times*.

Worldlyinvestor.com
New York, NY

Correspondent/Mutual Funds Editor
1998-2001

- Analyzed market trends and mutual fund industry analytics in support of investing content.
- Reported on financial/investment topics, especially mutual funds, on daily basis.
- Created/developed investing-oriented content for online financial content site.
- Edited mutual fund content daily, assigned articles and managed freelancers.

Self-Employed Consultant
1995-1998

- Managed new product launch, developed newsletter/catalog for a handheld computer firm, provided financial consultation for TV production company, extensive market research in various industries.

Republic National Bank of New York
New York, NY

Forward/Spot Foreign Exchange Trader
1990-1995

- Priced swap and outright forward contracts; up to $500 million for major corporate customers.

- Traded short-dated futures contracts: including EuroUSD, EuroDM, EuroSTG.
- Analyzed yield spreads for short-term and long-term trading opportunities.
- Made markets in spot Swiss and DM/Swiss; more than 200 trades per day.

Associate Institutional Sales/Trading—International Capital Markets
1988-1990

- Marketed and traded international fixed-income products (Eurobonds, foreign bonds and foreign currency government bonds) to major international client base (Central banks, mutual funds, insurance companies, bank trust departments and pension funds). Generated profits of $1,000,000 annually.
- Monitored all major international markets and worked with UST, money markets, FX, futures and options.
- Performed analysis for swaps, yield spread comparisons and hedging.

Rafidane Corporation
New York, NY

Import/Export Coordinator—Strategic Planner
1986-1988

- Coordinated activities for all aspects of merchandising; purchase and sales, import/export documentation, transportation, warehouse and storage, and futures hedging.
- Developed strategic marketing plan for major foreign product introduction in U.S.

EDUCATION

New York University. New York, NY
Graduate School of Business Administration. *1985-1987*
M.B.A. Finance/International Business

University of Vermont. Burlington, VT
B.S. Accounting. *1979-1983*
Extensive coursework in engineering

RELEVANT INTERESTS AND COMPUTER SKILLS

Proficient in Microsoft Windows and Office software
Comfortable with HTML and Internet publishing systems
Working knowledge of French and Spanish
Extensive independent international travel

Veronica Silvestri, CNM, FACCE
1 Smith Street
Waldwick, NJ 07100
Home: (201) 444-1000●Cell: (201) 447-1000●E-mail: VS11@optonline.net

---

Objective
To develop and/or expand Holistic Health Department, especially in birthing, by utilizing 25 years' experience as delivery nurse, published writer and teacher.

Experience   **1999-Present**
St. Barnabus OB/GYN PC, Bronx, NY. Certified Nurse Midwife for OB/GYN clinics and Labor and Delivery. Adjunct faculty for NY College of Osteopathic Medicine. Instructor in Clinical Nursing for Columbia University School of Nursing. Perinatal educator for Lamaze classes and teen health program. Director of "Pain Management Strategies" workshops.

1997-1998
Valley Center for Women's Health, Midland Park, NJ. CNM for OB/GYN practice. Full scope midwifery at Valley Hospital Obstetrical Clinic. Private Lamaze classes for expectant parents.

1979-1996
Valley Hospital, Ridgewood, NJ. Began as Registered Nurse. Promoted to Staff Nurse in Labor and Delivery. Childbirth Educator for last nine years as well. Career Ladder Level IV.

1977-1979
ECCR, Wyckoff, NJ. Charge Nurse for developmentally disabled children.

1962-1963
Valley Hospital, Ridgewood, NJ. Licensed Practical Nurse. Nursery.

Education   **2002-Present**
University of Medicine and Dentistry of New Jersey, Newark, NJ. Enrolled in Master of Science in Health Science Program. Projected Graduation: June 2004. GPA to date: 3.7

1995-1996
UMDNJ, Newark, NJ. Graduate of Nurse Midwifery Certificate Program. **Honors:** Cum laude

1992-1995
UMDNJ, Newark, NJ. Bachelor of Science, GPA: 3.5

1974-1992
Bergen Community College, Paramus, NJ. General Curriculum/Coursework in field of nursing.

1976-1977
Rockland Community College, Suffern, NY. AAS degree. Registered Nurse, licensed in NY and NJ.

1951-1961
Bergen Pines School of Practical Nursing, Paramus, NJ. Diploma. LPN.

Certifications	**October 1996**

Certified Nurse Midwife by ACNM Certification Council

1979-Present

CPR, IV, NCC (Inpatient obstetrical nursing) Lamaze International, Childbirth Educator, Neonatal Resuscitation, Defibrillation certification, Limited Third Trimester OB Ultrasound.

Honors/Continuing Education	**2001-2003**

Planned, designed and conducted "Pain Management Strategies" workshops, evaluated by New York Nurse Associate and designated as 4.2 CEUs.

1995-1997

New Jersey State Nurses Association, provider of continuing education for childbirth education workshops given at Valley Hospital, Ridgewood, NJ.

1993

Honors Fellow in American College of Childbirth Education by Lamaze International.

1979-Present

500 hours of continuing education programs. Many conferences were sponsored by Lamaze International, ACNM, ICEA and universities in New York and New Jersey. Certificates are available upon request.

Publications	**1996**

"Patient Satisfaction Survey." Research project. Abstract and research of nurse/midwifery clients at Maternal Infant Care Center. Poster presentations at UMDNJ on May 20, 1996, and Perinatal Association of NJ on October 4, 1996.

1994

Author of *Childbirth Education: A Handbook for Nurses.* Continuing education module for 8 CEUs, published by Professional Education Associates and Nurses Spectrum.

Professional Organizations/Community Service	**1995-Present**

Member of American College of Nurse-Midwives

1988-Present

Eucharistic Minister at St. Luke's Church, HoHoKus, NJ

1986-Present

Member of Lamaze International, ICEA

1993-1996

Member of Board of Directors of Northern NJ ASPO/LAMAZE

1972-1979

Coach of Girls' Track Team at St. Luke's Grammar School, HoHoKus, NJ

Terrence DePhillips   (937) 444-1000
10 Oak Street   (937) 445-1000, ext. 1000
Dayton, Ohio 46100   DeP1990@yahoo.com

CHIEF TECHNICAL OFFICER

CAREER PROFILE:

- Senior information technology professional with extensive experience managing large-scale development projects and organizations. Personal strengths focus on understanding business objectives, organizing teams and delivering solutions.
- Highly developed skills in organizational leadership, specifically in areas of staff and project management, organizational planning, budgeting, and staff development and the development of "best practice" policies.
- Development efforts focused on highly integrated applications that included revenue/yield management (pricing and discounts based on trends), sales and marketing (CRM-type focus on tracking customer activities), financials (General Ledger, Accounts Payable, ATMs).

Development technologies have included:
- Web – Java, XML, Sybase
- Client/server – PowerBuilder, C++, SAS, Sybase
- Mainframe – COBOL II, Assembler, IMS, DB2

PROFESSIONAL EXPERIENCE

NCR Corporation, San Jose, CA
Managing Director, Applications Development   *2002 - Present*
Director, Applications Development   *2001 - 2002*

NCR provides global IT infrastructure. Led organization that developed and supported applications for multiple business lines as member of senior management team. Direct management responsibilities including development staff that supported project activities across IT services and a management staff that supported department planning, budgeting and staff support.

- Managed development staff that supported ATM deployers that now easily transition to a complete application platform. This business unit sells technology/ATM services to various industries. The development team:
  - ➢ Developed, rolled out and supported products that provided customers with Internet Distribution Systems (IDS) and Global Distribution Systems (GDS) connectivity.
  - ➢ Developed a Web-enabled product (Easy Access) that allows customers to update information in multiple GDS databases through a single transaction.

- Managed development staff that supported customer information and billing systems.

- Managed a team of dedicated project managers assigned to manage selected efforts across business lines. These managers used MS Project and PowerPoint on project efforts for:
  - ➢ Managed Web-hosting, data center and network project activities associated with implementation of several Internet-based applications.
  - ➢ Implemented the Help Desk product in Phoenix.
  - ➢ Managed the data analysis associated with a major system conversion project.

- Managed a team responsible for department planning and financials. Corporate Finance required that all department expenses be quantified on an hourly basis. Actions taken:
  - ➤ Created new team composed of manager and analysts.
  - ➤ Developed budgeting processes that gathered plans from all business units.
  - ➤ This team and processes created resulted in year-end recoveries within 1% (positive) of total expenses.

- Managed team responsible for department people issues. Development staff grew significantly. Serious attention was paid to recruitment, retention and training.
  - ➤ Created a new team with technical experience and strong interpersonal skills.

- Selected by NCR Corporation management to participate in cross-organizational management teams that addressed IT best practices.
  - ➤ The Project Management team developed a "best practices" handbook.
  - ➤ The Human Resource team developed new policies and procedures.

EDAaptive Computing

Director, Applications Development	*1999 - 2001*
Manager	*1998 - 1999*
Project Leader	*1997 - 1998*

EDAptive Computing is an award-winning company that deals with complex electronics systems in aircraft and space vehicles. Expanding leadership responsibilities included supporting global systems. Direct responsibilities included management of projects and systems that included business relationships, systems analyses and designs.

Led teams that developed highly integrated systems supporting full business cycle. They included:

- Yield Management
- Sales
- Marketing
- Operations
- Financials

Recognized by management as leader and team player by selection to participate in key organizational teams:

- Selected by management as one of 40 people from corporation to drive and manage corporate re-engineering efforts.
- Selected by IT management as one of the lead people to work with consultants to identify department issues and to implement change.
- Selected by IT management to create a Project Review committee that evaluated larger scale development efforts and provided guidance and assistance to project teams.

EDUCATION

Ohio State University (Bachelor of Science, Psychology)

Mary Frances McKiernan

100 Waldwick Avenue • Waldwick, NJ 07100
(201) 444-1000 (H) • (212) 555-100 (W)

mfk100@optonline.net

EXECUTIVE SUMMARY

Senior Developer/Manager excels in financial business applications. Possesses analytical, design and programming experience — combined with excellent communication skills — with more than 13 years' experience. Technical expertise includes, but is not limited to, DB2/CICS and MQ Series

---

CAREER OBJECTIVE

Senior Manager in systems analysis and development at financial services organization

---

TECHNICAL SUMMARY

Software: MQ Series, COBOL II, CICS, DB2 (SPUFI, QMF, BMC, FD), VSAM, OS/JCL, IBM MQ Utilities, File-AID, OS/MVS/XA, SDF-2, INTERTEST. **System:** XPEDITER, SHADOW SERVER DEBUGGING FACILITY, STROBE, CATS, ENDEVOR, MS Office, TSO/ISPF

SKILLS, EXPERIENCE AND CONTRIBUTION

10/93 - Present • METROPOLITAN LIFE INSURANCE • New York
Manager - Programmer/Analyst

• Promoted to manager after one year. Each year responsibility increased. Currently managing 12 people in department.
• Designed, developed and implemented Excess Claims (ECS) and Environmental and Toxic Tort (ETT) Systems.
• Adept at ECS, which provides Excess Claim Department personnel with the ability to view policy and claim information as well as automate the processes of creating, abstracting and segmenting claims, financial activities, claim and policy indexing.
• Redesigned the Loss Management System (LMS), which was replaced by ECS and ETT systems, preparing system flow charts for the user review. Reduced costs significantly.
• Monitored performance of all newly created modules using STROBE prior to its implementation, which circumvented performance problems in production environment.
• Supervised group that created VB screens.
• Conduct production turnovers in ENDEVOR environment.
• Monitored bases ETT Replication on daily basis and resolved all issues concerning the process, which required user interface (QMF, SQL Server, Shadow Server).

2/92 - 10/93 • DEAN WITTER • New York
Programmer/Analyst

• Member of team that developed the Unit Trust Automated Redemption System (ARS) and Equity Information System (EIS)
• Expedited the redemption process by providing UIT personnel with complete information concerning redemption based on risk factors.
• Created, designed and analyzed flow charts on tight deadline.
• Wrote detailed program specifications and designed online screens, which required user interface.
• Handled daily transactions and production support for newly created and existing systems.
• Created VSAM files.

1/89 - 12/91 • CHASE MANHATTAN BANK • New York
Programmer

• Designed and maintained business applications, including payroll, human resources and transaction control information systems.
• Wrote program specifications.
• Participated in software development, starting with system design and finishing with detailed program specifications, coding, testing, implementation and production coverage.
• Prepared and designed economic tasks for financial applications.

EDUCATION

1982-1987 • Bachelor of Science • Pace University

ADDITIONAL TECHNICAL TRAINING

Advanced software analysis • Tel Tech Education (New York) 1991
Certificate of completion of CICS Command Level Programming

MARY WARD
171 Belmont, Jersey City, NJ 07100 (201) 432-1000 (201) 333-1000 <u>Mar@hotmail.com</u>

OBJECTIVE

Marketing Director at large daily newspaper in metropolitan area where management, creative and leadership skills will have positive impact on community and create revenue-building programs for company

---

CAREER HISTORY

NEWHOUSE PUBLICATION - EVENING JOURNAL ASSOCIATION: 1996 - Present

Marketing Director

- Develop highly successful publicity campaigns for daily newspaper:

    The Jersey Journal

    Plus five weeklies:
    Go Out!
    Coming Up.
    El Nuevo Hudson
    This Week in Bayonne,
    This Week in Jersey City

- Create revenue-building programs for newspaper.
- Supervise internal resources and outside agencies in the management of marketing projects; provide writing, editorial and creative concepts.
- Supervise and train circulation customer-service representatives.
- Plan and coordinate all trade shows/special events and conduct related research.
- Direct creative staff of eight responsible for artistic and creative input.

MARCH OF DIMES   1994 - 1996

Community Director

- Coordinated two major *"WalkAmerica"* sites, company's largest fundraising event.
- Responsible for marketing, fundraising, special projects and events for nonprofit organization
- Spokesperson for national nonprofit agency

FREELANCE JOURNALIST   1992 - 1994

- Hosted on-air fundraising for WNJT, New Jersey Network.
- Researched and interviewed published authors; worked as media consultant for dental practice.
- Conducted interviews, assisted assignment editor with future stories for daily news programs.
- Designed script for restaurant voice-over tape.

FOX TELEVISION, "A CURRENT AFFAIR"   1992 - 1993

Production Assistant

- Assisted reporters in all aspects of production, including topic research, screening story ideas for future productions.
- Facilitated and coordinated on-site taping and interviewing.

FLORIDA STATE LOTTERY   1987 - 1991

Promotional Director

- Became member of original start-up team.
- Developed, organized and implemented Florida State Lottery procedures.
- Managed promotional events, such as lottery-sponsored 1991 Super Bowl.

ORGANIZATIONS/AFFILIATIONS

- Chairman–Hudson County Chamber of Commerce Small Business Committee   1999 - present
- Member–National Federation for Female Executives   1998 - present
- Committee Member–St. Joseph's School for the Blind, Phil Rizzuto Golf Classic   1996 - present
- Board Member–Hudson Cradle, Home for Infants   1995 - present
- Committee Member–Valerie Fund, Children with Cancer   1995 - present

EDUCATION

Rutgers College of Arts & Sciences, Bachelor of Arts, Journalism

KAYLA ADAMS

PHYSICAL THERAPIST

100 MAPLE AVENUE
RIDGEWOOD, NJ 07100
201-447-1000 (H)

Marad@worldnet.att.net

PROFESSIONAL SUMMARY: Diversified and progressive experience in physical therapy, concentrating on geriatric home-care services. Provided pre- and post-prosthetic training for amputees; specialized in spinal cord injuries and orthopedic problems. Highly proficient at teaching in-service programs in mobilization. Adept at low-back and upper-quarter evaluations. Extensive supervisory experience.

OBJECTIVE: Plan and oversee the physical therapy program in geriatric facility and coordinate these activities with other instructional programs; train students and technical and nontechnical assistants; assign and oversee their work; administer active, passive and resistive therapeutic exercises, muscle training, and corrective exercises and coordination work; oversee the administration of hydrotherapy treatments; administer various types of electric therapy, including ultraviolet, infrared, diathermy and inductothermy; observe the physical conditions and reactions of clients.

EXPERIENCE

Valley Home Care   **October 1989 to Present**
Ridgewood, NJ
Physical Therapist

- In-house home care for the elderly, treating stroke victims, patients with orthopedic problems (especially hip and knee replacement), balance dysfunction, patients with musculoskeletal pain, patients with adult hemiplegia.
- Administered passive and resistive therapeutic exercises.
- Administered general muscle, transfer and gait training.
- Observed physical conditions and reactions of patients and prepared reports.
- **Relevant Coursework:** Evaluation and Treatment of Balance Dysfunction in the Elderly (July 28, 29, 2002); Neurological & Geriatric Rehabilitation: Implications for Balance Dysfunction (May 19,20, 2001). Geriatric Orthopedics, by Carole Lewis (November 1997); Stroke: The Continuum of Care (April 5, 19997).

Holy Name Hospital   **1986 to 1989**
Teaneck, NJ
Physical Therapist/Teacher

- Besides working with geriatric patients, acted as therapist for patients with burn, cardiac, stroke, wound care, respiratory, spinal cord injuries and orthopedic patients. Train assistants. Prepare evaluations.

- **Relevant Coursework:** PT Review for Therapists, III (November 14, 1987)

Englewood Hospital   **1982 to 1986**
Englewood, NJ
Senior Therapist

- Student coordinator. Taught "Back School" to adults, a course about proper body mechanics.
- Administered various types of electric therapy.
- Oversaw assistant therapists.
- Prepared evaluations.

Elmhurst General Hospital   **1980 to 1986**
Elmhurst, NY
Physical Therapist

- Physical therapy for geriatric, stroke, cardiac, spinal cord and other orthopedic patients.
- Trained assistants. Prepared evaluations.
- Oversaw work of trainees.
- **Relevant Coursework:** Lower Limb Prosthetics (May 16-27, 1983); Cardiac Fitness: The Facts and the Future (October 1, 1982); Examination and Rehabilitation of Cervical Spine (December 11,12, 1982); Practical Pharmacology for Physical Therapists (November 7, 1981); Clinical Management of Adult Hemiplegia (August 3-8, 1981); High Voltage Galvanic Stimulation (May 2, 1981)

PROFESSIONAL DEVELOPMENT

U.S. Public Health Hospital (Staten Island, NY) Student Physical Therapist	1980
Hillside Public Health Hospital (Staten Island, NY) Student Physical Therapist	1980
St. Agnes Hospital, Burn Center (Philadelphia) Student Physical Therapist	1980
Heywood Valley Nursing Home (Worcester, MA) Student Physical Therapist	1979

EDUCATION

University of Pennsylvania, Philadelphia, PA
    Certificate in Physical Therapy   1980
    GPA: 3.5
Clark University, Worcester, MA
    B.A. in Biology   1978
    GPA: 3.8

PROFESSIONAL AFFILIATION

American Physical Therapy Association Member

Kim Hilton
100 Lincoln Avenue
Ridgewood, NJ 07450
Telephone: (201) 447-1000 (H)
Cell phone: (201) 522-1000
E-mail: Khil@worldnet.att.net

Profile

Highly qualified mathematics teacher adept at building rapport with — and motivating — middle- and secondary-school students. Demonstrated strengths in test preparation, innovative teaching techniques and integrating technology skills into curriculum

Professional Qualifications

- New Jersey Teaching Certificate of Eligibility with Advanced Standing in Mathematics, K-12 (2002)
- M.Ed., Teaching Children Mathematics
- Results-oriented preparation of students for statewide testing and SAT
- Proficient knowledge of written and oral Spanish

Professional Experience

Union High School, Union, NJ • September 1999-Present • Mathematics Teacher
- Designed/implemented comprehensive units in Algebra I, Geometry and Basic Skills.
- Integrated technology as well as cooperative activities in lessons.
- Prepared students for statewide mandated testing with excellent results.

Cliffside Park School #4, Cliffside Park, NJ • April-June 1999 • Substitute Teacher
- Taught seventh- and eighth-grade students as full-time, long-term Substitute Mathematics Teacher.
- Managed to gain respect of students and maintain atmosphere conducive to learning.
- Developed daily lesson plans involving manipulatives and cooperative learning.

Ridgewood Public Schools, Ridgewood, NJ • February-March 1999 • Substitute Teacher
- Demonstrated versatility and flexibility while teaching at various schools in the Ridgewood Public School System.
- Developed skills in building student/teacher relationship quickly and effectively.

Clay Middle School, South Bend, IN • Fall 1998 • Eighth-Grade Student Teacher
- Taught both Algebra and Math classes on eight-block schedule.
- Gained experience with reform mathematics curriculum.

- Prepared students for mandated statewide testing with good results.
- Asked to teach Geometry and Honors Algebra II classes to tenth- and eleventh-grade students at Clay High School.

Field Experience, South Bend, IN • 1995-1998 • Observer
- Observed classroom teaching and management techniques.
- Worked individually and in small groups with students at various middle and high schools.
- Developed varied techniques and skills on encouraging students in class participation, homework completion, test preparation and cognitive readiness.

Related Work Experience

Camp David, Deal, NJ • Summer 1998 • Swim Instructor and Lifeguard
- Supervised and taught group swim lessons to campers, ages 9 to 14.

South Bend, IN • September 1997-May 1998 • Tutor
- Privately tutored middle-school students in mathematics.

Hamilton Adult Education Program, South Bend, IN • August-December 1995 • Tutor
- Prepared adults for GED.
- Prepared students for SAT.

Allendale Swim Club, Allendale, NJ • Summers 1994-1997 • Lifeguard
- Taught private and group lessons to children.
- Promoted to Head Lifeguard in 1997.

Education

William Paterson University, Wayne, NJ • M.Ed., Teaching Children Mathematics • 2002
University of Notre Dame, South Bend, IN • Bachelor of Science (Mathematics-Middle and Secondary Teacher Education Program) • May 1998
- Sophomore Class Council: Chaired Community Service Committee
- Junior Class Council: Elected to represent all junior class and off-campus students.

Spanish-American Institute, Seville, Spain • Spring 1997 Semester • Language Proficiency in Spanish (oral and written)

Technology Skills

Skilled at Microsoft Word, Excel, Internet, TI-82, TI-83, Geometer's Sketchpad and C

Related Activities

- Intramural Soccer: **Captain** and organizing member of off-campus women's soccer.

Interested in coaching position at middle- or high-school level, especially soccer

Sean Kowalski
100 Thompson Street, Apartment 1, New York, NY 10010
Home Phone 212.473.1000   **Cell Phone 917.687.1000**   **E-mail lkow@optonline.net**

Objective

Become an integral part of a sales team while providing quality outside sales by generating revenue and achieving set goals for an Internet media or media company

Experience

Sales Manager, Salon Media Group (6/00-3/04)

Recruited based on sales background, adaptability and strong communication skills. Identified and cultivated new clients in undeveloped sales territory. Exceeded expectations and grew territories while congruently building relationships with top national and New York advertising agencies and brands. Adept at listening to clients' needs and developing mutually beneficial relationships.

- Sold 31% of entire company sales team's revenue in first quarter of 2002.
- Generated 21% of all sales in 2001.
- Awarded raise as reward for strong performance.
- Ranked Number One East Coast Salesman last fiscal year.
- Promoted for continual success and highest sales-growth rate in company.
- Awarded raise based on accomplished goals.
- Designed and sold customized marketing opportunity that did not previously exist.
- Achieved sales goals 83% of time since being hired.
- Won Top Performer Award, 4th Quarter (2002).
- Won two of the four company-wide sales contests in 2001.
- Won lead generation contest both months eligible.

Sales Representative, GV Publications (6/99-9/99)
- Provided print advertising opportunities for clients while achieving set sales goals.
- Conducted outside sales with local businesses in community.

President, GLG Promotions (12/97-12/98)
- Promoted local bars and clubs and recruited 500 to 1,200 people nightly.
- Built company from ground up and developed new images and perceptions for existing venues.

Manager/Waiter, El Charro Café (3/98-5/00)
- Operated as headwaiter and promoted to manager after increasing food/beverage sales.
- Provided basic facilitator and server duties.

President, Sigma Phi Epsilon Fraternity (10/96-10/97)
- Operated as liaison between local chapter, national headquarters and University Dean of Students.
- Maintained daily operations for 120 men while organizing weekly chapter meetings and events.

Education

The University of Arizona, Tucson, Arizona (1994-1999)
Degree: Bachelor of Fine Arts
Major: Media Arts
Minor: Communications and Sociology

Communication Skills

Language: Speak, read and write Spanish
Computer: Operate Microsoft Word, Works, PowerPoint, Outlook, ACT, Excel, Salesforce, Palm

Sabina Smith

1000 Washington Ave., Apt. 1.   201.435.1000
Hoboken, NJ 07100   ss000@yahoo.com

PROFESSIONAL QUALIFICATIONS: Dynamic Publicist eager to use press knowledge, media contacts and communication skills to represent artists

EMPLOYMENT HISTORY

2002 - Present   **Office Manager, The New Teacher Project**
                        New York, New York
• Developing and maintaining HR- and finance-related databases and tracking sheets, such as comprehensive staff census, time-off tracking and grant-related tracking.
• Managing internal news/press cataloging system.
• Assisting HR Manager with processing employee benefit forms.
• Assisting Accountant with expense reporting and invoicing.
• Assisting CTO with technical support and Web site maintenance.
• Maintaining supplies, postage, marketing materials and filing systems.
• Distributing internal and external communications.

1993 - 2001   **PR Account Coordinator, Harron & Associates**
                        Boston, Massachusetts
• Assisting in the planning, organization and execution of various events for clients, such as The Shops at Prudential Center, Top of the Hub Restaurant, Boston Symphony Orchestra, Riverdeep Interactive Learning and BT Global Challenge.
• Writing press releases. Producing and maintaining databases, filing system, compiling and cataloguing press clips, training new staff, maintaining office equipment, reception, conducting project research and executing large-scale mailings.

1998 - 1999   **Assistant Director, The Harbor Art Gallery**
                        Boston, Massachusetts
• Assisting the Gallery Director with planning exhibitions, hanging artists' work, striking shows and organizing opening receptions.
• Managing gallery during hours of operation, providing visitor information, maintaining databases, distributing mailings and answering telephone inquiries.

COMPUTER SKILLS
• Proficient in both Macintosh and PC programs, including MS Word, Office, Excel, Access, Filemaker Pro, Gallery Pro, QuarkXPress and Photoshop 5.5.

EDUCATION
1995 - 2001   **University of Massachusetts,** Boston (Major: Fine Arts)

TRISH MURPHY
10-00 Dogwood Lane
Greenbrier, TN 37073
615/643-1000
MBB10@aol.com

Career Objective:
College-educated Office Systems Assistant with more than ten years' experience at Fortune 500 company seeks Administrative Assistant position at large Engineering firm where technical and communication skills as well as computer savvy can be used for preparation of reports and specs

Work History
> *Travelers Insurance,* Nashville, TN. 1993-present
> *Littlejohn Engineering Associates,* Nashville, TN. 1993
> *Brentwood Professional Center,* Brentwood, TN. 1992-1993
> *ProCuts Inc.,* Antioch, TN. 1991-1992

Summary of Qualifications
- Develop specialized safety reports used to aid in prevention of employee illness and injuries.
- Proof and edit project contracts and proposals.
- Complete highly protected risk reports that require high degree of accuracy and technical knowledge.
- Complete real estate contracts and proposals.
- Develop billing reports.
- Resolved issues with engineers regarding completion and content of reports.
- Schedule and maintain appointment calendars.
- Address customer complaints and resolve quickly.
- Maintain high volume switchboard.

Computer Skills
- Proficient with Word 97, Word 98 and Word 2000
- Proficient with Windows 3.1, Windows 95 and Windows 98.
- Knowledge of Flow Chart 3.2
- Knowledge of Excel 5.0, Excel 97 and Excel 2000
- Knowledge of WordPerfect 5.1
- Knowledge of Lotus 1, 2, 3
- Proficient with Internet research

Education
Murray State University, 1990
Bachelor of Science: Agriculture
Minor in Office Systems Administration

Raymond Thomas   *Public Relations*

1 Licoya Bay, Nashville, TN 37215 • (615) 677-1000
FAX: (615) 677-1001 • RT100@worldnet.att.net

ATTRIBUTES

- Excellent communication and interpersonal skills
- Capable of meeting tight deadlines
- Works independently to complete assignments with limited supervision
- Pays close attention to details
- Positive attitude and outlook

HIGHLIGHTS OF EXPERIENCE

- Promotions given in each position
- Reduced printing costs with quality control measures
- Brought new clients aboard with creative marketing strategies
- Member of team that made ergonomically correct adjustments to office space
- Consistently selected to attend Web page development seminars and courses

---

RELEVANT EXPERIENCE

R.D. Murray Communications, Nashville, TN
Marketing Manager
January 1999 to Present
Wrote all marketing materials. Part of a team that created ad campaigns that increased revenue by 22 percent. Supervised six people. Promoted from marketing coordinator in 2001. Created new business opportunities, some with Fortune 500 companies.

CloudNine Graphics, Columbia, SC
Marketing Coordinator
September 1995 to November 1999
Developed Web site and wrote marketing materials, both online and hard copy. Reduced mailing and printing costs by 5 percent. Worked on tight deadlines and was responsible for proofing all marketing materials while supervising freelance writers and editors. Promoted from marketing assistant in 1997.

EDUCATION

University of Tennessee, Bachelor of Arts (Communications) 1995.
Computer Skills: Microsoft Word, Access, WordPerfect, HTML. Web Page Development Certification from Waldon Community College (2000)

CONFIDENTIAL

CHARLES AHERN
10 America Avenue
Babylon, NY 11000
(718) 652-1000
cax2130@aol.com

QUALIFICATIONS: TECHNICAL STAFF MEMBER
More than 10 years' systems and programming experience in **Brokerage** and **Financial** applications. Wide background in IBM hardware, software and programming languages. Experienced with **full project life cycle** and **project control methodologies.** Extensive experience with **COBOL, COBOL II, VSAM, CICS,** and **DB2. Extensive user contact.**

Hardware:	IBM 3094, 3090, 3083, 3033, 4381
Software:	IBM MVS/ESA, DOS/VSE, TSO/ISPF, VM/CMS, Arthur Andersen Foundation and IEF (CASE), **CICS, DB2,** SPUFI, ISQL, QMF, IMS, IDMS, **VSAM,** INTERTEST, EDF, XPEDITER, PRO-EDIT, File-AID, Data Expert, SDF, UTILITIES; IDCAMS, SYNCSORT, COMPAREX, Panvalet, Librarian; Windows, WordPerfect
Languages:	**IBM COBOL II,** SQL, BAL, OS/JCL, DOS/JCL, PC-DOS, EASYTRIEVE

EXPERIENCE

Port Authority of New York and New Jersey   **11/97 - Present**
Senior Manager — Programmer/Analyst
Code and modify programs that combine the BARAMIS and AVPS systems. Daily system analysis and program development utilizing ADABAS, **COBOL II, CICS,** SDF, **VSAM,** QSAM, OS/JCL. Key member of the BARAMIS System Y2K conversion team. Changed **COBOL II batch and online programs,** record layouts and SDF maps; converting **VSAM** and QSAM files, and OS/JCL date parms. **CICS** programs were tested using INTERTEST and Xpediter used for batch programs. **Environment:** MVS/ESA, TSO/ISPF, VM/CMS, ADABAS, Xpediter, Panvalet: Windows, WordPerfect

Credit Suisse, New York   **6/93 - 9/97**
Senior Manager — Programmer/Analyst
Worked on pilot project to convert part of Warehousing System from Texas Instruments IEF (Information Engineering Facility) to standard **COBOL, CICS, DB2.** System processes and displays global customer information utilizing both batch and online programs. Analyzed the IEF high-level program code and converting the programs to native **COBOL, CICS, DB2** source code. Also tested and documented each program. Promoted from Manager to Senior Manager in 1995. Platinum, QMF and SPUFI used for accessing **DB2** tables and creating test data. File-AID and IDCAMS for creating and changing **VSAM** files. **Environment:** MVS/ESA, TSO/ISPF

Lehman Brothers, New York   **10/92 - 5/93**
Senior Programmer/Analyst
Worked on Maintain Securities Information (MSI) process of Multi-Currency Accounting and Reporting System (MARS). This large global security system processed corporate actions and pricing information received from financial organizations. Analyzed, designed and coded programs that performed validation of the vendor input data and creation of output transaction tables used to update the MARS database. Programs were written in **COBOL II** and **CICS** with embedded **DB2.** Platinum, QMF and SPUFI were used for testing **DB2** queries, ad hoc reports and creating test tables. **Environment:** MVS/ESA, TSO/ISPF

EDUCATION: Bachelor of Arts, Queens College

IZABELA KIESLOWSKI

100 Avenue E, Apt. 1   (201) 432-1000
Edgewater, NJ 07100   IzzyK@yahoo.com

OBJECTIVE: *Multi-lingual college graduate melds strong communication and interpersonal skills with leadership and computer savvy to management-training position in human resources*

- Hard working and well organized; able to work with little supervision
- Detail-oriented and analytical; able to see whole picture
- Highly adaptable in solving problems and working in multitask environment
- Demonstrated leadership in training/supervision
- Creative but able to meet deadlines
- Ability to master new skills, concepts and ideas quickly
- Computer proficiency in Windows 95/98, Microsoft (Word, Works, Excel, Access, PowerPoint), Internet Explorer, Claris Works, WordPerfect and Netscape Navigator

EXPERIENCE:

2002
Office Assistant
Liberty State Park, Jersey City, NJ
Greeted visitors at front desk. Answered customers' queries relating to park activities.
Received Employee of the Month award.
Handled bank transactions; issued boat launch permits; collected appropriate fees.
Performed office-related duties — such as data entry, answering telephones, filing, and faxing — in timely, positive and efficient manner.

2001-2002
Job Coach
Hudson County Occupational Center, Jersey City, NJ
Educated students in occupational setting on work ethics.
Trained students to perform basic job functions.
Developed lesson plans and scheduled events related to job placement, such as résumé writing and interviewing-skills workshops.
Assisted in research projects, utilizing Internet skills.

2000-2001
Student Intern
Jersey City Housing Authority, Jersey City, NJ
Assisted supervisor in various office-related activities, such as data entry, proofreading, organizing monthly statistical data, filing, copies and faxing.
Gathered information to update various spreadsheets for upper management's use.
Accurately and responsively coordinated flow of work.
Reduced costs and updated inventory of supplies.

1999-2000
Office Assistant
Academic Affairs, New Jersey City University, Jersey City, NJ
Maintained administrative and personnel records.
Entered and verified data in appropriate formats.
Responded to students' inquiries and requests.
Managed incoming and outgoing correspondence.

LANGUAGES: *Multilingual — Fluent in English, Polish and Ukrainian, some Russian*

EDUCATION: *Bachelor of Science, Management, May 2001*
New Jersey City University   Deans List, Fall 1996 and Spring 1997
Senior Class Vice President   Pre-Law Society member

David J. Rosen
100 Glenwood Avenue, Leonia, NJ 07100
Home: (201) 461-1000 Cell: (646) 431-1000 E-mail: <u>djr100@nyu.edu</u>

STATEMENT OF PURPOSE
Recent college graduate responsive to deadlines and with multifaceted intern experience seeks entry-level administrative and editorial support position at publishing house that requires the ability to multitask; has strong writing, proofreading and editing skills.

EDUCATION
- B.A., 2003, New York University, Gallatin School of Individualized Studies Concentration in English and Communications: 3.3 GPA

SKILLS
- Proficient in Microsoft Word, Works and Excel
- Familiar with Macintosh

EMPLOYMENT
Intern, *Show Business Weekly,* February 2003 – June 2003
- Proofread articles
- Phone duties
- Wrote casting notices
- Data entry
- Proposed cover concepts
- Wrote photo captions

Human Resources Intern, Time Warner Cable, Palisades Park, NJ, summer 2000
- Improved organization of office materials to upgrade efficiency.
- Assisted reporters at press conferences.

Clerical Assistant, NYU Undergraduate Admissions Office, October 1999 – May 2001
- Advised prospective students of upcoming events and off-campus functions.
- Filed important and confidential documents.

Customer Relations, Corporate Investor Communications, summer 1999
- Entered data and performed telephone duties.

STUDENT ACTIVITIES: Co-Junior Class Representative, Gallatin School Student Council: Helped initiate student council and implement new programs. Staff Member, *Minetta Review,* NYU Literary Magazine, 3 years: candidate for Editorial Position. Treasurer, Gallatin First Friday Organization: Helped organize monthly arts festival.

Terrence Martz
WIRE ROPE ENGINEER
100 Breuhaus Lane
Seaville, NJ 08230
(609) 624-1000 (Cell)
Tmar@hotmail.com

Objective: Managerial position in Wire Rope Industry where engineering expertise in suspension bridges can further advance the application of new wire rope technologies

➤ More than 10 years' experience as engineer in Wire Rope business
➤ Specialized in contract negotiation and specifications for pre-stressed products in bridges and cable-supported structures

---

J.A. Good Consultants, Cape May Courthouse, NJ   **1992-Present**

Manager/Field Engineer   **1997-Present**
Prepared and **tested** socketed strand assemblies to develop an approved methodology for subsequent field application.
Developed marketing strategies to increase customer base and increase usage of structural strand and wire rope products within construction sector.
Managed contracts for Warrior River RR Lift Bridge, Burlington Northern RR Life Bridge, Camas Prairie RR Lift Bridge, Texaco Pipeline Suspension Bridge, Capitol Center Sports Arena, Denver Sports Arena.
Provided estimates and then managed contracts for McKenzie River Bridge, Point Pleasant Canal Lift Bridge, Ben Franklin Bridge.
Recent field work includes:
➤ Replaced suspenders and handropes on Golden Gate Bridge.
➤ Made corrective repairs to suspender assemblies and handropes on Golden Gate.
➤ Inspected wire ropes on Harlem River 125th Street Lift Bridge.

Assistant Manager   **1994-1997**
Coordinated three warehouses and inventory management. Conducted transportation cost-analysis studies. Negotiated freight rates and developed national transportation policies that improved time-to-market and reduced costs by 20%. Wrote specifications for pre-stressed products in bridges. Proficient in Microsoft Office.

Senior Wire Rope Product Engineer   **1992-1994**
Provided engineering services to original equipment manufacturers and strip mining companies while acting as National Customer Technical Service Representative. Highly skilled in field investigation, negotiation, settlement of claims.

EDUCATION: Stevens Institute of Technology, Hoboken, NJ   **1990-1992**

MORGAN RIGG, RN
100 Lincoln Avenue, Ridgewood, NJ 07100
(201) 447-1000 Cellphone (201) 981-1000 mri@oal.com

PROFESSIONAL OBJECTIVE
Corporate Services Clinician or Substance Abuse Counselor in corporate setting

STRENGTHS AND AREA OF EXPERTISE
Certified substance abuse counselor. Able to help addicted through the entire recovery process, from initial crisis intervention to referral to treatment programs to counseling in halfway house situations and aftercare with full reintegration into a substance abuse–free life. Strengths include writing, organization, project management, fundraising and building trust with and developing motivation for people in distress. Career foundation as registered nurse. Fluent in oral and written Spanish and German

EDUCATION, PROFESSIONAL TRAINING AND LICENSURE
CADC (Certified Alcohol and Drug Addiction Counselor) June 2003
RN (Registered Nurse), State of NJ, 1982; license current
AAS in Nursing, Bergen Community College, Paramus, NJ
BA in Spanish and Sociology, Trinity College, Burlington, VT
- Dean's List
- Triple Key Honor Society
- Who's Who in American Colleges and Universities

VOLUNTEER SERVICE
Volunteer Counselor at a battered women's shelter and halfway house
- Counsel battered women with drug and alcohol abuse issues, as well as recovering women. 1998 to present.
Eucharistic Minister at Valley Hospital, Ridgewood, NJ.
- Regularly served the Eucharist to patients in hospital. 1987 to present.
Home School Association member and leader, Glen Rock and Ridgewood, NJ
- Successfully raised money for grade school, junior and senior high school classes through at least 20 functions, including auctions and fundraising dinner events; Senior Ball Team Leader (1982); continued work on committee (to 2003).
- Organized first Glen Rock House Tour for senior class of 1994. This event has become a yearly tradition, generating more than $45,000 per year for the HSA.
CCD Teacher at St. Catharine's Roman Catholic Church, Glen Rock, NJ
- Taught weekly religious education classes. 1984 to 1994.

NURSING EXPERIENCE
Wayne General Hospital, Wayne, NJ
Pediatric and Medical/Surgical Nurse. 1982 to 1985
Also served as registered Nurse at hospital clinic in Paterson, NJ.

COMPUTER SKILLS
Microsoft Word; Internet; adept at managing client records in pre-existing database

Myles Byrne
WEBMASTER
1 Northland Avenue
Appleton, WI 54100
(920) 444-1000 (Home)
(920) 445-1000 (Cell)
Mylie111@msn.com
www.mylie.com

OBJECTIVE: To combine expertise as **editor** and **writer** with computer skills as highly proficient **Assistant Webmaster** for **Webmaster** position at large corporation in Wisconsin

---

Assistant Webmaster, SYS-CON Media, Montvale, NJ. 2001-2004

SYS-CON Media, listed in *Inc. 500* three years in a row as the fastest-growing, privately held publishing company in America, is leading publisher serving the i-technology markets.

As **Assistant Webmaster,** maintained and enhanced various publications' Web sites, including *Wireless Business & Technology, Java Developer's Journal, XML-Journal, Web Services Journal and ColdFusion Developer's Journal,* where it was necessary to type, scan, import and edit text. Additionally, wrote, edited, researched and solicited as well as acquired additional information for Web sites.

Skills and **qualifications** necessary to successfully fulfill requirements were knowledge of Macintosh, WYSIWYG and graphics software, HTML, QuarkXPress.

Expertise in Internet technologies, such as CGI and JavaScript, Adobe GoLive. Proficient in Word, WordPerfect, MS Works, PowerPoint.

Sports Editor/Copy Editor, *North Jersey Herald & News,* Passaic, NJ. 2000-2001

Worked as **Assistant Editor** and **Copy Editor** at metropolitan newspaper covering Paterson and surrounding area. Competently met daily deadlines in high pressure atmosphere. Wrote sports news briefs and copyedited daily section.

Skills required for position: thorough knowledge of AP style; thorough knowledge of sports (even minutiae); acquired skills in Macintosh, Quark, PhotoShop. Honed skills as writer and editor, with emphasis on accuracy and clarity.

Unrelated experience:

South Coast Deli, Santa Barbara, CA 1995-1998.

Prepared sandwiches and worked cash register 20 hours per week during school semesters. Developed **skills**
- interacting with public
- working long hours
- taking direction from four supervisors simultaneously

EDUCATION: University of California, Santa Barbara, Bachelor of Arts, **English.** Minor in **Computer Science.** 1998. GPA: 3.2.
- Involved in many intramural sports (volleyball, basketball).
- See www.mylie.com for sample work.

Sharon M. Smith
559 Holly Court
Mahwah, NJ 07100
(201) 760-1000
Suz559@aol.com

OFFICE MANAGER *with definitive strengths in managing day-to-day administrative and financial operations*

Traphagen & Traphagen, CPAs, Oradell, NJ
October 1981 to Present

Office Manager/Administrative Assistant/Administrative Partner
- Supervise front office staff.
- Supervise entire staff for firm policy compliance.
- Manage time accounting and billing system.
- Accounts Receivable
- Accounts Payable
- Liaison between partners and clients
- Prepare firm financial reports.
- Facilities maintenance (250-year-old historic structure)
- Equipment maintenance
- Property management for rental properties
- Prepare promotional material.

SUMMARY OF ACCOMPLISHMENTS

- Led computer conversion for firm's billing and accounts receivable system.
- Assisted in restoration of historic structure.
- Assisted state-funded program for victims of September 11th in receiving nonprofit organizational status — worked directly with governor's office.
- Volunteer for March of Dimes

SKILLS

MS Windows, Word, Excel, PowerPoint, Peachtree, Quickbooks, Unilink TB Plus, Lacerte and Steno

EDUCATION

Berkeley Secretarial School, Executive Secretarial Program
Graduate of Dale Carnegie Effective Communications Course

ALICE A. THOMAS
15 East 10th Street, Apt.10, New York, NY 10100 (212)533-1000
E-mail: Alito@aol.com

PROFESSIONAL OBJECTIVE
College-educated and bilingual Administrative Assistant with 14 years'
experience seeks to support management at architectural firm with
excellent accounting, communication and computer skills.

- Proficient in MS Word, Excel, PowerPoint, and Lotus and Internet
- Fluent in Spanish

EXPERIENCE
Ambassador Construction, New York, NY   1995-2004

Administrative Assistant
- Promoted to Administrative Assistant in Insurance Department.
- Streamlined accounting procedures.
- Created highly workable file structures.
- Assigned special projects.

Executive Secretary
- Composed and prepared routine correspondence.
- Liaisoned between immediate managers and high-level executives.
- Organized official company documents for prospective clients.
- Edited and proofread reports.
- Maintained accounting procedures.

Dow Jones & Co., Inc., New York, NY   1993–1994
Executive Secretary at NBEW's Advertising Department
- Composed and prepared routine correspondence. Adept at bookkeeping,
  filing, typing, heavy phones and customer service.
- Coordinated and created promotional materials.
- Maintained personnel attendance log.
- Arranged reservations and travel.

Globus/Cosmos Tourama, Rego Park, Queens, NY   1989–1993
Word Processor/Travel Documentation Assistant
- Initiated procedure to coordinate travel documentation with issuance
  of airline tickets to clients; **process was instituted nationally by
  the company's Documents Department.**
- Prepared travel itineraries and hotel lists worldwide.

EDUCATION Hunter College. Projected graduation: 2007

CHARLES HENRY

100 Walnut St. • Brookline, MA • 02100 • (617) 277-1000

henry.cat@verizon.net

Education

Tufts University, Medford, MA   *1988-1990*
University of Massachusetts, Amherst, MA   *1990-1992*
- Bachelor of Arts, Psychology, December 1992
- Cum laude graduate

Experience

May 2000 - present
Program Analyst
Vaxgen, Inc., Brisbane, CA

- Provide SAS programming support for Phase III clinical trial involving experimental AIDS vaccine.
- Perform validation and creation of summary tables supporting Phase I/II reports submitted to FDA.
- Create semiannual summary tables for submission to Data Safety Monitoring Board.
- Act as sole support for contract laboratory data.
- Create and maintain Contract Payment System responsible for quarterly payments made to 61 participating clinical sites for Phase III clinical trial.
- Maintain company intranet with respect to summary tables and subject listings for Clinical and Data Management departments and remote staff

November 1998 -
May 2000
Consultant
Statistical Programming Consultant *for* **Trilogy Consulting** and **Atlantic Search Group**
Programmer/Data Manager, Warner-Lambert Company, Morris Plains, NJ (*Trilogy*)
Analyst, Pharmacyclics, Inc., Sunnyvale, CA (*ASG*)

- Provided consulting services/SAS programming support for clinical study applications and NDA submissions of Phase I/II clinical trials.
- Inspected existing systems, SAS code and report generation for accuracy.
- Created data warehouse through the construction of SAS data sets and analysis files from source data (e.g., SAS, ASCII, spreadsheets, transport, text, etc.).
- Executed database queries on protocol specifications and

follow-up for resolution with clinical/data
management groups.
- Generated complex data reports.
- Assisted in the development of department-wide SOPs
  and the standardization of SAS code generation.
- Created finalized status reports for related programming
  and data management activities.
- Trained/developed new staff for all data management
  aspects and auditing data listings.

April 1998 -
November 1998   ***Programmer Analyst***
                     Abt Associates, Inc., Cambridge, MA

- Represented Law and Public Policy area in all
  company-wide programming issues.
- Wrote reports of study results for funding agencies.
- Cleaned and analyzed data for Senior Scientists in Law and
  Public Policy Area and investigators at federal offices.
- Wrote and debugged SAS code for several projects.
- Served as internal resource adviser and mentor in
  statistical programming for junior staff.
- Interviewed and evaluated prospective Abt employees in
  programming and statistical skills.

July 1995 -
April 1998   ***Senior Research Associate (1997-1998)***
                     Research Associate (1996)
                     Senior Research Assistant (1995)
                     New England Research Institutes, Watertown, MA

- Conducted site visits to study centers in New York, DC,
  Chicago, San Francisco and Los Angeles to monitor adherence
  to study laboratory protocols.
- Tracked central specimen repository containing 400,000
  specimens.
- Used SAS to select specimens to be retrieved from specimen
  repository for individual substudies.
- Acted as primary contact with central repository staff.
- Served on protocol development team for substudy involving NIDA.
- Worked directly with NIAID Program Officer during study
  renewal.
- Performed exploratory statistical analysis and analysis for
  eventual manuscripts in SAS for a multicenter study of women
  and HIV disease progression.
- Served as primary contact to multiple working groups, including
  Epidemiology-Statistics, Retention, Shipping, Laboratory and all
  lab-related subgroups.

- Collaborated directly with principal investigators and site project directors on data management and analysis issues.
- Produced monthly reports on protocol compliance, accrual and retention of study participants.

June 1994 -
July 1995

Research Assistant
Medical Research International, Burlington, MA

- Programmed in SAS on multiple studies involving pharmaceutical companies.
- Provided database management support for multiple studies.
- Acted as primary contact with overseas office regarding international study status.
- Assisted in coordination and implementation of database construction using SAS.
- Assisted in development and implementation of internal quality assurance procedures.
- Collaborated with systems development staff on design of study-specific data-management systems.

December 1991 -
January 1993

Senior Team Leader
Laboratory for Behavior Assessment, University of Massachusetts

- Recruited subjects for laboratory behavior studies.
- Distributed and monitored tasks performed by research assistants.
- Oversaw all activities performed in laboratory.

Professional Organizations

Golden Key National Honor Society
Psi Chi (The National Honor Society in Psychology)

Computer Skills

SAS through 8.01; basic methods (sort, merge, retain, formats, freq, etc.), macros, report generation (data null, tabulate, report, graphics, etc.), statistics (proc means, tabulate, univariate, etc), arrays (implicit, explicit), SAS SCL programming, AF Frame creation, SAS/Graph, time series graphing, Shell scripting, SPSS, S-Plus, FoxPro, Paradox, WordPerfect, Microsoft (Word, Access, Excel, PowerPoint, Outlook), Quattro Pro, Netscape, Internet Explorer, Eudora Pro, FTP, Windows NT and UNIX environments

BARRY MITCHELL

100 Baxter Avenue   Home: 516-437-1000
New Hyde Park, NY 11010   E-Mail: mitch@msn.com

PROFESSIONAL EXPERIENCE

THE DEPOSITORY TRUST & CLEARING CORPORATION (DTCC)
1998-2003
Manager, Corporate Communications

> Conceive and write/edit annual reports, policy papers, talking points,
> internal/external newsletter articles, speeches and press releases while
> also creating marketing collateral material for trade shows, industry
> conferences and direct-mail pieces. Respond to media inquiries and pitch
> stories to trade publications. Converted complex topics into readable
> copy for all business units.

ANTON COMMUNITY NEWSPAPERS OF LONG ISLAND
2001-Present
Syndicated Columnist, "Eye on the Island"

> Write weekly public affairs column for 18 Nassau County, Long Island,
> newspapers. The Anton papers have a subscription base of more than
> 75,000 households. The current piece is online at
> http://www.antonnews.com/feature.

THE NEW YORK STATE BANKING DEPARTMENT
1996-1998
Public Information Officer

> Primary media relations contact for agency that regulates much of New
> York's financial services industry. Wrote speeches, press releases,
> talking points and other key correspondence for governor and
> superintendent of banks. Managed staff that processed hundreds of
> Freedom of Information Act (FOIA) requests each year.

CORPORATE COVERAGE
1992-1996
President

> Operated a public and governmental relations firm that included among
> its clients Jamaica Water Supply (a subsidiary of Emcor, a publicly
> traded corporation), the Oyster Bay-East Norwich, New York, public
> schools and Jay Leno's Big Dog Productions.

TOWN OF NORTH HEMPSTEAD
1989-1991
Public Information Officer

> Primary media relations contact for municipality of 210,000 in northern Nassau County, Long Island. Wrote press releases, speeches, issue backgrounders, legislative memoranda and constituent correspondence for town's elected officials.

MANHASSET PRESS
1984-1988
Editor

> Edited and wrote hard news and features for Nassau County weekly newspaper with a circulation of more than 3,500 households. Supervised freelance writers. Broke numerous stories before daily news media.

ELECTIVE OFFICE
Village of Manorhaven
1991-1993
Trustee

> Elected to two-year term with more than 60 percent of vote in village that is home to almost 7,000 in Port Washington, New York. Voted in favor of garbage contract that increased recycling and against largest property tax hike in Manorhaven's history. Moved out of village and did not seek re-election in 1993.

EDUCATION

> *Fordham University*
> Bachelor of Arts (Communications)
> Earned Dean's List honors and was catcher on varsity baseball team.

SELECTED ACHIEVEMENTS

Public & Media Relations

- Created DTCC's first-ever Recruitment Brochure, Code of Ethics manual, and employee guide to Customer Support Center.

- Developed marketing collateral materials that boosted sales for DTCC products, such as Security Position Reports and its Data Delivery Service.

- Served as key media relations contact for DTCC's Board of Directors and frequent speechwriter for DTCC's Chairman/CEO.

- Generated story ideas and was major editorial contributor to *@dtcc*, the company's external newsletter — and *The View*, its internal publication.

- Business units requested reprints of numerous *@dtcc* articles for sales-generation purposes and to keep current customers up-to-date.

- Coordinated Harvard's Henry Louis Gates's DTCC appearance (press release, Chairman's speech, company-wide publicity) as part of company's African-American history month celebration.

- Served as primary point of contact for DTCC Managing Directors seeking assistance with correspondence and presentations. Edited for content, style and readability.

- Supervised all of New York State's regulatory media relations activities pertaining to the Chase Manhattan-Chemical merger and the one between Union Bank of Switzerland (UBS) and Swiss Bank Corporation (SBC).

Governmental Affairs

- Developed remarks and position papers for Governor Pataki and New York's Superintendent of banks regarding their financial regulatory policies.

- Interacted with the New York Bankers Association (NYBA), trade groups, and key legislators on the "wild card" law, the ATM Safety Act, and the creation of the state's Holocaust Claims Processing Office.

- Monitored Freedom of Information Act (FOIA) requests closely, recognizing that some would generate subsequent media inquiries.

- Edited the *Weekly Bulletin*, a document that summarized branch bank closings/openings as well as Mortgage Broker and Banker activity statewide.

Journalism

- Write/research weekly column that covers politics, government, sports, and entertainment— and profiles Long Island personalities.

- Appeared as frequent guest on WLIW-TV's "The Editor's Desk," a current events program aired on Long Island's public television station.

- Acted as guest lecturer, St. Joseph's College, Patchogue, New York.

- Have a wide array of editorial contacts at various news outlets, including the *Wall Street Journal* and the Associated Press.

LiAnn Chu
100 Cinder Road
Edison, NJ 08100
Telephone: (H) (732) 744-1000

Email: LiAn@hotmail.com

Work History

September 2002 - Current
Senior Consultant
Technovision Inc., Clark, NJ

Project: Post-Trade Transaction Processing System for SIAC
- Familiar with new Post-Trade Transaction Processing. Analyze and test performance of newly developed programs using MQ Series and JCL.
- Design and develop new batch programs to identify and process Gaps during the Post-Trade Processing.
- Test performance of new programs.

Oct. 1998 - June 2002
Senior Programmer Analyst
Company: **(i) Structure, Inc.,** Parsippany, NJ

Project: Customer Information Database for Pershing, Credit Suisse First Boston
- Analyzed and specified Cash Management, IRA and COD account business editing rules.
- Designed and developed Cash Management editing, creating, viewing and bridgeback programs to interface with PONA (CICS,VSAM System), and other Web-based Front-end using CICS, COBOL II, DB2 and MQ Series.
- Analyzed, designed and developed Cash Management Batch Conversion and Bridgeback Processing to convert the existing Cash Management information from PONA to CID tables and to bridgeback information from CID tables back to temperate files for verification.
- Tested and supported all developed programs in DEV, SIT and UAT by using Message Manager Tester, XMLLink MsgExplorer and InterTest.

March 1999 - December 1999

Project: Paradigm (Integration System for Online Brokerage) for Pershing, DLJ
- Developed new Inquiry, Add and Update programs for Investment Objectives to Interface with the GUI Front-end (MQ Series) in Paradigm system.
- Analyzed, designed, developed new programs and modified old programs of PONA (Online Name and Address) system to interface with the GUI Front-end (Planetwork) for New Accounts Approval Processing in Paradigm.
- Supported the GUI Front-end team with PONA Knowledge.

Environment and Resources: IBM mainframe, CICS, COBOL II, DB2, INTERTEST, MQ Series and ENDEVOR.

October 1998 - March 1999
Company: **ETS**

Project: DANTES, GMAT Y2K Renovation Projects for Educational Testing Service.
- Coordinated the Renovation Team, Testing Team and the Customers for Y2K Renovation of DANTES and GMAT testing systems.

Main tasks were:
✓ Managed the progress of renovation and testing.
✓ Documented and solved issues raised by renovation, testing team and customers.
✓ Liaison between renovation, testing team and customers

Environment and Resources: CICS, COBOL II, VSAM, IDMS (ADSO)

April 1997 - September 1998
Programmer Analyst
Company: **Andersen Contracting,** Melbourne, Australia

Project: FLEXCAB (Flexible Charging and Billing System) for Telstra, Australia
As *Migration Coordinator and Data Representative*
Main tasks were:
✓ Maintained and controlled the versions of programs and data elements.
✓ Reconciled updated programs and data elements with production versions.
✓ Defined new programs and data elements in Design/1 and Endevor.

As *Lead Programmer Analyst*
Main tasks were:
✓ Analyzed the Change Requests.
✓ Designed detail solutions for Change Requests for each quarterly release.
✓ Coded and unit tested the programs for Change Requests
✓ Documented all new changes in the Design/1.

Environment and Resources: MVS JCL, CICS, COBOL II, DB2, SAS, SPUFI, ProEdit, Access for DB2, SCLM, SmartEdit, SmartTest and DESIGN/1, ENDEVOR

November 1995 - July 1996
Software Consultant
Company: **TaskForce Computer Service,** Melbourne, Australia

Project: GRCS for State Revenue Office (Ferntree Computer Corporation) VIC Australia (GRCS is a Generic Revenue Collecting system developed under MVS, COBOL II, DB2, CICS and GUI interface.)
Main tasks were:
✓ Maintained Land Tax and Payroll Tax collection programs.
✓ Solved User Requests and Production problems.
✓ Designed and developed new reports within existing programs.

Environment and Resources: MVS, COBOL II, DELTA (Cobol Generator), DB2, CICS and SPUFI, File-Aid for DB2, ENDEVOR.

May 1994 - Oct. 1995
Programmer Analyst
Company: **Andersen Contracting,** Melbourne Australia

Project: FLEXCAB (Flexible Charging and Billing System), Telstra Australia.
Environment & Resources: MVS JCL, COBOL II, DB2, SPUFI, File-Aid, SAS and Design/1, ENDEVOR, MS Project, CTM

January 1989 - April 1994
Programmer Analyst
Company: **NEXUS Business Software Pty. Ltd.,** Melbourne, Australia

Project: NEXUS (Integrated Accounting System)
Environment & Resources: IBM-PC, C++, DATAFLEX

IT SKILLS SUMMARY

IBM mainframe DB2 SQL	Excellent	8 years
IBM mainframe MVS JCL, COBOL II	Excellent	8 years
IBM mainframe CICS COBOL	Excellent	5 years
IBM mainframe IMS(DL/1)	Familiar	1 year
UNIX COBOL	Good	2.5 years
PASCAL, GW-BASIC	Familiar	
MS-DOS DATAFLEX	Good	5 years
SAS, C++	Familiar	1 year
Software Utilities (Package)		
ENDEVOR	Very Good	8 years
DESIGN/1	Very Good	2 years
File-AID	Good	7 years
SPUFI, PROEDIT	Good	7 years
File-AID for DB2, Access/DB2	Good	6 years
SmartEdit SmartTest	Good	1 year
SCLM	Familiar	1 year
MQ Series	Familiar	1 year
MS Project	Familiar	0.5 year
Microsoft Word, Excel	Excellent	6 years

Education:
- Master of Science: Software Engineering **ZhongShan University,** China 1985
- Bachelor of Science: Computer Science & Software **ZhongShan University,** China 1982

JOHN SMITH
100A EXETER STREET
BOSTON, MA 02100
(617) 266-1000

JS100@worldnet.att.net

EDUCATION:	Babson College, Master of Business Administration (1981) Villanova University, Master of Science Math (1969) Villanova University, Bachelor of Science Electrical Engineering (1965)

EXPERIENCE

1997-PRESENT   **SKYCADY**
BOSTON

Principal
Involved in variety of consulting assignments both for venture capital groups and with small and medium-size companies. A member of the BOD of Savior Technology, Campbell, CA.; Finale Inc, Boston, MA; Asic Alliance, Woburn, MA; and Site Technology, Sunnyvale, CA. Completed several acting CEO assignments.

Boston University, Boston; Dean College, Franklin, MA; and University of Phoenix, Braintree, MA

Part-Time Instructor
Taught undergraduate/graduate level in Computer Science Department.

1989-1998   **DATA GENERAL CORPORATION**
WESTBORO, MA

Vice President Worldwide Channels
Responsible for all activities associated with DG's distribution channels. This includes P&L, credit, technical support, account management, training, advertising and promotion. Budgets in excess of $1 billion. Member of operations committee, which approves product directions, sets marketing strategies, determines corporate expense plans and partner investment.

Vice President of Americas Sales and Service
Managed all sales, support, field marketing, customer service and national account activities in North and South America. Built a $600M open system business from scratch in five years while simultaneously

increasing sales productivity by 50% and generating more than 70% of this business from accounts new to Data General. Completely restructured field function to integrate VARs, OEMs, ISVs, telesales, teleservice, agents, subcontractors, integration channel partners, major accounts and end users. Responsibilities included revenue budgets in excess of $700M, associated profit budgets and professional staff of more than 2,000 people.

1985-1989   **APOLLO COMPUTER CORPORATION**
CHELMSFORD, MA

Vice President of North American Sales Operations
Managed all sales, support, field marketing and national account activities. Sales, revenue and profit responsibilities for all markets through all channels. Took over sales when 85% of sales were to OEMs and expanded sales into major accounts, new accounts and VARs. Grew major accounts 40% and doubled new accounts each year. Member of operations committee, which approves product directions, sets marketing strategies, determines corporate expense plans and partner investment.

1983-1985   **DIGITAL EQUIPMENT CORPORATION**
MAYNARD, MA

Northeast Regional Sales Manager
Managed all the field and sales marketing activities in the Northeast. Sales and revenue responsibilities for all markets through all channels. Fastest-growing and #1-performing region in the company in 1984.

1981-1983   *United States Distribution Manager*
Managed the operations activity for all distribution channels. Group consisted of approximately 60 people involved in operations, technical support, account management, training, advertising and promotion.

1969-1983   *Sales and Sales Management*
Various sales and sales management positions in Manhattan and Boston. Overachieved goals in every year of eligibility. Managed Digital's top district for three consecutive years.

1976-1977   **NEW YORK INSTITUTE OF TECHNOLOGY**
WESTBURY, NY

Adjunct Faculty
Instructor for undergraduate statistics course

1965-1969   **TECHNITROL INC., & U. S. ARMY (Civilian Employee)**

Electrical Engineer
Various electrical engineering assignments in test equipment design

CATHERINE SMITH
1 Madison Street #1C
Hoboken, NJ 07010
Telephone: 201-792-1000
E-mail: csss10@hotmail.com

Professional Experience

2000 - Present **TD SECURITIES (USA), Inc.**   New York, NY
Associate, Media & Communications Group

• Active member of several four-person deal teams that structured, originated and executed six new/amended and restated senior leveraged credit facility transactions within the cable, programming and publishing sectors for which TD Securities acted as Agent Bank and earned more than $7.5 million in fee income. Responsibilities included performance of due diligence, preparation of credit and valuation analyses, construction of transaction terms, negotiation of loan documentation and frequent interaction with prospective investors during syndication phase to support due diligence initiatives.

• Acted as primary Transaction Manager for 13 accounts totaling $600 million within Media & Communications Portfolio, which involves active monitoring of financial and operational performance, reassessment of credit risk and enterprise valuation as well as preparation of formal analyses used to regularly update senior credit committee members.

• Serve as bank's primary representative in workout phase and Chapter 11 filing of an Internet broadband company. Responsibilities included the development and update of credit analysis and recovery scenarios, calculation and recommendation of loan loss provisions and frequent direct communication with key credit committee members, including the Chief Credit Officer.

• Negotiated with domestic and international counsel and with client management to remedy loan defaults of two Argentine cable companies caused by extreme local economic and political conditions, which resulted in partial receipt of interest payments and loan principal.

Summer 1999 **ARGUS RESEARCH CORPORATION**   New York, NY
Summer Associate, Sell Side Equity Research

• Constructed quantitative models used to project earnings and equity valuations for several telecom service companies.

• Researched and prepared written analyses of a telecom equipment company and a telecom service company to initiate research coverage of its equities.

- Composed daily and monthly client reports that summarized current events in telecom services/equipment and cable/media industries and projected their potential impact on equity prices.

1996 - 1998   **BANKERS TRUST COMPANY**   New York, NY
Assistant Vice President, Internal Audit Department

- Evaluated accuracy of market and credit risk statistics used by derivatives trading desks.

- Composed audit reports directed to senior management, including Chief Information Officer and Senior Managing Director of Sales and Trading.

1992 - 1996   **DELOITTE & TOUCHE LLP**   Parsippany, NJ
Senior Accountant, Accounting and Auditing Services

- Analyzed quarterly and yearly financial statement balances related to investment activity and researched material differences.

- Identified and substantiated variances in client portfolio performance vs. market trends.

Education: **NEW YORK UNIVERSITY**   New York, NY
Leonard N. Stern School of Business
Master of Business Administration, May 2000
Emphasis in Finance/Economics

- GPA: 3.77/4.0: Graduated *with Distinction*

LEHIGH UNIVERSITY   Bethlehem, PA
Bachelor of Science, Accounting, June 1992
- GPA: 3.5/4.0: Graduated *cum laude*
Minor in American Literature

Certification: Certified Public Accountant since 1993, Series 7/Series 63

Language: Fluent Spanish

Caryn Andrea
100 10 Street
New York, NY 10003
(212) 674-1000
cary@aol.com

Film Production Experience

Muse Film and Television, Co-ordinating Producer of *Civilization*   Present
by Subway, proposed pilot for professional development video series
involving New York City cultural institutions and serving New York City
public school teachers

Magic Box Productions, Associate Producer of documentary on
the *School Arts Rescue Initiative*, commissioned by the 9/11 Fund and
the *New York Times* Foundation

Intern, Researcher, WCBS-TV News   1982

Development, Marketing, and Management Experience

Management Consultant, Advisory Committee Member,   Present
Dancenow/NYC. Work with directors to create marketing and funding
strategies to facilitate the organization's expansion. Assist with all
aspects of producing two-week dance festival.

Work for various cultural organizations, including: 1998 - 2003

Educational Outreach at the 92nd Street Y. Developed and
implemented strategy; researched potential clients to increase
number of schools participating in "Musical Introduction Series."
Assisted with administration of arts education programs reaching
thousands of New York City public school students.

New York City Museum School. Created "white paper" to explain
its alternative model to educational community.

The Pearl Theatre Company, Co-Chairperson, Development
Committee, Trustee. Developed and implemented fundraising
strategies with development staff and fellow board members.
Researched potential high-net-worth individuals, corporate, and
foundation funders.

Barnard Business and Professional Women, President. Oversaw general operations of alumnae membership organization and planning for conferences and events.

Shearman & Sterling, Marketing Specialist. Worked with partners to win new business. Researched potential clients and competitors. Wrote/edited letters, brochures, and other marketing material. Created models for development of practice group brochures and proposals and developed systems to manage and disseminate information.

1995 -1998

Altman Foundation, Program Officer. Evaluated prospective grantees through site visits, interviews, and analysis of written materials. Researched best practices in the four fields of interest to foundation – arts, education, health, and social welfare. Prepared written and oral reports regarding potential grantees.

1989 -1993

Victoria Marks Performance Company, Manager. Managed all aspects of the dance company's fiscal and general management. Developed and implemented fundraising, marketing, and touring strategies. Created a not-for-profit entity with a board of directors to oversee the company.

1988 -1989

Shearman & Sterling, Corporate Legal Assistant Coordinator. Managed team of legal assistants. Researched and reported on current and potential clients.

1987-1988

Assemblywoman Louise Slaughter, Senior Legislative Aide, Louise Slaughter for Congress, Fundraising Coordinator. Managed Assemblywoman Slaughter's Albany office. Researched and developed legislative proposals. Served as liaison between the Assemblywoman and constituent groups and lobbyists. Managed all fundraising for Assemblywoman Slaughter's successful congressional race.

1985 -1986

Jacob's Pillow Dance Festival, Associate Director of Development. Developed and implemented corporate, foundation, and government solicitation strategies. Analyzed potential funding sources for specific projects.

1983 -1985

Education

1983   Bachelor of Arts, English. Barnard College, Columbia University

Computer Skills

Microsoft Word, Access, Excel, PowerPoint, Netscape and Internet Explorer, Windows NT

EILEEN BERGEN

100 Knoll Drive   (650) 740-1000
San Carlos, CA 94100   eeb100@aol.com

PROFESSIONAL EXPERIENCE AND ACCOMPLISHMENTS

Stanford Hospital and Clinics, Stanford, California   1987 - 2002

Director of Patient Care Services (6/95 - 6/02)

Provided seven years of leadership in clinical departments consisting of 500 FTEs with an operating budget of $40 million, and 12 patient care units. Clinical areas include 10 Medical/Surgical Units, Rehabilitation Unit, Skilled Nursing Facility, Psychiatric Services, Antepartum, Labor and Delivery, Postpartum, Well Baby Nursery and Rehabilitation Services.

Accomplishments

- Monitored quality improvement efforts for an average daily census of 240 patients.
- Decreased the 2001 operating budget by 12% ($4.5 million), exceeding budgetary requirement.
- Planned the communication strategy for employees regarding the UCSF/SHS merger resulting in a unified informational approach between two distinct medical center sites.
- Created and implemented the *Lucile Packard Johnson Center*, a comprehensive mother-baby center, consisting of 160 FTEs, in collaboration with nursing management as well as adult and neonatal physician groups.
- Built productive working relationships with managers and staff resulting in an 8% vacancy position rate and high job satisfaction ratings.
- Decreased admissions to intensive care units by designing and implementing a nursing unit with short-term EKG monitoring capability for acute surgical patients.
- Designed and implemented a hospital-wide plan to facilitate the professional and competent return of the nursing workforce at the conclusion of an eight-week nursing strike.

Nurse Manager of Emergency Department (6/90 - 6/95)

Directed operations for five years at the Emergency Department (a level one trauma center), with annual patient visits of 35,000. Hired a highly regarded management team, recruited specialty trained staff and implemented a new graduate nurse training program resulting in a department vacancy rate of less than 2%. Responsible for 75 FTEs and an operating budget of $9 million.

Accomplishments

- Assured the delivery of quality and cost-effective care to patients in collaboration with pediatric and adult physicians.
- Expedited patient care delivery and operations by implementing an automated laboratory and supply order entry system.
- Implemented an automated patient instruction program (Logicare), resulting in detailed discharge information for patients and families providing for continuity of care and internal departmental data.
- Designed and oversaw the construction of a $2 million Emergency Department patient lobby, which improved patient flow and access, working with multidisciplinary teams, including physicians and staff.
- Communicated with media, police, fire department, campus police to maintain positive working relationships.
- Provided community linkage with government personnel, including the Secret Service.

Registered Nurse Recruiter (10/89 - 6/90)

- Recruited exempt and non-exempt staff for Stanford Hospital; representing Nurse Managers and unit needs to applicants.
- Assessed nurse applicants for experience and aptitude for unit requirements, maintaining data via recruitment software.

<u>Senior Staff Nurse/Emergency Department</u> (7/87 - 10/89)
- Responsible for direct patient care in trauma, triage, critical and non-acute-care areas
- Rotated charge nurse responsibilities.
- Preceptor for new staff members

Holy Name Hospital, Teaneck, New Jersey   1984 - 1987
<u>Senior Staff Nurse/Emergency Department</u> (1/84 - 2/87)
- Responsible for direct patient care in trauma, triage, critical and non-acute-care areas.
- Rotated charge nurse responsibilities.
- Assisted with orientation, evaluation and education of new staff.

Memorial Sloan-Kettering Cancer Center, New York, New York   1979 - 1984
<u>Senior Staff Nurse/Radiation Oncology Unit</u> (5/80 - 1/84)
- Conducted oncology patient/family sessions in coordination with social workers
- Taught nursing curriculum to student Radiation Therapy Technologists.
- Responsible for direct in-patient care, including clinical research support
- Responsible for planning, organizing and teaching outpatient care to patients and families in radiation oncology

<u>Staff Nurse/Neurology Unit</u> (1/79 - 5/80)
- Rotated charge nurse responsibilities.
- Evaluation, orientation and education of new staff
- Coordinated patient discharge on a multidisciplinary health care team.

Valley Hospital, Ridgewood, New Jersey   1975 - 1978
<u>Staff Nurse/Orthopedic Unit</u> (1/75 - 12/78)

EDUCATION
University of San Francisco, San Francisco   1993
    <u>Master's in Public Administration, Health Science focus</u>
Marymount Manhattan College, New York   1981
    <u>Bachelor of Arts, Psychology</u>
Helene Fuld School of Nursing, New York   1977
    <u>Associate Degree in Nursing</u>
St. George's Hospital, School of Nursing, London   1974
    <u>State Enrolled Nursing License</u>

LICENSES AND CERTIFICATIONS
- New York, New Jersey and California nursing licenses
- Certified in Advanced Cardiac Life Support, Basic Life Support; Trauma Nurse Course
- Mobile Intensive Care Nurse (MICN)

PUBLICATIONS AND PRESENTATIONS
- Co-author of "Emergency Department Management," a chapter in *Emergency Nurses Association Core Curriculum* (W.B.Saunders Company, 1994).
- Co-author of "The Patient with Acute Myocardial Infarction: Assessing the quality of care in one emergency department," *Journal of Emergency Medicine,* May/June 1990.
- Co-author of "The Role of the Nurse in Radiation Therapy," A Century of Oncology Nursing 1884-1984, Memorial Sloan-Kettering Cancer Center.
- Presentation, "How Safe Are You at Work?" Stanford's Trauma Symposium, 1993.

Roseanna Pollack
1 Main Street
Newton, NJ 07100

Telephone: (973) 300 1000
Fax (973) 300 9100
E-mail: R10@aol.com

EDUCATION
Graduate of Montclair State University, January 1994
Received Bachelor of Arts (Language)
Graduated in 3½ years with 4.0 GPA

PROFESSIONAL HIGHLIGHTS

Customer Follow-Up Coordinator
April 1999 - Present

> *McGuire Chevrolet:* July 2001 - Present
> *Franklin Sussex Auto Mall:* April 1999 - Present
> *Condit Ford World:* April 2001 - April 2003
> *Prestige Volvo:* February 2001 - October 2001

Sales • Marketing • Service Skills

Contact customers who have visited each dealership via telephone and **document** respective Sales/Service experiences. **Answer** customers' questions regarding dealers' policies and procedures. **Chart** results of telephone calls, as well as dates and times of attempted calls, making sure three attempts are made to contact customer — all within three business days. **Write** Customer Feedback Reports whenever there is a concern. **Verify** that each report is immediately forwarded to appropriate manager and it is promptly **resolved, documented** and **reviewed** with personnel involved. **Draw up** Trend Analysis Reports for each dealer based on information **collected** from customers, **evaluating** where each dealer is strong and where each requires improvement. **Design** reports that correspond to and reflect each vehicle manufacturer's specification (e.g., Chrysler's Five Star Program, Ford's Blue Oval Certification, etc.). **Acting as liaison** so that these reports are available for inspection by each vehicle manufacturer. **Remind** customers to fill out and return manufacturers' surveys. **Improve** each dealership's CSI score each quarter.

Jump Lumber Company, Inc. Newton, NJ
June 1997 - Present

Bookkeeper • General Office
Balance books at end of business day. **Adjust** computer inventory to match physical inventory, entering customer payments and purchase orders. **Match** purchase orders with receivings and bills to ensure all figures are correct. **Print** checks, making sure bills and taxes are paid on time. **Run** customer statements at end of each month. **Mail** out in timely manner, **filing** customer receipts, **backing up** the computer after closing, **updating** the computer system at end of each month, quarter and fiscal year. **Input** weekly payroll each week and verify that hours have been added up correctly.

United Parcel Service, Inc. Parsippany, NJ
May 1993 - February 1997

Customer Service Account Executive
Youngest woman **promoted** to Management in North Jersey District; directly responsible for 11,000 shippers in Morristown area. **Set up** new accounts. **Sold** UPS services. **Persuaded** customers from using competition. **Inspected** damages, **settling** claims, **responding** to customer concerns, **maintaining** solid relationships with customers, as well as **establishing** new contacts. **Taught** customers to utilize new technology. **Wrote** and **submitted** logistic study analysis to **improve** customers' shipping procedures. **Initiated** and **approved** incentive pricing. Coordinated donations to United Way. **Oversaw** customer counter that is open to the public during Christmas holiday.

UPS Customer Service Intern
Discovered good locations for UPS overnight letter boxes. **Set up** contracts with property owners and **coordinated** placement of letter centers. **Canvassed** areas and **created** new overnight/international shipping accounts. **Worked** on various advertising projects for UPS letter centers. **Qualified** driver leads and assisted Account Executives in customer follow-up.

Marissa Capelli
Cape3@bc.edu

Current Address
1000 Commonwealth Avenue
Apartment 100
Brighton, MA 02100
(617) 787-1000

Permanent Address
1 Monroe Court
Harrington Park, NJ 07000

(201) 767-1000

EDUCATION

Boston College
College of Arts and Sciences
Bachelor of Arts, projected graduation: May 2004
Major: Communications
Cumulative GPA: 3.6/4.0
Honors: Dean's List (5 semesters); Golden Key International Honor Society

---

WORK EXPERIENCE

The Brunswick Group
London, England
Research and Information Intern
June 2002

✓ Assembled specific information regarding clients using programs, such as Bloomberg, Lexis Nexis, Multex, Hemscott and Reuters.

✓ Created a media overview and press analysis of particular company, tracking national and regional coverage, and third-party comments on company funding.

✓ Researched quarterly reporting dates and figures for many Brunswick clients and their competitors.

✓ Summarized controversial AGMs (annual general meetings) and compiled a casebook to serve as a reference guide for Brunswick's future client situations.

Boston College Career Center
Chestnut Hill, MA
Peer Adviser
Academic year 2001

✓ Training in communication skills, résumés, cover letters and interview skills.

Boston College Career Center (continued)

✓ Conducted résumé, cover letter and interview workshops for undergraduate students and provided individual assistance to teach basic skills.

✓ Directed recruitment project by creating advertisements for Boston College newspaper, mass e-mails and fliers to recruit peer advisers for next academic year.

The Lily Pad Academy
Hackensack, NJ
Day Care Assistant
Summer 2001

✓ Planned and ran activities for children ranging from 1 to 5 years of age.

✓ Assisted in personal development of each child through activities and individual nourishment.

The Limited & Co.
Paramus, NJ
Salesperson
Winter 2000

✓ Assisted in the visual display of merchandise, exceeded daily sales goals, managed client relationships.

ACTIVITIES
BC-GESS Mentoring Program, Thomas Gardner School
Allston, MA
Mentor
Fall 2000

✓ Promoted academic achievement and instilled values in child at academic and social risk.

✓ Received training on mentor tasks and roles, communication skills, child abuse prevention and cultural diversity.

SKILLS

Computer: Proficient in Microsoft Office, Knowledgeable in Multex, Bloomberg and Reuters
Language: Conversational in Spanish

Nicholas Murray   **1 Mount Walley Road**
Nicmc@yahoo.com   Waltham, MA 02100
(781) 899-1000

EDUCATION
Harvard University
Bachelor of Arts, with honors (cum laude) in 2003
GPA: 3.25 (3.30 in major)
Relevant Coursework: Introduction to Investments, Political Economy of Japan, Calculus

RELATED WORK EXPERIENCE

Morgan Stanley (Boston)   6/02 - 9/02
Financial Services Intern
- Identified potential market strategies by contacting outside fund companies. Presented these strategies to upper management.
- Researched current market conditions and fixed-income industry segments.
- Analyzed portfolios, using Bloomberg and Nasdaq information services. Made suggestions to identify strengths and weaknesses.
- Attended research meetings over live video feed from New York.
- Prepared client reports using Microsoft Excel.

Fidelity Investments (Boston)   6/01 - 9/01
Trade Analyst
- Acted as liaison between 40 Investment Managers and custodian bank to research and answer client inquiries. Provided quick resolution to problems. Answered inquiries in efficient and timely manner.
- Compiled and analyzed variety of securities, failed trades and trade metrics for company's database to streamline operations.
- Forecasted potential overdrafts by monitoring global cash balances.

Sullivan and Cogliano Companies (*Staffing Solutions,* Waltham, MA)   6/00 - 9/00
Research Analyst
- Located and contacted potential candidates for recruiting firm.
- Researched client company profiles for sales division. Familiarity with Macintosh. Proficient in Microsoft Windows and Internet research.

OTHER WORK EXPERIENCE

Harvard University Athletic Operation   09/01 - 09/03
Facilities Staff: Monitored facilities after hours and assembled facility equipment prior to athletic competitions. Committed 15 hours per week to defray cost of education and maintained high GPA.

Harvard College Fund   9/00 - 12/00
Student Fundraiser: Raised more than $20,000 each semester by contacting alumni by telephone for various branches at Harvard. Honed telephone and customer service skills. Learned value of following up with customers.

ACTIVITIES
Member of Harvard Varsity Baseball Team, 09/99 - 2003. Member A.D. Club, Harvard Finals Club, 09/01 - 2003, Harvard Student Thank-a-Thon Committee Member, 09/00 - 09/02

100 DARTMOUTH STREET, BOSTON, MA 02100
TELEPHONE (617) 901-1000 CELL PHONE (617) 901-1010 E-MAIL HC2@HOTMAIL.COM

HEATHER CASH

EDUCATION

Boston College
Arts & Science
Majored in communication. Honors
GPA: 3.8. Projected graduation: 2004

Fordham University
Liberal Arts
Cumulative GPA: 3.3
1999-2000

WORK EXPERIENCE

WCVB-TV Channel 5   **Newton, MA**
Intern   **5/02 - 8/02**
- Conducted daily station tours, interacting with public and exhibited excellent communication and people skills.
- Wrote press releases and viewer response letters, meeting all deadlines.
- Assisted with public service effort, *Keeping Kids on Track*.
- Worked with Director of Programming, using computer skills, such as Microsoft Word, Excel, Access.

Reagan Communications Group   **Boston, MA**
Intern   **6/01 - 8/01**
- Wrote calendar listings, press releases, feature stories. Honed proofreading and editing skills.
- Worked at special events, exhibited communication and people skills.
- Updated contact information, using computer skills.
- Scheduled photo opportunities, bringing together an assortment of people on a timely basis.

Dirtpile.com   **South Boston, MA**
Public Relations and Sales   **5/00 - 8/00**
- Acquired new customer base; maintained customer relations and satisfaction.
- Maintained continual customer contact through telephone, computer and mail correspondence.
- Research, update and input in Web pages; familiarity with HTML.

Sterling Equipment   **East Boston, MA**
Salesperson   **6/99 - 8/99**
- Sold construction equipment.
- Advised customers on purchases.
- Managed flow of new merchandise.
- Maintained basic accounting (cash register, sales slips, book balancing), utilizing computer skills.

Many books have been written on résumés and cover letters, but because the digital age has had such a profound impact on job seeking, I found myself referring to some books more than others. A bibliography of all the sources used follows, but the books (and column) mentioned here were particularly helpful when researching this new digital territory. One book that did not cover electronic submittals is also mentioned here because it provided readable and insightful information that distinguished it from the rest. The books are not listed alphabetically but according to my preference.

eResumes, by Susan Britton Whitcomb and Pat Kendall (McGraw-Hill, 2002), covers the full range of the electronic submission process. Whitcomb's previous book, *Résumé Magic* (JIST Works, Inc.), is comprehensive (at 596 pages!) and valuable too. In addition, *Electronic Resumes & Online Networking* (Career Press), by Rebecca Smith, also covers the full range of electronic submission and provides step-by-step tutorials. *The Everything Resume Book* (Adams Media), by Burton Jay Nadler, doesn't focus on electronic résumés, but it is useful on the overall process of finding a job.

Finally, the Sunday "Job Market" column in the *New York Times* consistently dealt with pressing issues confronting job seekers in the recent "jobless recovery" and published, week after week, excellent articles that addressed everything from the new electronic hiring process to what to wear during an interview in a downturned economy. The individual articles are listed in the bibliography.

BOOKS

Bermont, Todd. *10 Insider Secrets to Job Hunting Success!* Chicago: 10 Step Publications, 2002.

Cunningham, Helen, and Brenda Greene. *The Business Style Handbook: An A-to-Z Guide for Writing on the Job with Tips from Communications Experts at the Fortune 500.* New York: McGraw-Hill, 2002.

Farr, Michael. *The Quick Resume & Cover Letter,* 2nd ed. Indianapolis: JIST Publishing, 2003.

Kotter, John P. *A Force for Change: How Leadership Differs from Management.* New York: The Free Press, 1990.

Nadler, Burton Jay. *The Everything Resume Book,* 2nd ed. Avon, MA: Adams Corporation, 2003.

Rosenberg, Arthur D., and David Hizer. *The Resume Handbook.* Avon, MA: Adams Media, 1996.

Smith, Rebecca. *Electronic Resumes & Online Networking.* Franklin Lakes, NJ: Career Press, 2000.

Whitcomb, Susan Britton. *Résumé Magic.* Indianapolis: JIST Publications, 1999.

Whitcomb, Susan Britton, and Pat Kendall. *eResumes.* New York: McGraw-Hill, 2002.

ARTICLES

Adelson, Andrea. "Big Job Sites Try to Think Small." *New York Times,* 29 October 2002.

Bing, Stanley. "How Not to Succeed in Business." *Fortune,* 30 December 2002.

Brooks, David. "A Nation of Grinders." *New York Times,* 29 June 2003.

DePalma, Anthony. "Tell Us About Yourself." *New York Times,* 27 July 2003.

Field, Anne. "When a Job Hunt Is Measured in Seasons or Even a Year." *New York Times,* 8 December 2002.

Fitzgerald, Thomas J. "Help Wanted: Customizing a Job Search." *New York Times,* 20 March 2003.

Fortune 500 List. *Fortune,* 15 April 2002.

Greenhouse, Steven. "Job Training That Works, and It's Free." *New York Times,* 10 August 2003.

"IBD's 10 Secrets to Success." *Investor's Business Daily,* 10 January 2003.

Kiviat, Barbara. "The New Rules of Web Hiring." *Time,* 24 November 2003.

Koeppel, David. "Unexpected Joys of a Workplace Seen the Second Time Around." *New York Times,* 11 May 2003.

Lemley, Brad. "Anything into Oil." *Discover,* May 2003.

Leonhardt, David. "Losers All: 'Egalitarian Recession' Keeps Anger at Bay." *New York Times,* 15 June 2003.

Lublin, Joann S. "College Students Make Job Hunting Tougher with Weak Résumés." *Wall Street Journal,* 29 April 2003.

Lublin, Joann S. "Job Hunters with Gaps in Their Résumés Need to Write Around Them." *Wall Street Journal,* 6 May 2003.

Maher, Kris. "Online Job Hunting Is Tough. Just Ask Vinnie." *Wall Street Journal,* 24 June 2003.

Milbourn, Mary Ann. "Job Hunt & Peck." *Orange County Register,* 30 December 2002.

Parnes, Francine. "New Interview Uniform: Gray Means Business." *New York Times,* 19 January 2003.

"New York-Area Hiring Managers Weigh in on Résumés." Beta Research Corporation/*New York Times,* 14 July 2002.

Tejada, Carlos. "Applicant Flood Makes It Tough to Hire Wisely." *Wall Street Journal,* 24 December 2002.

WEB SITES

I examined all company Web sites of the Fortune 500 participants, but a few of them need to be cited for material. They are listed below, as well as any other career-related Web sites that provided information.

www.alltel.com

www.bartleby.com

www.business2.com

www.careerbuilder.com

www.editoral.careers.msn.com

www.heinz.com

www.hoovers.com

www.hotjobs.com

www.jobweb.com

www.jvsjobs.org

www.lehman.com

www.mindtools.com

www.monster.com

www.m-w.com

www.nytimes.com/marketing/jobmarket

www.ohio.edu

www.onrec.com

www.owl.english.purdue.edu

www.pg.com

www.resumes.com

www.siac.com

www.edison.com

www.ups.com

Brenda Greene is a writer, author, and editor. She is married and the mother of three children. Her publishing experience includes working as an editor at *Working Woman* magazine and as an editor at the *North Jersey Herald & News*. She began her career at Whitney Communications, where she was a senior editor. She is coauthor, with Helen Cunningham, of *The Business Style Handbook, An A-to-Z Guide for Writing on the Job with Tips from Communications Experts at the Fortune 500* (McGraw-Hill, March 2002).

On the corporate side, Brenda worked as a marketing manager for a business-to-business venture. She was also the writer and editor for a project to create a health and fitness manual for children with asthma, jointly sponsored by Theracom Communications and Pfizer Pharmaceuticals. She worked on various projects at Dugan Farley Communications, Agora Publications, and the University of Maryland.